GARFIELD OF OHIO

The Available Man

Books by John M. Taylor

Garfield of Ohio

Korea's Syngman Rhee:
An Unauthorized Portrait

From the White House Inkwell

GARFIELD OF OHIO

OF OHIO

The Available Man

JOHN M. TAYLOR

W·W·NORTON & COMPANY·INC·

NEW YORK

For Alice, Kathy, and Jimmy

CONTENTS

9

CONTENTS

Illustrations appear between pages 160 and 161.

FOREWORD

---·◆·---

In the Department of State library in Washington, on a remote shelf apparently reserved for memorials to departed statesmen, there is a leather-bound volume of tributes to President James A. Garfield following his death in 1881. The browser cannot help being impressed with the depth of the nation's grief over its second martyr president in a generation. There are proceedings of services in New York, Buffalo, Washington, and Denver. There is even a sermon by the Chaplain of Congress, the Rev. Mr. Byron Sunderland, who once opened a session of Congress with the plea, "Vouchsafe them brains, O Lord!"

As the decades passed, however, Garfield and his brief administration slipped easily out of memory. It became the conventional wisdom that the post-Civil War period was dominated by political mediocrities of dubious moral standards, and a particular opprobrium was reserved for those who, like Garfield, had supported the Republican reconstruction program for the "prostrate" South. Even after he was elected president, the brevity of his term invariably led Garfield to be consigned to essentially the same limbo as the other little-known chief executives who followed Lincoln.

But Garfield deserves more than a statue in the park, if only because he was a very human person with an unusual assortment of strengths and weaknesses. He was something of a puzzle even to his contemporaries. Albert G. Riddle, an Ohio politician and historian who was by no means unfriendly to Garfield, asked rhetorically in 1878, "What is the lack in Garfield? What is the thing wanting? Not large obviously. Some little thing wanting to completeness. . . ."

Garfield was, in fact, a man of contradictions. A brave and capable general with the Army of the Cumberland, he carried on a clandestine correspondence which contributed to the dismissal of his friend and commanding officer, William S. Rosecrans. A devoted husband and father, he felt a need for feminine companionship which came close to ruining his marriage. An earnest and hard-working congressman, he had a blind spot for conflict of interest in both legal and financial matters which almost forced him out of politics. And throughout his career Garfield felt obliged to repress his own driving ambition in order to conform to the convention of the day that the office must seek the man.

In terms of source materials on the twentieth president, there is almost nothing "wanting to completeness." Garfield was a compulsive diarist, and from the first day of 1848, when he was sixteen, until he was shot down as president thirty-three years later, Garfield kept a journal in which he rarely failed to write at the end of each day. His other papers in the Library of Congress total among the largest volume of any president. To these materials I have been able to add some unpublished Garfield letters in my own possession. The problems which have arisen in connection with this work have been those of interpretation rather than of locating primary sources.

With regard to sources, all Garfield letters not otherwise cited are to be found in the Garfield Papers, Library of Congress. To avoid a proliferation of footnotes, very short quotes of a noncontroversial nature have not been specifically referenced. The bulk of such brief quotes are in fact from Garfield's diary.

Although I would not recommend that anyone attempt to

FOREWORD

write a presidential biography from half way around the world, I have been fortunate in the long-range assistance which I have received in the writing of *Garfield of Ohio*. Professor Robert C. L. Scott of Williams College and Professor Walter B. Posey of Agnes Scott College were most helpful in calling my attention to recent publications pertinent to Garfield's career. I am indebted also to Mr. Thomas W. Bleezarde, editor of the *Williams Alumni Review*, Mr. John Y. Simon, Executive Director of the Ulysses S. Grant Association, and to Mssrs. Burt McKee and George Porter of the United States Information Service, Singapore, for their assistance in obtaining source materials.

Two very able scholars, Professors Bell I. Wiley of Emory University and Jack M. Holl of Williams, were good enough to read for me those chapters dealing with Garfield's war service and his congressional years, respectively. In addition to recommending specific changes, they were able to provide reassurance that I had not overlooked any recent scholarship which would significantly alter my conclusions. To Mr. Evan Thomas of W. W. Norton & Company I am indebted not only for his perceptive recognition of the need for a new biography of Garfield but for his valuable suggestions concerning both organization and content.

Finally, I wish to acknowledge a very special debt to my wife Priscilla—companion, editor, and historian—who has devoted to this latest manuscript the same scholarly attention which she brought to its predecessors.

John M. Taylor
Rangoon, Burma
September 1969.

ACKNOWLEDGMENTS

The author wishes to thank the following authors and publishers for permission to quote from the books cited: the Michigan State University Press, *The Wild Life of the Army: Civil War Letters of James A. Garfield,* edited by Frederick D. Williams; McGraw-Hill Book Company, *Carp's Washington* by Frances Carpenter Huntington; Oxford University Press, *The Republican Party: 1854–1966* by George H. Mayer; Harper & Row, Publishers, *The Assassins* by Robert J. Donovan; Yale University Press, *The Life and Letters of James Abram Garfield* by Theodore C. Smith; Charles Scribner's Sons, *Autobiography of Seventy Years* by George F. Hoar; University of Illinois Press, *Outlawing the Spoils* by Ari Hoogenboom; Harcourt, Brace & World, Inc., *The Edge of Glory* by William M. Lamers, and *The Politicos* by Matthew Josephson; University of Michigan Press, *The Garfield-Hinsdale Letters;* the University of Chicago Press, *The Trial of the Assassin Guiteau* by Charles E. Rosenberg; Little, Brown and Company, *Reunion and Reaction* by C. Vann Woodward; University of Pennsylvania Press, *Jeremiah Sullivan Black* by William N. Brigance; Mr. Donald B. Chidsey, *The Gentleman from New York: A Life of Roscoe Conkling;* Mr. Harry Barnard, *Rutherford B. Hayes and His America;* Mr. Tyler Dennett, *John Hay: From Poetry to Politics.*

GARFIELD OF OHIO

The Available Man

Chapter One

A CONVENTION
IN CHICAGO

———————◆———————

Few political gatherings before or since have equaled the Republican convention of 1880 for excitement and pure drama. These elements are not always present, for under different circumstances the presidential nominating exercise can be a rather empty ritual, involving little more than the personal fortunes of a few participants. But in a year of peace and prosperity, fifteen years after the close of the Civil War, the Republican convention had in its power to determine the direction to be taken by the party—and most probably the country—for the next four years.

This is not always the case, for more often than not an outgoing president has an heir apparent, and the main function of the party convention becomes that of legitimizing the succession. So it was in 1960, when the Republican convention routinely accepted Richard Nixon as political heir to President Dwight D. Eisenhower. But in 1880 the party's convention promised to be wide open. The administration of President Hayes had been an eventful one, highlighted by the withdrawal of federal troops from the South, but Hayes had spurned renomination and

19

was virtually without influence in his own party. In terms of the G.O.P.'s future, Hayes' four years in the White House had served no purpose beyond delaying the political bloodletting now planned for Chicago.

Even before the gavel fell, there were three recognizable factions at the convention. Numerous and vocal were supporters of the "silent soldier," former President Ulysses S. Grant. His coterie was led by two prominent senators, Don Cameron of Pennsylvania and Roscoe Conkling of New York. The Pennsylvanian, whose father had served briefly as Lincoln's secretary of war, was the tactician of the Grant forces. Soft-spoken and reserved, quite unlike the prototype political boss, Cameron probed the convention rules for chinks which might be exploited by the Grant forces. Roscoe Conkling was quite a different story. Tall and domineering, a masterful orator whose bearded good-looks made him seem the embodiment of a senator, Conkling stood in the van of the Grant delegates and defied all comers.

Ranged against the Grant forces, though hardly in alliance, were supporters of James G. Blaine and John Sherman. The senator from Maine was in all likelihood the most popular man in the country with the Republican rank and file. Brilliant in debate and beloved by his supporters, Blaine had come within an ace of his party's nomination four years earlier. Only the abrupt adjournment of a convention seemingly prepared to stampede to the "plumed knight" had given his rivals the time they needed to coalesce behind the candidacy of a dark horse, Rutherford B. Hayes. A key to the 1880 Convention, however, was the long-standing enmity between Blaine and Conkling which made co-operation between their two factions impossible.

Finally, a variety of elements opposed to both Grant and Blaine had found refuge in the candidacy of John Sherman. The slightly built Ohioan with the "wise, eager little head" had been a competent secretary of the treasury for Hayes, and had long been prominent in the politics of his state. But Sherman was totally lacking in the charisma of a Blaine or a Conkling, to say nothing of the appeal of his brother, General William Tecumseh Sherman. "People will be knocked down for calling Blaine a thief," wrote one perceptive observer, "but whoever heard of anyone knocked down for calling Sherman a thief?" [1] It was perhaps symptomatic that even Sherman's manager, Congressman James A. Garfield, was personally more inclined toward Blaine than to his fellow-Ohioan. But Garfield wanted to move up to the Senate, and had agreed to manage Sherman's presidential bid in return for the latter's support.

Inside the mammoth Interstate Exposition Building, all was in readiness for the first Republican convention at which every state would be represented. The G.O.P. still counted itself the party of Lincoln, and the Civil War motif was very much in evidence. Many of the veterans in attendance wore their old uniforms, while one after another the bands broke out with "The Battle Hymn of the Republic," "We Are Coming, Father Abraham," and "Marching Through Georgia." Generals Phil Sheridan, John A. Logan, and Benjamin Harrison were among the delegates, and the 400-foot-long hall was dominated by a great portrait of Lincoln. More than 500 of the 15,000 gallery seats had been allocated to veterans—the "Boys in Blue" who continued to represent one of the bulwarks of the party.

The business of the convention began on June 2, after Don Cameron, chairman of the national committee, had brought the assemblage to order. Already, however, there was an air of crisis. Two nights before, public meetings of the pro- and anti-Grant groups had been held, one at Dearborn Park and one at the baseball field. The anti-Grant meeting drew a crowd of more than 10,000, and onlookers had listened attentively to speakers who denounced "boss rule" and who attacked any third term for Grant. These outdoor proceedings lent zest to a secret meeting of the national committee being held in the august Palmer House. There Cameron, as a tactic favorable to Grant, had pressed for a so-called unit rule, under which each delegate would be bound to support whatever candidate was favored by a majority of his state delegation. A majority of the national committee was anti-Grant, however, and insisted that the question be put to the floor. When the Pennsylvanian hedged, his committeemen insisted that unless they had more satisfactory assurances "he would be removed from the office of chairman, and a person who would carry out the wishes of the committee be substituted." [2]

Under the circumstances, Grant's supporters had no alternative other than to back down, and in so doing lost a key trick. The unit rule was defeated by the assembled delegates, who then went on to choose Senator George F. Hoar of Massachusetts as convention chairman. In the balloting for committees which followed, the Grant forces experienced further reverses. They were unable to control either the committee on credentials or the committee on rules. The chairmanship of the rules committee went to Sherman's manager, Garfield.

Stung by these early setbacks, the Grant forces attempted to regain the initiative. At the opening of the third session Conkling introduced a resolution to the effect that every delegate "is bound in honor to support the nominee, whoever that nominee may be; and that no man shall hold a seat here who is not ready to so agree." This innocuous resolution was passed with only three dissenting votes, but Conkling, seemingly overestimating his strength, haughtily demanded the expulsion of the dissenting delegates. This second resolution was roundly defeated, with Garfield among those speaking against it. "We come here as Republicans," he declared in his measured baritone, "and as one of our rights we can vote on every resolution 'aye' or 'no'. We are responsible for these votes to our constituents, and to them alone." [3]

Garfield's remarks were received with loud applause, a tribute both to their content and to the man who uttered them. The blue-eyed Ohioan, with his dark beard and athletic build, cut an impressive figure among the frock coats and well-filled vests on the delegates' platform. Garfield had served in Congress since 1863, where his intelligence and capacity for hard work had overcome the handicap of his association with some unsavory affairs of the Grant era, and had enabled him to reach the post of minority leader. At the convention, he was widely regarded as representing the best in orthodox Republicanism, and he probably had more personal friends among the delegates than anyone except Blaine.

Garfield was not comfortable in his role as Sherman's advocate, but he was determined to get through the job in a manner which would leave no room for criticism. Garfield was a worrier, and from his suite in the Grand Pacific Hotel he worried about his yet-unwritten speech for Sherman, the bad temper among the

Grant men, and the growing prospect of a deadlock among the supporters of Grant, Blaine, and Sherman. The Ohio congressman had a genuine distaste for the clashes of personality which so often characterized his party's conventions, and he looked forward to a seat in the U. S. Senate as affording opportunities for advancement as well as providing a select audience for the carefully researched speeches which he dearly loved.

By the time the convention was ready for nominations, Garfield was fairly widely regarded as the leader of those anti-Grant delegates who did not actively support Blaine. His role as Sherman's manager, his successful opposition to the unit rule, and his defense of the three dissenting delegates all showed him at his conciliatory best. There were, in fact, some in the hall who saw him as the party's eventual nominee. A small but noisy claque cheered Garfield's appearances, a fact which prompted Conkling to send the Ohioan a sarcastic note congratulating him on being the convention's dark horse.[4]

The nominating speeches began on June 5. Blaine, who had a tremendous following in the galleries, was first to be nominated. Four years before, the same ritual had inspired one of the memorable orations of American politics when Robert Ingersoll had nearly stampeded the convention for the "plumed knight" from Maine. But this year there would be no such oratorical flights. Passing over Ingersoll, Blaine's managers chose an unknown Detroit industrialist, James Joy, to deliver the address. Ungrammatical and seemingly apathetic, Joy apologized for having been chosen to make the speech, promised to be brief, and then stumbled through a text in which he once referred to the candidate as James *F.* Blaine.

After Blaine's nomination came several favorite sons including the senator from Minnesota, William Windom. A lawyer and a high-tariff man, Windom was one of a comparatively small number of Western spokesmen whose fiscal views were acceptable to the Eastern financiers whose backing was so critical to the G.O.P. The chair then recognized Senator Conkling of New York. Climbing upon a reporter's table in the middle of the hall, Conkling began with a bit of doggerel verse his speech nominating Grant for an unprecedented third term:

And when asked which State he hails from,
  Our sole reply shall be,
He hails from Appomattox
  And its famous apple tree.

The uproar that greeted these lines lasted for a full ten minutes. When the speaker resumed his address, his audience remained enthralled. "Every word, perfectly enunciated, reached every person in the hall; finished, polished phrases, exquisitely balanced periods, all were delivered in the manner of a master." [5]

Consider, then, the formidable Conkling. A native of upstate New York, he had first become prominent as a Republican congressman during the Civil War. He was elected to the Senate in 1867, where he opposed Andrew Johnson, supported President Grant, and through the latter made himself the arbiter of patronage throughout the state of New York.

It was evident almost from the first that there was not room enough in the Senate chamber for both him and James G. Blaine. There were no important policy differences between the two, and their *modus operandi* was strikingly similar. Their rivalry, rather, was a classic conflict of personality, fueled by the famous reference by Blaine to his rival's "turkey-gobbler strut." Each controlled the Republican machinery in his state; each was a master of the spread-eagle oratory of the day; each was ambitious up to and including the presidency. But whereas Blaine gained much of his strength through the warmth of his personality, it was for Conkling to command. The New Yorker was a complex personality:

> A musical voice heightened the attractiveness of a face with finely chiseled features and glittering steel-blue eyes, while wavy yellow hair made Conkling seem even taller than his six feet three inches. A careless elegance in dress and a fondness for exotic colors vaguely suggested a Byronic temperament, but his ruthless pursuit of power dispelled any illusion that Conkling was a dreamy nineteenth-century romantic. Behind an arrogant manner lurked a gnawing sense of inadequacy. Not only was Conkling abnormally sensitive to slights, but he brooded over unimportant remarks that most men would have ignored. . . . His defense mechanism was a haughtiness unprecedented in American politics.[6]

Haughtiness may not have been his only defense mechanism. For several years there had been rumors of intimacy between Conkling and the legendary Kate Chase Sprague, by then the wife of a retired senator from Rhode Island. (Conkling was a physical culturist of sorts, and it was said that he possessed the most "magnificent torso" in the U. S. Senate.) This was the Conkling who now waited for the chairman to bring the convention to order so that he might resume his paean to Ulysses S. Grant. The orator continued with the vibrant resonance of one who would have spurned an amplifier even had such a contrivance been known in 1880:

> Having tried Grant twice and found him faithful, we are told that we must not, even after an interval of years, trust him again. My countrymen! My countrymen!—What stultification does not such a fallacy involve. . . . From the man who shoes your horse to the lawyer who tries your cause . . . what man do you reject because by his works you have known him, and found him faithful and fit?
>
> Gentlemen, we have only to listen above the din and look beyond the dust of an hour to behold the Republican party advancing, with its ensigns resplendent with illustrious achievement, marching to certain and lasting victory with its greatest Marshal at its head.[7]

The roar which greeted this oratorical tour de force far eclipsed the response to any of the preceding nominating speeches, and threw consternation into the anti-Grant forces. Was Conkling to do for Grant what Ingersoll had so narrowly missed doing for Blaine four years before? As Chairman Hoar gaveled the convention back to order, there was no way of knowing that Conkling's oration had represented the high-water mark of Grant's drive, or that factional lines were so tightly drawn on the convention floor that few if any delegates were in a mood to be swayed by oratory.

After Conkling it was Garfield's turn. Faced with the task of overcoming Conkling's spell, he delivered, with only a occasional glance at his notes, the most memorable rebuttal of his debating career. "I have witnessed the extraordinary scenes of this convention with solicitude," he began deliberately. "Nothing touches my heart more quickly than a tribute of honor to a great and noble character; but as I sat in my seat and witnessed this demonstration, this assemblage seemed to me a human ocean in tempest." There followed one of Garfield's drawn-out nautical similes. Conkling, who had heard the convention's occasional cheers for Garfield with suspicion, rose and left the hall. "The man's making me seasick," he snorted. Garfield moved on. "And now, gentlemen of the convention, what do we want?"

A voice from the floor interrupted, "We want Garfield!"

The speaker moved on to a recapitulation of the triumphs of the Republican party, the party of Lincoln and free men. New mandates could be won only by a united party, he insisted, and he made capital out of Conkling's taunts at the Blaine forces. Victory could not be won by "assailing our Republican brethren. . . . To win this victory now, we want the vote of every Republican, of every Grant Republican in America, of every Blaine man and every anti-Blaine man." Only after this plea for unity did Garfield move on to his discussion of Sherman, whose virtues he outlined with eloquence but without great passion:

> He has shown himself able to meet with calmness the great emergencies of the Government for twenty-five years. He has trodden the perilous heights of public duty, and against all the shafts of malice has borne his breast unharmed. . . .
> I do not present him as a better Republican, or a better man than thousands of others we honor, but I present him for your deliberate consideration. I nominate John Sherman, of Ohio.[8]

Garfield was never in better form than for this joust before a national audience, with the presidential nomination as the prize. But mixed with the praise of the Republican press was a dose of cynicism. The *New York Times* reported that "those who were unable to recognize the Secretary of the Treasury as the ideal man whose picture he drew, begin to think that the picture was Gen. Garfield's picture of himself. Suggestions to this effect have been made by men who are in no way hostile to Gen. Garfield, and who see in the course he has pursued during the Convention indications of an honest desire to advance his own fortunes." [9]

Two more favorite sons were placed before the convention,

which then adjourned for the night. When voting began on June 7, it seemed relatively tame by comparison to the impassioned oratory which had gone before. The first roll call saw Grant take a small lead over a divided field:

U. S. Grant	304	George Edmunds	34
James G. Blaine	284	Elihu B. Washburne	30
John Sherman	93	William Windom	10

These figures were to remain almost static throughout the day, except that on nearly every successive ballot Garfield received one or two votes from either Pennsylvania or Alabama. By the end of the day, after twenty-eight ballots, the convention was tightly deadlocked, with the three leaders claiming 307, 279, and 91 votes respectively.

The rules did not permit debate between ballots, and this fact, plus the fact that the three main factions were mutually antagonistic, forced the convention into a sequence of ballots which saw little change. On the morning of the 8th, Grant fluctuated between 302 and 312, Blaine between 275 and 285, and Sherman between 91 and 120. Only the latter enjoyed any sort of a "boomlet," but his total fell off after reaching 120 on the thirtieth ballot.

The fact that Sherman was not acceptable as an alternative to Grant and Blaine finally led to a break on the thirty-fourth ballot when sixteen delegates from Wisconsin—largely Blaine and Washburne men—switched to Garfield, who was increasingly talked about as a compromise candidate. His comings and goings had become a signal for whistles and cheers from a claque of admirers whose number had grown as the deadlock in the balloting had become pronounced. With the move by Wisconsin, Garfield felt it incumbent on him to reiterate that his candidacy, such as it was, was a passive one. The result was a memorable dialogue between Garfield and Chairman Hoar.

'Mr. President.'
'For what purpose does the gentleman rise?'
'I rise to a question of order.'
'The gentleman from Ohio rises to a question of order.'

'I challenge the correctness of the announcement. The announcement contains votes for me. No man has a right, without the consent of the person voted for, to announce that person's name, and vote for him, in this convention. Such consent I have not given.'

'The gentleman from Ohio is not stating a question of order. He will resume his seat. No person having received a majority of the votes cast, another ballot will be taken. The clerk will call the roll.' [10]

In his memoirs Hoar wrote,

This verbatim report is absolutely correct, except that where there is a period at the end of Mr. Garfield's last sentence there should be a dash, indicating that the sentence was not finished. I recollect this incident perfectly. I interrupted him in the middle of his sentence. I was terribly afraid that he would say something that would make his nomination impossible.[11]

The chairman need not have been so anxious. Garfield was not about to slam any doors; he did, however, want to make it clear that his behavior was above reproach. In any case, the stampede began on the next roll call. The thirty-fifth ballot saw Garfield's total reach 50, largely as a result of the switch of twenty-seven Blaine men in the Indiana delegation. On the next roll call, with 378 votes required for nomination, Garfield went over the top with 399 votes. Only the Grant delegates—the Stalwart 306—stood by their candidate to the end.

On the floor and in the gallery, all was pandemonium. Cannons were fired on the Exposition grounds, while weary delegates pressed to congratulate the party's new standard bearer. There were a variety of impressions of how Garfield reacted to the occasion. Some spoke of his poise and composure; others saw him as the most surprised person on the floor. One of his first acts was the somewhat embarrassing chore of assuring the Sherman delegates that he had done all he could for their candidate. One by one, spokesmen for the various delegations rose to move that the nomination be made unanimous.

In accordance with political tradition, a committee headed

by Senator Hoar called upon Garfield that evening at his hotel to formally advise him of his nomination. The candidate replied briefly and modestly that "I have felt, with you, great solicitude concerning the situation of our party" during the convention, but expressed confidence in the prospect of a united party for the campaign. That same evening he cabled to his wife, "If the result meets your approval I shall be content. Love to all the household."

The news of Garfield's nomination was received in much of the country with pleasure and surprise. Although few Democrats would cross party lines to vote for him in November, the public loves an underdog, and not even Democrats were entirely immune from the excitement of the Ohioan's unexpected victory. His party had every intention of exploiting this appeal, and Republican papers were already setting type which would extol Garfield's career as the embodiment of the American Dream. He had received his party's highest honor; now it remained only for the electorate to provide a happy ending to the saga which had begun in a log cabin in Ohio's Western Reserve.

Chapter Two

THE WESTERN
RESERVE

James A. Garfield was forty-eight when he was nominated for the presidency, younger than all but three major party candidates up to that time, but then he had always been something of a prodigy. He was born on November 19, 1831, a few miles south of the city of Cleveland in that part of northern Ohio popularly known as the Western Reserve. Although scarcely developed in the 1830s, the Reserve was a fertile land dominated by virgin forests which in time would give way to homesteads and dairy farms, and eventually to railroad cuts and iron mills.

It was in the second and third decades of the eighteenth century that the first few settlers moved into the Reserve, primarily from southern New England. The Garfields were originally from Massachusetts, and traced their residence there as far back as 1630. In 1760, Solomon Garfield became the first of the family to make the trek westward, moving in that year from eastern Massachusetts to the area of Cooperstown, New York. Nearly forty years later his grandson, Abram Garfield, joined the post-Revolution migration west of the Alleghenies. The Western Reserve at that time was

30

hardly the inviting land which it would later become. Not until William Henry Harrison broke the power of Tecumseh at the Battle of the Thames would the Reserve achieve the measure of security necessary to attract settlers in significant numbers.

In 1819, Abram Garfield met and married Eliza Ballou, herself a New England immigrant to Ohio. It was she who was the great influence on their children, for she more than made up for her lack of formal education with self-reliance and imagination. Abram Garfield brought to their union a dogged diligence and a robust physique; it was said that "he could take a barrel of whiskey by the chime, and drink out of the bung-hole." Eliza, for her part, brought an ear for music and a strong religious faith.

When Jim Garfield was born the Western Reserve was largely wilderness. Its largest town, Cleveland, had scarcely one thousand inhabitants. Living was never easy, even for those who prospered, and Abram Garfield never really prospered. At times during the 1820s he had abandoned farming for land speculation, gambling that the success of the Erie Canal might lead to a similar route between Cleveland and the Ohio River. By 1831 he had returned to a 20-acre farm near Orange, where he first erected a modest log cabin to house his family. Thus it was a father's straitened circumstances that caused James A. Garfield to become the last president of the United States to be born in a log cabin.

Jim Garfield had no clear recollection of his father, who died of a fever when the boy was not yet two, and scarcely better recollection of his own birthplace. Later, however, when he was twenty-three, Garfield stopped at Orange. The sight of the old cabin, long since fallen into disuse, stirred memories which might otherwise have escaped a young man who was constantly being lured by new vistas. "The old stone backwall to the chimney is still standing," Garfield wrote, "and as I stood there and looked upon those stones it brought vividly to my mind the days of my childhood, when that wall served as a screen against which the blaze of the log fire was leaping and crackling . . . in all the imaginations of a childish fancy." [1]

The death of her husband in 1833 left Eliza Garfield with the responsibility of bringing up four children, the eldest of whom, Thomas, was ten. The two sisters, Mehitabel and Mary, were seven and four respectively, while Jim was still an infant. Although Tom was both strong and devoted, the stilted prose of later campaign biographies fails to do justice to the responsibilities shouldered by the Widow Garfield.

> She lost no time in irresolution, but plunged at once into the roughest sort of men's labor. The wheatfield was only half fenced; the precious harvest which was to be their sustenance through the winter was still ungathered, and would be destroyed by the roving cattle, which had been turned loose during the forest fires. The emergency had to be met, and she met it. Finding in the woods some trees, fresh fallen beneath her husband's glittering ax, she commenced the hard work of splitting rails. . . . Day by day the worm fence crawled around the wheat field, until the ends met.[2]

Clearly, the farm was approaching viability at the time of Abram Garfield's death. But even allowing for this factor, and for the assistance provided by neighbors, Eliza Garfield emerges as a woman of considerable fortitude. The winter of 1833–34 was one of privation for the Garfields. But in the following spring the soil began to yield, and the family improved its finances through the sale of 50 acres of undeveloped land. The problem became one of storing the harvest of corn and potatoes.

Once stomachs were full, there was the question of schooling. Immigrants to the Western Reserve brought with them much of the New Englander's preoccupation with education, and when the township of Orange sought land for a rude schoolhouse, it was the Widow Garfield who offered a corner of her own farm. Her motives were not altogether altruistic. It was becoming rapidly apparent that young Jim was a precocious child, and she probably hoped that a school nearby would allow time for both school and farm chores. Meanwhile, Tom Garfield was the man of the house. When Jim and his sisters set out across the fields to the schoolhouse, Tom stayed home to work the farm. This appears to have been a sensible arrangement, for Jim never was particularly handy about the barn. His wife wrote in later years, "In many ways he was a blundering, careless boy. To learn the use of an axe, he was obliged almost a score of times to . . . hobble on crutches, disabled by fearful gashes made through his carelessness.

Once he came near killing his cousin Silas Boynton by heedless use of an axe, and within a hair's breadth of ending his own life by plunging headlong down through a mill." [3]

By the time he was sixteen, a boyhood on the farm had given Garfield a sturdy physique and a reputation as a diligent if not dexterous worker. He had not developed any aptitude for farm life, however, and when the first adventure beckoned he took his leave, at some cost to his mother's feelings. As Garfield recalled the episode, he was determined to become a sailor.

> Nautical novels did it. I had read a large number of them, all I could get in the neighborhood. My mother tried to turn my attention in other directions, but the books were considered bad and from that very fact were fascinating. I remember especially the "Pirate's Own Book" which became a sort of bible or general authority with me at that period. In the spring of 1848 I chopped 100 cords of wood upon a farm in Newburg, Cuyahoga county, within sight of the Lake, and the passage of a ship made me almost insane with delight.[4]

Eliza Garfield was bitterly opposed to her son's departure. Hittie and Mary were married and gone, while Tom, having helped in the building of a frame house to replace the old cabin, had just departed to seek his fortune in Michigan. But Jim was not to be dissuaded, and in July 1848 he set out for the Cleveland waterfront. Rebuffed in his first attempt to land a berth in one of the lake vessels, Garfield sought employment on a canal boat, apparently out of some vague idea that such employment might constitute an apprenticeship for the sea.

The Ohio and Pennsylvania Canal was part of the network of waterways that connected the Great Lakes with the industrial towns of Pennsylvania and New York. Major items of trade were iron and copper ore, which came to Cleveland from the West by schooner and then were shipped to manufacturing centers such as Akron and Pittsburgh. The barges returned with coal and, occasionally, manufactured goods. The canals themselves were fairly primitive. The barges were towed by teams of horses or mules on a towpath, and the "seamanship" required was minimal.

Life along the canal was also fairly primitive, but the barge on which he signed—the *Evening Star*—happened to be owned by another Garfield cousin, Amos Letcher, who took a paternal interest in the boy. Even so Garfield was repeatedly obliged to defend himself, and his later biographies abound with stories of how the sea-struck teenager stood his ground against the ruffians of the canal. Garfield stuck with the *Evening Star*, and in the course of one trip to Pittsburgh was promoted from the lowly task of mule-driver to work on the deck of the barge.

In the early part of the year Garfield had begun keeping the diary which, after several false starts, would become the daily journal which he kept with only occasional lapses for the rest of his life. Writing of his four months on the canal, however, he limited himself to a skeletal outline:

> Aug. 16 Wed. went to Cleveland hired on Canal boat Evening Star to my cousin A Letcher started up the Canal. 17 Thur we pursued our journey up the canal through Akron &c &c our loading consisted of fifty-two tons of Copper ore taken on at Cleveland and destined for Pittsburg. From Akron we turned East on the Cross cut which passes through Cuyahoga Falls, Franklin, Ravenna, Warren, Youngstown and a short distance [from] the latter place it forms a junction with the Erie extension and from there we went to Beaver on the Ohio River. hired a steamboat to tow us up the river to Pittsburgh where we arrived on the 26th. Sun 27 took a stroll [about] the place listened to two sermons in the street by men hired by the authorities of the place. . . .
> Wed. 30 arrived at Youngstown took 60 tons Coal and started for Cleveland where we arrived September second. Staid over Sunday unloaded Monday and started up the Canal again. My business is bowing which is to make the locks ready, get the boat through trim the lamps &c I get 14 dollars per month.[5]

Garfield's enthusiasm for the sea was not complemented by knowledge of how to swim, and it soon developed that he was in as great danger from drowning as from the ruffians who sailed the canal. By Garfield's own count, he took fourteen tumbles into the water while tending the lines. One night, while alone on the deck, he once more lost his balance, and found himself in the water unable either to swim or to make his cries heard. Floundering, he seized the line which had gone over with him, only to have it continue to pay out over the side of the barge. Providentially, the line hit a snag, and held fast. All but exhausted, Garfield pulled himself back into the boat.

After such an escape, Garfield can hardly be blamed for concluding that his future lay on dry land. Early in November he parted amicably with his friends on the *Evening Star* and returned to his mother in Orange. The rigors of canal life appear to have taken their toll; once home, Garfield came down with a fever that prostrated him for five months. But his stint on the canal had been more than a lark, for Garfield had seen more in a few months than many of his neighbors would see in a lifetime spent in northern Ohio. The canal had forced him to develop self-reliance, while at the same time convincing him that his future lay elsewhere than on the Ohio and Pennsylvania Canal.

Garfield's bout of fever put him largely at the mercy of his mother, who renewed her importuning that he stay closer to home. A feeling of responsibility toward his mother, together with a feeling that he had "had his fling," led Jim to accept her suggestion that he return to school. In the neighboring town of Chester, east of Orange, there was a new school, with the somewhat pretentious title of Geauga Academy. By the criteria of the Reserve, Geauga was a clear cut above the log schoolhouse in Orange; it boasted a faculty of six, a student body of more than a hundred, and a library of 150 volumes.

Thus in March 1849 Garfield began his first formal schooling. With him were two close friends—a cousin, William Boynton, and a neighboring youth, Orrin Judd, with whom Jim initially shared lodgings. By all accounts, Garfield was a diligent student. After the spring term he took on farm chores in order to pay his tuition and to meet the doctor's bills of the past winter. Returning to Geauga for the fall term, he worked out an arrangement with a local carpenter whereby he would receive board and lodging for $1.06 per week. In two terms at Geauga, he picked up the rudiments of grammar, algebra, and "philosophy."

In November, under an arrangement common in that day, Garfield applied for and received a certificate of his fitness to teach school. He had himself studied under instructors who were scarcely a chapter ahead of their students in the text; now it would be Garfield's turn to pursue the few dollars to be earned by teaching at some country school. After several rebuffs, the eighteen-year-old Garfield found a position at the Ledge School that paid $12 per month and board. But the lot of the frontier teacher was no bed of roses. On January 4, 1850, Garfield wrote in his diary,

> Compositions and declamations. A boy sixteen years old refused to obey me and was very saucy. I flogged him severely and told him to take his seat. He caught a billet of wood and came after me and we had a merry time. He vamosed [sic].[6]

With the money thus hard-earned, Garfield took his first trip outside the Reserve since his canal-barge days. Traveling with his mother early in 1851, he took his first train ride from Cleveland to Columbus on a newly opened line. There, the legislative delegate from Geauga County, Gamaliel Kent, showed mother and son the sights of the capital. After having seen the legislature, where he would one day sit, Garfield was unimpressed with the members on the floor. "Their rubicund, bloated faces spoke plainly of the midnight bowl," he wrote, "and in my opinion unfitted them for representing the free people of a great state."

Garfield subsequently returned to Geauga Academy for the final of the four terms which would constitute his principal preparation for college. In his later writings, the often-sentimental Garfield noted with satisfaction "the work which was accomplished for me at Chester. . . . While there I formed a definite purpose and plan to complete a college course. It is a great point gained when a young man makes up his mind to devote several years to the accomplishment of a definite work." [7] Actually, Garfield appears to have become restless in his final year at Geauga. He had, during the previous year, been baptized into his mother's church, the Disciples of Christ, and he took to his new faith with fervor. Not surprisingly, he found the Baptist atmosphere at Geauga distasteful.

One offshoot of this new religious zeal was to have considerable bearing on his later choice of careers. Philosophical subjects had always interested young Garfield, but heretofore this interest

had manifested itself in omnivorous reading and in occasional reflections in his diary. With his conversion, however, he became
increasingly interested in the science of debate, and became quite
at home on the speaker's platform. His immaturity, however, led
him down strange byways. In March 1850, he opposed in debate
the immediate emancipation of slaves and, to confirm that his
stand was one of conviction rather than happenstance, noted in
his diary that "the simple relation of master and slave is not un-
christian." A later entry suggests that Garfield had discovered the
joys of debate for debate's sake:

> I have engaged to support in debate the following proposition;
> viz., that Christians have no right to participate in human gov-
> ernments. . . . It creates some excitement. Never mind. I love
> agitation and investigation and glory in defending unpopular
> truth against popular error.[8]

When he entered Hiram Institute that fall, Garfield in effect
turned his back on the frontier for what then looked like a career
in teaching or in the ministry. Nevertheless, he regarded himself
as a son of the frontier, and never overcame a nostalgia for his
boyhood on the farm. His attitude was in no sense unusual. In a
eulogy delivered not long after Garfield's death, his friend Jacob
Cox articulated the pastoral ideal in terms of which Garfield
would doubtless have approved:

> I can think of few more healthy places for the growth of mind
> and body than a farming community in Northern Ohio fifty
> years ago. . . . The country was just passing from the rude
> condition of first settlements in the wilderness to that of a
> thriving industrial region, dotted with prosperous villages.
> . . . Under such circumstances poverty had none of the degra-
> dation which too often accompanies it in old and populous
> communities. Here was no squalor, no vice, no loss of caste. It
> involved no closing of any career to a boy who had health and
> courage, brains and will.[9]

One gathers from Cox's remarks that, even as he spoke, he
mourned the passing of an era. Many of his contemporaries, even
then, doubtless did likewise. For when Garfield entered politics,

and especially when he campaigned for the presidency, one of his strongest assets would be his appeal to those who saw in his rise a vindication of the American Dream: from the farm to the White House.

Chapter Three

THE YOUNG
ZEALOT

———◆———

An attempt to make Garfield's life out to be the typical American success story would not be inappropriate, for many of the elements are there: intelligence, persistence, and good luck. But Garfield's was not a "typical" boyhood, even should one concede that there is such a thing. He was good-natured, and capable of being outgoing on occasion. But for the most part he was introspective, and one is conscious of an absence of creditable anecdotes concerning his youth. At a time when many boys were discovering the opposite sex, or at least enjoying a pipe behind the corncrib, Jim Garfield was undergoing a religious awakening.

The Disciples of Christ were the creation of two Scottish immigrants, Thomas Campbell and his son Alexander, who had separated from the Baptists in the 1820s. Theologically, the Campbellites were fundamentalists in that they rejected all "interpretations" of the Scriptures—"Where the Bible speaks, there we speak; where the Bible is silent, there we are silent." The Campbells were zealous propagandists. Although the new denomination originated in western Virginia, it spread rapidly into frontier areas where the Campbellite emphasis on simplicity of worship struck a responsive chord.

The Campbellite mecca was Bethany, Virginia, where Alexander Campbell had founded Bethany College in 1840. Emulating their leader, the Disciples established schools and colleges elsewhere. One such school was at Hiram, Ohio, where an energetic Campbellite community inaugurated a typical single-building "college" with the pretentious title of the Western Reserve Eclectic Institute. * The principal, A. Sutton Hayden, was a Campbellite preacher, and the six-man faculty consisted entirely of Disciples. The curriculum was patterned on the classic model of the day, but little importance was attached either to the course of study or to the qualifications of instructors. In the revivalist atmosphere of Hiram, the emphases were on fraternity and Christian teaching.

Garfield's two years as a student at the Eclectic are of little interest in terms of their influence on him as an adult. He entered as a notably immature twenty-year-old and left, after two years of emotional and spiritual ferment, little changed in outlook. Nor was there any significant intellectual awakening; the rigidly classical curriculum, together with the pervasive religious zeal, made such an experience unlikely. In terms of personal relationships, however, the years at Hiram were important ones. In his years there, he formed more lasting personal attachments than in any comparable period in his life. Partially as a result of these friendships, Garfield began an association with the Eclectic which was to prove a durable one.

"My first impression of him," wrote his friend Corydon Fuller, "is as a young man . . . about 6 feet in height, powerfully built, with a head of bushy hair and weighing about 185 pounds." Presumably it was the entire Garfield, not just the head, that weighed 185 pounds; nevertheless, his friends recalled that Garfield's head was proportionately large for one of his build.

As is often the case, Garfield's emotional maturity was far behind his physical maturity. The bond that developed between him and his religious brothers and sisters at Hiram became a

* The Eclectic survives today as Hiram College, a coeducational institution with a student body of over 1,000 and still affiliated with the Disciples of Christ.

deep psychological attachment. He filled his diary with rhapsodic entries and even occasional flights of poetry, which in later life he would read with some amusement. When, after his first semester at Hiram, he was invited to deliver a "valedictory," the address which resulted was a commentary both on the speaker and on the accepted literary standards of the day:

> Three short months have been chronicled since a band of strangers met within these walls. We had left the society of friends and parents, the endearments of home, to seek the sparkling gems of science, to expand and elevate the mind, to raise the soul and point it to the skies. . . . [But] what one of our number, ere another sunny spring visits the earth, shall have gone to inhabit the silent city of the dead? We part. Death does his work and we sink down into his dark domains.[1]

Later, in 1874, Garfield wrote in his diary,

> In the evening got out my journals of 1851–4 and read till after midnight. I am amazed at the gush and slush of those days. I was a very pulpy boy till I was at least twenty-two years old. But . . . I was dead in earnest and was working by the best light I had. In looking over it now I am not ashamed of the most of it.[2]

Garfield was justified in speaking about his earnestness, for the same enthusiasm which took such maudlin form on the printed page drove him to excel in his studies at the Eclectic. He devoured all that his instructors had to offer—Latin, Greek, mathematics. He was able to continue the debating which he had found so congenial at Geauga and, since the Disciples had no ordained clergy, was able to indulge his religious bent in the pulpit. Had the same opportunities been combined with a more stimulating intellectual climate, the years at Hiram might have been definitive.

In his first year, Garfield once more helped support himself with work as a carpenter's assistant. His friend Fuller, who was also working his way, recalled how he and Garfield would "talk of the past and the future and build air-castles; we were both young

. . . and spent little time in regretting that we had not plenty of money we had not earned." Fuller was a close friend, more so than William B. Hazen, another Disciple who, like Garfield, would end up as a Union general. But the person who exerted the greatest influence on Garfield at Hiram was Almeda Booth. The formidable Miss Booth had arrived at the Eclectic at the same time Garfield did. Like him, she had a taste for the classics; she was reputed to have digested Gibbon's *Decline and Fall of the Roman Empire* at the age of twelve, and to have taught school at seventeen. She had boarded with President Hayden from the time of her arrival at Hiram, and when Garfield was similarly invited to live in the president's house he and Almeda became fast friends. In the summer of 1853, Garfield, Almeda Booth, and several others decided to spend their holiday in study of the classics. Garfield's later description of this interlude tells much of the standards of the day:

> Miss Booth read thoroughly, and for the first time, the *Pastorals* of Virgil . . . and the first six books of Homer's *Iliad*, accompanied by a thorough drill in the Latin or Greek Grammar at each recitation. I am sure that none of those who recited with her would say that she was behind the foremost in the thoroughness of her work, or in the elegance of her translation.
>
> During the Fall Term of 1853, she read one hundred pages of Herodotus, and about the same amount of Livy. During that term also, Profs. Dunshee and Hull and Miss Booth and I met, at her room, two evenings of each week, to make a joint translation of the Book of Romans. . . . How nearly we completed the translation, I do not remember.[3]

The dominant influence on Garfield during his first year at Hiram appears to have been the intellect of Miss Booth, and it is a commentary on his zeal that Garfield's preoccupation with ancient Greek overshadowed the first flutterings of romance. One of his contemporaries at Hiram was Lucretia Rudolph, called "Crete" by her friends, with whom Garfield had first shared a classroom at Geauga Academy. Like Garfield, she was a Disciple whose parents had moved to Ohio from New England. In 1852 the Rudolphs had moved to Hiram, where their daughter was en-

rolled at the Eclectic. But even as they resumed the role of school-
mates, there was no love at first sight between Garfield and his future wife. In fact, for several months in 1852 Garfield was
infatuated with a girl from Warrensville, Mary Hubbell. According to his official biographer, Theodore Clarke Smith, this torrid
romance was "utterly naïve and youthful and, as might have
been foreseen, written in water." The fact was, however, that only
after he had broken off this affair, which had reached a point
where marriage could be cautiously discussed, could Garfield,
after a protracted period of emotional self-examination, turn his
attention to Lucretia Rudolph.

This young lady, however, was quite a remarkable person in
her own right, a dark-eyed brunette whose outward shyness concealed an affectionate nature and remarkable strength of character. Her relationship with Garfield was in many respects a case of
opposites attracting. The devout Lucretia was inclined to conceal
her feelings and outwardly did little to encourage Garfield's interest. He, on the other hand, could be suffocating in his affections.
"I am so constituted," he wrote in his diary, "that I cannot enjoy
a cold formal friend . . . but must be as familiar as to a brother
or to a sister." [4]

The one thread which runs strongly through Garfield's writings at this time is his intense religious conviction. Indeed, anyone meeting him would probably have concluded that he was
headed for the ministry. But his prowess in the classroom again
brought teaching opportunities, and he and Almeda Booth were
invited to lecture in some subjects while reciting in others. One
suspects that, by the standards of the Reserve, Garfield was above
average as a teacher. In one of his earliest known letters Garfield
wrote from Warrensville, Ohio, in 1852, "Oh, that I possessed the
power to scatter the firebrands of ambition among the youth of
the rising generation, and let them see the greatness of the age in
which they live and the destiny to which mankind are rushing.
. . ." [5] Garfield was nothing if not a romantic. Even after he
learned to cool his metaphors, the romantic strain would persist.
But it was an idealistic age, and Garfield was hardly unique in his
romanticism. At about the same age another future president,
Rutherford B. Hayes, was writing in his diary, "What a world of

time and brains are wasted in idle daydreams, castle-building visions of happiness too rapturous for reality. Am I in love, that it grows on me, or is it habit rising unchecked? . . . If in love, where's the sweetheart?" [6]

By the spring of 1854, Garfield was engaged in a cautious courtship of Miss Rudolph. Garfield was full of self-doubt. "I hope," he confided in his diary in February, "by the assistance of my Heavenly Father to move cautiously and judiciously in reference to the sacred subject of matrimony." But Garfield persevered, and before he left for Williams College he and "Crete" had reached an understanding tantamount to engagement.

During his second and final year at Hiram, Garfield gave considerable thought to his further education. In the summer of 1853 he had made a pilgrimage to Bethany College. It was a curious visit. On the one hand, Garfield was enthusiastic over his first meeting with Alexander Campbell, concluding that he was "a living wonder." But he was less impressed with Bethany College. The debating society was a disappointment, and debating was rapidly becoming Garfield's principal intellectual diversion. Nor did the faculty impress the young visitor from Ohio. Without attending a class, he rather surprisingly decided that Bethany would not do.

Although Garfield's decision was ostensibly made on pragmatic grounds, it appears likely that sectional bias played a part. Bethany was at that time located in the slaveholding state of Virginia. Although there were comparatively few slaves in the western portion of the state, the atmosphere was still a good deal more Southern than that of the Western Reserve. Garfield was not politically aware at this time. Unlike the majority of his neighbors, he took no interest in the Underground Railroad, the key sectional compromises of the day, or even local politics. Thus his initial political predilections appear to have grown out of an intuitive dislike of some of the trappings of "Southern" society which he saw in Virginia. After observing commencement at Bethany, Garfield wrote in his diary in July 1853, "There was a vein of flattery running through almost every speech, i.e., flattering the ladies,—and a kind of noisy patriotism which ill comports with the feelings of our Ohio people. . . . I cannot endure that southern dandyism, so interwoven with the manners of many of the students there."

So Garfield determined to go East, arguing in part that "I thought best for the sake of liberalizing my mind, to spend some time in the atmosphere of New England, which is so different from our Western institutions." He wrote to the presidents of Brown, Yale, and Williams, describing his studies to date and asking what would be required of him to graduate. In his diary, Garfield told how he reached his final decision.

> Their answers are now before me. All tell me I can graduate in two years. They are all brief, business notes, but President Hopkins concludes with this sentence: "If you come here, we shall be glad to do what we can for you." Other things being so near equal, this sentence . . . has settled the question for me. I shall start for Williams next week.[7]

With his arrival at Williams in the fall of 1854 Garfield left behind him the frontier haunts of his youth for what passed for the mainstream of American education. Williams was a venerable institution as American colleges went. Founded as a free school in 1793, it had led a hand to mouth existence until 1836, when it chose as president a member of the faculty, Mark Hopkins, who was to become one of the legendary figures of American education. The new president infused new blood into the faculty, gained the confidence of the surrounding communities, and transformed a struggling country college into a respected citadel of the conventional wisdom of the day.

Garfield arrived at Williams at a time of gradual but significant change. For three decades Williams—along with many liberal-arts institutions—had modeled its curriculum after that of Yale, with emphasis on mathematics, the classics, and intellectual and moral philosophy. Rejecting any suggestion that colleges should adapt their curricula to "the business character of the nation," the Yale trustees emphasized the disciplining of the mind and character development. Williams, under Mark Hopkins, followed closely the example set by Yale, but the period of Hopkins' presidency saw a gradual modification of the "classic" curriculum. A semester of American history had been offered since 1843. German became an elective three years later. History and political economy had become a standard portion of the curriculum.

For most students, however, the subjects taught at Williams were of minor interest alongside the inspiration of Dr. Hopkins. "The object of the college," said Hopkins, "is to make men." He himself was no scholar, although his senior-year course in moral philosophy was one of Williams' drawing cards. In his scheme of things, Christian influence was far more important than subject matter, and the great aim of education was to help the student to perceive religious truth. "As he moved through the lectures on moral philosophy," Hopkins' biographer has written, "the president approached each spring the question of choice, at which time he made abundantly clear to every senior that within his own power lay the opportunity to choose God or reject Him." [8]

Hopkins, of course, was not alone in placing such stress on religion. Where he stood out was in his effectiveness as a teacher. He was unwilling for classes to be mere exercises in memory and recitation, although by present-day standards there was no shortage of either. The responsibility of the teacher, according to Hopkins, was "to watch the progress of the individual mind, and awaken interest, and answer objections." It was into this paradoxically stimulating citadel of conservatism that Garfield bounded in the summer of 1854, still wet behind the ears.

For young Garfield this new phase in his education was both an adventure and a challenge, and any misgivings which he may have had were lost in a general euphoria. It rained in the course of his steamer trip from Cleveland to Buffalo, a fact which caused Garfield to note in his diary that "the murmuring cadence of the deep had swelled into the storm's pealing anthem." He delighted in the trip down the Hudson from Albany, as he once more experienced a scenic grandeur so different from his native Ohio. Following a visit to New York City, Garfield traveled by train to Hoosick, New York, and hence by stage the remaining 17 miles to Williamstown. For decades previous, student hearts had sunk at the thought of the enforced isolation brought by each new term at Williams. But to Garfield, Williamstown was quite civilized. In his eyes, the college town of some 3,000 persons was a "beautiful little village" whose mountainous surroundings made it seem "like a diamond in an emerald casket."

Garfield came to grips with academic reality when he presented himself to Dr. Hopkins for examination. He appears to have had some idea of graduating in less than a full two years, but Hopkins quickly disabused him. Nevertheless, the Ohioan was impressed with what he saw, especially the faculty. An academically qualified faculty was something new for him, and Williams would be the first school he had attended where he was not invited to join the faculty after a semester or two.

There were other adjustments, also. In a letter to his mother he complained of the high cost of living ("Board, room, washing and all cost me $3.00 per week now"), and there was the lack of feminine companionship. "I have the best of board," he wrote to his friend Fuller, "but the boarders happen to be about the roughest in college. . . . The absence of females from table and society takes away a very wholesome restraint and leaves roughness in its stead." Nor did Garfield adjust quickly to the fairly cosmopolitan student body, drawn primarily from the urban centers of New York and New England. Having arrived a full two months before the beginning of the fall term, he passed the time in private study, particularly to bring up his mathematics. There was much to interest him, even between semesters. He wrote in a letter to Fuller, "On Tuesday I listened to an address from Ralph Waldo Emerson of Boston, and I must say he is the most startlingly original thinker I have ever heard. . . . I could not sleep that night after hearing his thunderstorm of eloquent thoughts."

Garfield encountered little difficulty with his first year's course of study. In a letter to Lucretia he described his daily schedule:

> Rise and attend prayers in the chapel at 5 and then recite one
> hour in Quintilian. Then go a quarter of a mile to breakfast.
> At 9 o'clock, three times a week attend lectures on Philosophy
> and at 11 recite in Mechanics. At 4 P.M. Greek for an hour,
> then prayers. In addition to these there are occasional exercises
> in themes, debates and orations.[9]

Garfield's adjustment to campus life was, initially, somewhat less successful. Like any transfer student, he moved into a social

47

orbit where friendships had already been made, and where in-
groups already existed. Garfield's problem in gaining acceptance
was underscored by his painful earnestness, as well as by self-con-
sciousness concerning his religious convictions. He found the Cal-
vinistic religious atmosphere at Williams uncongenial, and probably found ways of registering his disapproval. Garfield's roommate
was a fellow Disciple from Ohio, Charles D. Wilber, and at first
the two were left largely to their own devices. According to one
classmate, "They made no attempt to conform to the ways and pe-
culiarities of college life or to ingratiate themselves with the students. . . . Their position at first was a very isolated and peculiar
one, and which was enhanced by a whisper that soon circulated
among the students that they were *Campbellites*. Now what that
meant, or what tenets the sect held, nobody seemed to know, but
it was supposed to mean something very awful." [10]

At the close of the fall term Garfield was invited to the
nearby town of Pownal, Vermont, where he helped to meet expenses by teaching a class in penmanship. (By a curious coincidence, one of the teachers at Pownal the previous year had been
Garfield's future running mate, Chester A. Arthur.) Since Garfield and Wilber were regarded at the Eclectic as "testing" Williams on behalf of other possible applicants from Hiram, there
was considerable correspondence between them and their friends
in the Western Reserve. Whatever misgivings he may have har-
bored about his classmates, Garfield spoke highly of the college
and of the economics of attending Williams. In one letter he
wrote,

> By next September you can both enter the Sophomore class
> in Williams College, and can live at college for $250 per
> annum, clothing included—perhaps cheaper. You can keep up
> with your classes and teach three months each winter. Being
> absent will lessen your college expenses and increase your
> funds.[11]

Predictably, Garfield wasted no time in joining college debating groups. Shortly after joining the Philologian he delivered
his first oration (on "Chivalry") and was moved to write home, "I
have never had so good an opportunity to improve in speaking as

48

now." The fraternities of the day were little more than debating societies, and Garfield found further speaking opportunities after he joined a new group, the Equitable Fraternity, which had been formed with a view to combatting the influence of the "secret" Greek-letter fraternities. By the spring of 1855, his aptitude for debate was sufficiently established so that he achieved recognition in a related literary field and was elected one of the editors of the *Williams Quarterly*, a literary magazine. Garfield took his new position seriously, as might be expected, and appears to have shouldered much of the editorial work in connection with the publication.

Garfield's debating interest is of more than passing importance, for out of it grew his first real interest in politics. As recently as the presidential contest of 1852 between Pierce and Scott, Garfield had expressed contempt for politicians and a total lack of interest in the political process. Gradually, this attitude changed. In 1855, a lecture by a Massachusetts congressman, John Z. Goodrich, on the subject of the Kansas-Nebraska Act caught his attention; to a classmate Garfield deplored the fact that Goodrich's subject matter was unfamiliar to him, and vowed to inform himself on the issue. Shortly before graduation, when news of Fremont's nomination reached Williamstown, Garfield is said to have made his first political speech at a "ratification" meeting for the Republican candidate.[12]

Meanwhile, Garfield continued to flourish under the tutelage of Mark Hopkins; on one occasion he wrote in his diary, "There is a mine opened in the College Chapel twice a day and the treasures are President Hopkins' great mind and heart." In a letter to Lucretia he wrote, "Have you seen Irving's 'Life of Washington?' It is a most thrilling work. Hard-hearted as I am, I cried more than a dozen times while reading the last 50 pages of the first volume." During his senior year, Garfield took up the study of Hebrew and immersed himself in Shakespeare, Tennyson, and Sir Walter Scott.

But Garfield was becoming somewhat anxious about his future, and so indicated in his letters to his fiancée. By the spring of 1856 he had become disenchanted with the career of a Campbellite minister, on both economic and theological grounds:

I want very much to talk with you in reference to my future
course of life and my duty in regard to choosing some calling.
. . . It is always disagreeable to talk of money in connection
with the Gospel, and yet I must and will say that I do not intend to abandon our earthly support to the tender mercies of
our Brotherhood. . . . I think I shall not become a preacher
now, if I ever do.[13]

On the other hand, the prospect of a teaching post at the Eclectic
—which Garfield had reason to feel would be offered him—held
few charms. Two years at Williams had made him critical of
standards at the Eclectic, and the $600 per annum which it was
prepared to pay him seemed paltry. In the winter of 1855–56,
Garfield appears to have been offered a teaching post in central
New York at $1,500 per year. He declined the post, on grounds
that his roots were in Ohio, but recollection of the offer colored
his attitude toward returning to Hiram.

In affairs of the heart, too, new horizons brought new problems. Periodically during his years at Williams Garfield had visited nearby Campbellite congregations for services and for fellow-
ship. On one such visit, to Poestenkill, New York, he met a pretty
and vivacious young girl, Rebecca Jane Selleck, to whom he
became greatly attracted. The feeling was mutual, and by the
spring of Garfield's senior year the whole question of his engagement to Lucretia was very much up in the air. Even after he returned to Hiram he could not get Rebecca out of his mind; the
self-doubt which he had felt on the subject of marriage since his
abortive romance in 1852 was underscored as he attempted to
choose between the sprightly Rebecca Selleck and the more de-
mure Lucretia Rudolph.

Meanwhile, there were final exams to consider. "For two
days," he wrote to Lucretia, "we were 'put through' by the Sach-
ems and Sages of New England, and at the conclusion of the second day the examining committee announced that 44 of the class
had creditably acquitted themselves and were accordingly admitted 'ad primum gradum liberalium artium.' " Garfield had acquitted himself sufficiently well that he was chosen to deliver the
"Metaphysical Oration" at commencement, one of an endless
round of declamations which brought the college year to a close

with a rhetorical flourish. When commencement arrived, Garfield performed creditably on the podium, but was so beset by the various graduation fees that he was obliged to borrow from several people, including his mother and President Hopkins.

In contrast to his earlier period at the Eclectic, Garfield's two years at Williams were formative ones. At Williams he was able to gain some insight into what lay outside of the Campbellite community on the Western Reserve. He had gained acceptance from a student body drawn from backgrounds quite different from his own, and had mastered a curriculum far more advanced than anything which he had known on the Reserve. But two years in the Berkshires had brought inner conflicts as well, and Garfield returned to Ohio a less fervent Disciple, and less certain as to his feelings for Lucretia Rudolph. The little world of Hiram, in which he had been so at home only two years before, suddenly seemed small and confining.

Chapter Four

POLITICS: THE FIRST STIRRINGS

When Garfield returned to Hiram, he found it little changed from four years before. It was still but a village, smaller than Williamstown, and located a full three miles from the nearest railroad. In its own way, though, Hiram was as pleasant a locale as all but a few in Massachusetts. With its hillside location, and its sixty-odd houses surrounding the central green, it simultaneously bespoke thrift and a modest prosperity. The Eclectic still operated from its single brick building on the green, but student enrollment had risen to nearly 300.

The trustees of the school quickly installed their returned protégé as a teacher of ancient languages and literature. But Garfield, in returning, experienced a tremendous letdown and entered a period of depression. "My stay here will certainly be very short," he wrote, "no longer at most than the year for which I have engaged." He passed through a period of doubt concerning his and Lucretia's suitability for one another, a period highlighted by her patience and forbearance. Garfield's anxieties appear to have derived from a variety of pressures: doubts concerning his readiness for marriage; fear that his return to Hiram represented a backward step in terms of his career; and a continuing restlessness on the question of what profession he should pursue. Nor was his position made easier by the fact that he was being advanced by one group among the school trustees as president of the college, while others favored either the retention of President Hayden or his replacement by an older, more mature member of the faculty.

The issue of who was to head the school came to the fore in the spring of 1857, when Hayden resigned in order to devote his full time to the ministry. The arrangement arrived at with respect to his successor reflected the differences among the trustees; Garfield was named "chairman" of the faculty, and as such assumed responsibility for the management of the school. But the presidency was left vacant, clear evidence that young Garfield had something less than a ringing mandate. The Garfield of later years would have attempted to smooth over differences among the trustees, and assure the widest possible base of support for himself among faculty and trustees alike. But in his first year as principal of the Eclectic he blundered in the matter of a faculty appointment in such a way that it colored his entire tenure at Hiram.

"Harry" Rhodes had been a student at the Eclectic before Garfield went to Williams, but it was not until 1857, when both were on the faculty, that they began to room together and became close friends. Rhodes was well-read and convivial, qualities which endeared him to Garfield, whose need at this time for a close confidant bordered on hunger. When Rhodes followed Garfield's example and determined to complete his education at Williams, there was some question as to whether there would be a position on the faculty for him on his return. But Garfield was determined that his friend should rejoin the faculty at Hiram, and following Rhodes' return in 1859 he negotiated with the trustees to discharge Norman Dundee, an able and popular member of the faculty who was one of Garfield's old teachers, in order to make room for his friend. Garfield had his way, and Rhodes his position, but at the price of bitter criticism from friends of the ousted Dundee.[1]

Although highly sensitive to the criticism which ensued, Garfield threw himself into his new work with characteristic energy. He raised money for a new fence around the college grounds and issued the first new catalogue in years. On the theory that Disciples needed little encouragement to come to the Eclectic, Garfield sought to gain community support by enrolling students from other denominations. At one time he wrote to Fuller that he was teaching seven classes, as well as handling the administration of the school "and its correspondence besides."

Notwithstanding his own self-doubt, Garfield appears to have been an excellent teacher-executive, able to maintain discipline yet equally capable of communicating his own enthusiasm to students. His methods were not always orthodox. One of his Hiram students, the Reverend J. L. Darsie, recalled how "Garfield always called us by our first names, and kept himself on the most familiar terms with all. He played with us freely, scuffled with us sometimes, talked with us in walking to and fro, and we treated him outside the class-room just about as we did one another. Yet he was a most strict disciplinarian, and enforced the rules like a martinet." Reverend Darsie, without the benefit of having read Garfield's diary, seems to have sensed his young teacher's hunger for human relationships. "If he wanted to speak to a pupil," wrote Darsie, "he would generally manage to get one arm around him and draw him close up. . . . He had a peculiar way of shaking hands, too, giving a twist to your arm and drawing you right up to him." [2]

Garfield had an enthusiasm for games which was not matched by any particular athletic gifts. To some, his being left-handed underscored Garfield's awkwardness on the playing field, and the same Reverend Darsie has left a memorable description of the future President's being hit on the head with a fly ball in a game of cricket. In any case, the unanimous recollection of young Garfield as outgoing and friendly contrasts with numerous gloomy entries in his diary. "I am succeeding in the school here better than I had any reason to hope," he wrote, "yet my heart will never be satisfied to spend my life in teaching." It was in this period that Garfield manifested his first interest in a career in law.

But not all was gloom even at Hiram. Garfield joined the

Masons in 1858, and although he never achieved exalted masonic rank he appears to have enjoyed its social activities. He continued to make enduring friendships. An association as close as that with Rhodes was Garfield's relationship with Burke Hinsdale. Whereas Rhodes was a close and confidential companion to the gregarious Garfield, Hinsdale, though six years his junior, was a friendly critic, whose advice Garfield would value increasingly as the years passed. Hinsdale was no more than a part-time student at the Eclectic in the years before the Civil War, but his connection with the college would prove even more enduring than Garfield's.

Still uncertain as to his career options, Garfield grew nervous at the prospect of marriage to Lucretia. Not until the spring of 1858 did his determination return, but by May he was actively looking for a suitable house conveniently located near the Hiram campus. The wedding took place on November 11, 1858, at the home of the bride's father. Garfield, typically, didn't know whether he was happy or not. On December 4 he wrote to Harry Rhodes, "I have felt very keenly over the isolating effects of marriage on my friends. There may be something of it unavoidable —but I am very sure it will not be a manifestation of my life." [3]

But for all such illustrations of his immaturity, Garfield was proving surprisingly adept around the college. He took pride in his successes in keeping several promising students at the Eclectic when family or financial problems threatened to take them out of school. In later years Garfield told of one meeting with a father who had come to pick up his son:

> When I got the letter of the son telling me, in the saddest language that he could muster, that he could not come back to school any more . . . I revolved the matter in my mind, and decided to seek an appointment to preach in the little country church where the old gentleman attended. I took for a subject the parable of the talents, and, in the course of my discourse, dwelt specially on the fact that children were the talents which had been entrusted to parents, and, if these talents were not increased and developed, there was a fearful trust neglected. After church, I called upon the parents of the boy I was beseiging, and I saw that something was weighing upon their minds. At length . . . the young man himself was discussed, and I gave my opinion that he should, by all means, be en-

55

couraged and assisted in taking a thorough course of study.
. . . The next term the young man again appeared upon
Hiram Hill, and remained pretty continuously till gradua-
tion.[4]

The fact was that Garfield was developing a liking for Hiram
which he would not have believed possible on his return from
Williams. In the spring of 1859 he turned down an offer to teach
at a Cleveland institution at a salary of $1,500 per year, observing
that "when I balance my freedom here against the few hundreds
of dollars & the restraints of these positions, I find that I love
freedom and friends best." He was troubled with jealousies on the
faculty, but was no longer unduly sensitive. The fact is that Garfield loved an audience, and enjoyed his dual role of teacher-ad-
ministrator more than he cared to admit. He continued to preach
when the spirit moved, and when he finally moved on to a profession which lay outside either teaching or the ministry it was in
the belief that politics would combine the attractions of both of
these esteemed professions.

Ever since he spoke for Fremont at Williamstown, Garfield
had identified himself with the fledgling Republican party. There
had been comparatively few opportunities for political speeches at
Hiram, but over the years he had nevertheless become one of the
best-known speakers in his area. In part Garfield's reputation derived from his connection with the Eclectic, and from his campaign to make it more representative of the surrounding community. But it was through his preaching—at a time when religion
was simultaneously evangelical, educational, and a chief form of
entertainment—that Garfield had become well-known. His friend
Hinsdale later observed,

> For full five years he preached somewhere nearly every Sun-
> day. . . . At the great 'yearly meetings' where thousands gath-
> ered under the old "Bedford tent" or under the shade, he was
> a favorite preacher. His sermons live only in the hearts of
> those who heard them. They were strong in the ethical rather
> than in the evangelical element. . . . His stricter brethren
> found much fault with him because he was not more denomi-

national, but the people, wherever he went, would turn out to hear Garfield preach.[5]

But Garfield was restless, and early in 1859 he let it be known that he was "available" for a debut in Republican politics. In the summer of that year he was approached by a group of Portage County Republicans, who invited him to allow his name to be put in nomination for the Ohio senate. Although Garfield was clearly interested, his decision was not without pitfalls. Many of his Campbellite brethren looked askance at participation in politics, and as early as July rumors of Garfield's impending plunge led one Disciple to write to him that "your best friends in Christ all shake their heads when you are named in connection with law or politics." Nevertheless, Garfield attended the Republican district convention on August 23, and heard himself unanimously nominated for the senate seat shared by Portage and Summit counties. He was anxious, however, to avoid any suggestion that he was seeking office. In a letter of September 12, in reply to some questions put to him, he stated, "I have not, nor shall I now, pledge myself to any men or measures; but shall, if elected to the State Senate, hold myself free to pursue any line of State legislation which my own judgment, aided by the advice of my constituents, may dictate."[6] It is interesting that, in what he doubtless felt to be a bold statement of his independence, Garfield experienced no hesitation about saying that he would be guided by the advice of his constituents.

Garfield was aided in his quest for the nomination by the fact that the Republicans were a new party, with no entrenched stable of proven vote-getters. It was almost too easy, and in a letter shortly after he received the nomination Garfield exuded a certain complacency:

Long ago, you know, I had thought of a public career, but I fully resolved to forego it all unless it could be obtained without wading through the mire into which politicians usually plunge. The nomination was tendered to me by acclamation, though there were 5 candidates. I never solicited the place, nor did I make any bargain to secure it.[7]

Once the die was cast, Garfield proved a vigorous campaigner. By his own count he delivered some thirty speeches, verbal marathons which averaged some two hours apiece. It is unfortunate that no record of these speeches has survived, for Garfield's first campaign coincided with John Brown's raid, and political passions were high. All in all, Garfield was probably a beneficiary of the sharpened antislavery sentiment in northern Ohio; Portage County—normally Democratic—went Republican by a substantial majority in 1859. In the balloting for the senate, Garfield defeated his Democratic opponent by 1,430 votes out of nearly 9,000 cast.

Thus Garfield arrived in the state capital at Columbus on the threshold of a new career. His teaching experience at Hiram would be of little use to him there. For all his inexperience, however, Garfield had two qualities which went far in the politics of the Civil War period: a good platform manner, and a capacity for legislative detail. As for political alignments, Ohio politics were in a state of flux. Prior to 1840, politics had centered on financial issues and the need of a frontier community for internal improvements. That was before slavery had become the critical issue in a state which bordered on Kentucky to the south and whose citizens were in many places active in the Underground Railroad for runaway slaves.

In Ohio as elsewhere, the emergence of the slavery issue had caused the old Whig alliance to fall on hard times. In the decade following the election of 1848, dissident Whigs combined with liberal Democrats and the splinter Liberty party to establish the Free Soil party, a realignment which initially did nothing but assure election victories for the regular Democrats. In 1849, however, Free Soilers in the state senate had found enough Democratic allies to send Salmon P. Chase to the U. S. Senate. By 1856, Ohio was solidly in the Republican fold. Not only did it go for Fremont in the presidential election, but it elected Chase governor in the first of eight successive gubernatorial victories which would keep the state house in Republican hands until 1874.

The Ohio senate would prove to be a good place from which to launch a political career, but its powers were not great even within the bounds of Ohio. Under a revised state constitution leg-

islative prerogatives were sharply curtailed; judges and key officials were made elective rather than appointive offices, and a ceiling was placed on the state debt. But with popular election of
U. S. senators still some time away, the Ohio senate retained the
politically sensitive function of electing the state's two senators.
In this connection, Garfield was somewhat suspicious concerning
the warm welcome which he received during his first call on Governor Chase, underscoring in one letter the statement "He is a
candidate for the U. S. Senate."

Inevitably, Garfield began to take a greater interest in national politics. Although he never attempted to justify John
Brown's raid, he sympathized with Brown's motives and referred
to him following his execution as a hero whose death "shall be
the dawn of a better day." [8] He established good relations with
two senators from adjoining districts, James Monroe and Jacob
Cox, both of whom were strong Republicans, and the three together came to represent a strongly antislavery bloc in the upper
chamber. Their paths would continue to cross through the years.
Monroe was a professor at Oberlin, who would later serve with
Garfield in Congress. With Cox Garfield formed a particularly
close relationship; after rooming together in Columbus, in the
home of Governor Dennison's private secretary, each went on to
become a Union major general and from there to positions of
prominence in Republican politics. Everywhere Garfield demonstrated his remarkable capacity for making friends. William Dean
Howells, whose father would later become one of Garfield's important political supporters, recalled how Garfield bounded into
his newspaper office in Columbus to share with him a favorite
passage from Tennyson. "The rich fullness of his voice," Howells
recalled, "and his fine self-forgetfulness as he read [were] impressive enough to a boy of twenty, who had looked up to him as a
law-giver." [9]

But on the senate floor, the boy orator of the Reserve had
only limited impact. His maiden speech, in defense of an appropriation for school libraries, was not enough to keep the bill from
being voted down. His other activities were routine: he drafted a
committee report on the Geological Survey of Ohio, another on
the regulation of weights and measures, and yet another on the

care afforded pauper children. A visit to Columbus by the legislatures of Kentucky and Tennessee helped to break the monotony. Garfield supported the request of the new governor, William Dennison, that the legislators invite their Southern colleagues and provide money for expenses. When the bill was passed Garfield was made chairman of the committee to escort the visitors, a task which he enjoyed immensely.

Garfield's two years in the Ohio senate gave him a useful introduction to legislative technique, and were an opportunity to make a favorable impression on his older Republican colleagues. But Garfield still had only a rudimentary understanding of national politics, and appears to have recognized none of the danger signals as the country moved toward civil war. A Fourth of July oration, delivered by Garfield in 1860, minimized the likelihood of secession and rang with the same platitudes which had been employed since the founding of the Republic. ("There is, deep down in the hearts of the American people, a strong and abiding love of our country and its liberty, which no surface-storms of passion can ever shake.") Essentially Garfield was still an orator, not a politician. The school still occupied much of his time, for Garfield's attendance at Campbellite meetings often meant much to the school in terms of donations and applications. "We must use the Summer weeks to the best possible advantage," he wrote to the Eclectic's financial agent in August. "Students are coming in and the work of a big term is upon me." [10] But he was also in demand for political gatherings, and noted to Fuller in October 1860 that he had made more than forty political speeches in the previous two months.

Garfield's influence was growing, and so was his self-esteem. He had become a father for the first time with the birth, on July 3, 1860, of a daughter Eliza, whom the delighted parents nicknamed "Trot." Not everyone who came into contact with Garfield, however, ended up as an admirer. Hattie J. Benedict, the daughter of a Disciple elder and a Democrat, was not only unimpressed with Garfield but contributed a number of newspaper articles over the years which were highly critical of him. In one article she recalled the Garfield of 1857 as fresh from college, with boundless energy and ambition large and general, with a charming sociability and freedom of manners which made him appear emphatically a man of the people. His cheerful good-fellowship had nothing in it offensively condescending to the 'great unwashed'—his ready hand was held out for the poorest to shake in those days with delightful democracy—his broad shoulders were thrown back for a deep-chested laugh with the most obscene joker. . . . His [religious] meetings were always well attended and were even more popular with the sinners of the world than with the saints of the church. There was a lack of spirituality about him that grieved the latter . . . but the sinners liked to hear his short, sparkling, logical discourses.[11]

By 1860 these qualities were very much in evidence as Garfield canvassed the state for the Republican national ticket. His political oratory was not in vain, but neither was it especially needed. For all its North-South cleavage Ohio went Republican once more, and Garfield was able to write in his diary on election night, "Voted for Lincoln and Hamlin. Went to Ravenna in evening; at midnight knew that L. and H. were elected. God be praised!" [12]

Although Garfield had learned much at his first legislative session, he did not react as one who had finally found his milieu. He never appreciated his family as much as when separated from them, and by 1861 he had, in addition to his wife and his mother, the young daughter to draw his thoughts home during dreary legislative sessions and to provide one more excuse for trips between Columbus and Hiram. In any case, short legislative sessions permitted Ohio legislators to keep up with their business and professions, and Garfield continued his itinerant preaching. He retained his position as head of the Eclectic, and kept up a voluble correspondence with Harry Rhodes, who acted for him during legislative sessions.

But Garfield was not content. In a letter to his wife, he duly counted his blessings but then confessed to an absence of inner serenity. "I know my restless nature so well that this picture brings no permanent joy, for, were I possessed of it, I should straitway sigh for the fiercest activities of life. . . . Do you suppose *real strong men* have such waverings?" [13] Yet for all his restlessness, Garfield did not appear eager to disturb the routine which permitted him to divide his time so agreeably between Columbus and Hiram. As a result, the issues which were about to divide the country intruded on him only gradually.

By the time of Garfield's second senate session in January 1861, the secession of South Carolina had made disunion a reality and had underscored divisions within the legislature. In Ohio, as elsewhere, there was a sharp cleavage between those who supported coercive measures and those who favored conciliation. Although Garfield had considered himself a moderate on the slavery issue—somewhat behind, perhaps, sentiment in his constituency —he returned to Columbus a full-blown hawk. "There is a strong warlike sentiment here," he wrote to Crete. "I expect in a few days Cox and I will be seen on the East portico of the State House learning the use of the light infantry musket." A letter from Garfield to Hinsdale underscored the change which had come over the young orator since his speech of the previous Fourth of July:

My heart and thoughts are full almost every moment with the terrible reality of our country's condition. We have learned so long to look upon the convulsions of European states as things wholly impossible here, that the people are slow in coming to the belief that there may be any breaking up of our institutions, but stern, awful certainty is fastening upon the hearts of men. *I do not see any way, outside a miracle of God, which can avoid civil war, with all its attendant horrors.* Peaceable dissolution is utterly impossible. Indeed, I cannot say I would wish it possible . . . I am inclined to believe that the sin of slavery is one of which it may be said that without the shedding of blood there is no remission.[14]

On January 24, Garfield introduced a bill to raise and equip 6,000 state militia. But the state which was to prove a major center of pro-Southern "Copperhead" sentiment during the war was not easily won to coercive measures, and Garfield's bill was defeated. He had better luck with a measure which he introduced to make "treason" against the state a punishable offense. To Rhodes he wrote, on January 26, "Today I introduced a bill to punish treason in Ohio, against the laws of the State or of the Union. . . . I fear some of our decisive, bold measures will be lost in the House by the nervousness of our timid men." [15]

On February 16, the new president-elect stopped off at Columbus as he made his way to Washington. Garfield does not appear to have met Lincoln on that occasion, but he observed him closely. He wrote his impressions to Crete:

> Mr. Lincoln has come and gone. The rush of people to see him at every point on the route is astonishing. He has been raising a respectable pair of dark-brown whiskers, which decidedly improve his looks, but no appendage can ever render him remarkable for beauty. On the whole, I am greatly pleased with him. He clearly shows his want of culture, and the marks of Western life, but there is no touch of affectation in him, and he has a peculiar power of impressing you that he is frank, direct and thoroughly honest. His remarkable good sense, simple and condensed style of expression, and evident marks of indomitable will, give me great hopes for the country.[16]

Although Garfield as a congressman would become a critic of Lincoln on certain issues concerning the management of the war, his initial assessment of the sixteenth president reflects credit on a young man whose judgment was not always so astute. Garfield was inclined to be charitable in his initial judgments of people. It was only when they failed to meet his rather exacting standards that he tended to become caustic.

Chapter Five

A CITIZEN ARMY

———————◆———————

The Ides of March brought to Columbus all the intrigue of a balloting for U. S. senator in the faction-ridden Ohio senate. In 1861, a vacancy was created by Salmon P. Chase's acceptance of a position in Lincoln's cabinet, and the competition to succeed him in the senate was fierce. Garfield supported the candidacy of his friend Governor Dennison, but in the end the victor was John Sherman, the brother of a promising Union general and one whose political career would often intertwine with that of Garfield. In ordinary times, the election of a U. S. senator would have been the highlight of a legislative session in Columbus. But the times were far from ordinary, and Chase's political advancement was of minor interest to Ohioans from all walks of life who observed the imminent dissolution of their country.

April brought the bombardment of Fort Sumter, and Garfield was caught up in the martial ardor of the day. In a letter to Harry Rhodes, he caught much of the flavor of a nation poised on the brink of war:

> I am completely exhausted. The Senate adjourned today at noon, and the chamber is nearly deserted. It is raining and dismal outside, and a little group of members is sitting and talking anxiously of the probable fate of . . . Sumter. . . .

64

The reflection is so very terrible, that Maj. Anderson has been kept there for 3 months with his hands tied while 19 tremendous batteries have been erected & brought to bear upon him, & now when they are all ready, he must certainly surrender to the traitors or perish. . . .

I am glad we are defeated at Sumter. It will rouse the people. I can see no possible end to the war till the South is subjugated. Better to lose a million men in battle than to allow the government to be overthrown. The war will soon assume the shape of Slavery vs. Freedom.[1]

Not until much later would the war assume the character of an antislavery crusade as desired by Garfield. Meanwhile, he wrestled with the dilemma of whether or not it was his duty to volunteer for military service. He could, of course, count on Governor Dennison's assistance in securing a commission. And it was of romantics such as Garfield that Mr. Lincoln's army would be made. But Garfield rarely made an impulsive decision, and he was not about to do so at this crossroads of his career. As he balanced the glory-potential of service in the field against its dangers and his own lack of military training, he became anxious and irritable.

At the end of April Garfield went on a mission for Governor Dennison to Springfield, Illinois, to discuss military problems with state officials there. By this time Garfield was seeking a colonel's commission, but he was anxious not to appear unduly "pushy" in doing so. On his return from Springfield he campaigned for the colonelcy of the Seventh Ohio Regiment, but with disastrous results. Despite the discreet backing which Garfield enjoyed from the governor's office, the regiment voted by more than 2 to 1 for his rival, a businessman and militia brigadier named Erastus B. Tyler. It was to be the last election which Garfield would lose, but at the time his rejection left him humiliated and depressed. The Democratic *Weekly Portage Sentinel* increased his misery with an editorial which attacked Garfield by saying that he was "without military education, experience or training," and that his ambitions were only "to leap from the walks of a private citizen to the position of a military chieftain." [2]

In June Dennison offered Garfield the lieutenant colonelcy of another regiment, but Garfield, still smarting from the debacle of the previous month, declined. He did not slam any doors, however, and wrote to a friend in Hiram that if he could get the appointment "without making a great effort" he might redeem himself "from the obloquy they have attempted to heap upon me." But he would "rather not succeed in it at all" than to open himself to further press attacks.[3] For much of Garfield's career there would be this conflict between his ambition and his sensitivity to criticism. Nevertheless, when Dennison once more tendered him a lieutenant colonelcy, Garfield was receptive. By virtue of settling for less than a full colonelcy, Garfield was signifying his willingness to serve under some more experienced soldier, and he set off confidently for Hiram to find recruits there for his "paper" unit, the Forty-second Ohio Infantry.

Busy weeks followed, but in the end Garfield was able to fill the ranks of the Forty-second almost entirely from among his constituents in Summit and Portage Counties. The new recruits traveled to Camp Chase, near Columbus, where the separate companies were formally mustered into service. When the regiment had completed its basic training, Dennison appointed Garfield as its commanding officer. The plan for the Forty-second to be commanded by a professional was not again raised.

Garfield threw himself into his new role with characteristic zeal and thoroughness. He memorized whatever military treatises he could lay his hands on, including the memoirs of Frederick the Great, and observed all that went on about him. The training at Camp Chase took place during the lull which had followed the Federal defeat at Bull Run, and the disorganization in that encounter had made both sides newly aware of the importance of training. No one took the training more seriously than Garfield, but he found the role of disciplinarian an uncongenial one:

> A late occurence has put a wider gulf between me and the men. I was so proud of them that I was willing to warrant that they were not engaged in any irregularities like breaking guard etc. But lately I found that a few had been engaged in it and last night I spent nearly all night in scouting. This morning found five of my men in the guard-house. It has touched my pride, roused all my determination, till I now feel that I must be the scourge of many rather than the cooperant friend and leader.[4]

66

After four months of training and drill at Camp Chase, the Forty-second Ohio was ordered to report to General Buell's headquarters at Louisville, Kentucky. There Garfield stayed behind while his regiment, under new orders, moved downriver to reinforce the Union garrison at Catlettsburg. On arriving at Louisville Garfield was almost immediately summoned by Buell, a somber, forty-three-year-old Army professional, whose bearded good-looks concealed a deliberate approach to military operations which would eventually cost him his command. At Buell's headquarters Garfield was thrown together once more with Buell's aide-de-camp, Almon F. Rockwell, who had been a classmate of Garfield's at Williams. The friendship resumed at Louisville would last for the rest of Garfield's life as Rockwell joined Hinsdale and Rhodes in the inner circle of Garfield's friends.

Over the next few days Buell and Garfield evolved a plan in which Garfield would command the smaller of two Union columns that had as their task the clearing of Confederate forces out of eastern Kentucky. The larger Confederate force, commanded by General Zolicoffer, was not Garfield's concern. But a smaller column, some 2,000 men under Brigadier General Humphrey Marshall, had entered Kentucky from Virginia and was entrenched south of Paintsville. There the Confederates were making desultory efforts at recruitment, while their commander wrote letters to Richmond complaining of the size and composition of the troops under his command.

Buell's orders to Garfield placed him in command of the Eighteenth Brigade, comprising some 3,000 men divided into four infantry regiments plus cavalry. In his official orders on December 17, Buell directed Garfield to place one regiment, the Fortieth Ohio, in a position "as will best give a moral support to the people . . . on the route to Preston and Piketon, and oppose any further advance by the enemy on the route." With the remainder of his force, which included his own Forty-second Ohio, he was to confront Marshall in the vicinity of the Sandy River "and drive the enemy back or cut him off." He was given no artillery, which Buell viewed as a liability in such rugged terrain, although the Confederates were known to have several pieces.[5]

That such a mission could be entrusted to virtually untrained recruits is a commentary on the state of readiness of both armies. Garfield himself characterized one of his regiments as "little more than a well-disposed, Union-loving mob." [6] But by December 23, the erstwhile preacher, who had never heard a shot fired in anger, had joined his own Forty-second Ohio at Louisa and begun a laborious advance. Garfield ordered Colonel Jonathan Cranor's Fortieth Ohio, then encamped at Paris, nearly 100 miles away, to march east toward the Big Sandy Valley and there attempt to place his force between Marshall's force and his return route to Virginia. Meanwhile, Garfield fretted about his lack of artillery. On Christmas Eve he wrote to his wife, "We are now within 18 miles of 2,500 rebels who have four guns. . . . We are waiting for our Ky. regts. to come up."

Not until December 31 did Garfield resume his march southward down the Paintsville road. He professed to have never seen such country, or such narrow, rutted roads. Adding to his problems were some 150 mules which had been pressed into service before they were fully broken to the yoke. Had it not been for his immobile adversary, Garfield's Big Sandy operation could easily have been a disaster, with rather adverse effect on his budding political career. But Marshall made no move either to attack or elude the Union column, but instead had his command entrench on the road between Paintsville and Prestonburg to the south.

When Garfield finally reached striking range on January 9, the opposing forces were numerically quite closely matched. This was, however, a result more of accident than design, for Garfield had originally hoped to place the Fortieth Ohio at Marshall's rear. His plan had proved to be abortive when Cranor, fearing that he might be turned on by Marshall's entire force, had chosen to rejoin the main Union column. Whatever the theoretical merits of Garfield's earlier plan, Cranor's arrival permitted him to match his adversary's numbers and to retrieve a possible blunder as a result of having divided his small force.

The "Battle of Middle Creek," which took place on January 10, was essentially a day-long skirmish in which neither side demonstrated any convincing superiority. According to Garfield's account, by 4:30 P.M. the Confederates had ordered a retreat, and by 5:00 P.M. had retired from the field. Marshall's report, by way of contrast, denied that he had been driven off and contended that only a shortage of food had prevented him from pursuing and destroying the federal force. As for casualties, neither commander knew the exact size of the force he had faced, and both came up with grossly inflated casualty figures. Garfield reported that the Confederates had carried off most of their casualties, but had left 85 dead on the field, including three officers. The loquacious Marshall, in his report, claimed 250 Union dead and 300 wounded. On the other hand, if one credits each commander's figures concerning his own casualties, Middle Creek appears somewhat less sanguinary. Total federal casualties were reported to be 21, only three of whom were killed. Confederate casualties totaled 24, with 10 killed and 14 wounded.

Notwithstanding Marshall's claims to the contrary, such strategic advantage which resulted from the battle was clearly with the federals. Marshall advanced no further into Kentucky, and eventually withdrew entirely; the end result was exactly what Buell had set out to achieve. Success of his design was assured when General George H. Thomas defeated Zolicoffer's army at Mill Springs on January 19, killing its commander and pursuing the Confederate force into Tennessee. Although Thomas' victory —the first notable Union triumph in the West—far eclipsed Garfield's little expedition in the public eye, the Middle Creek campaign nevertheless gave Garfield his first major publicity throughout his own state. General Buell, in a general order commemorating this affair, observed that the Middle Creek campaign "called into action the highest qualities of a soldier— fortitude, perseverence, and courage." Garfield had, in fact, demonstrated all these qualities plus a concern for the welfare of his men on a long and difficult march. But he had also been extremely lucky. Marshall's cannon shells were so defective that only one was observed to explode. And although Garfield, in exuberant letters written two weeks apart, credited Marshall first with 4,000 and then with 5,000 men, the Confederate commander claimed in his report to have had only 1,500 men in action.[7]

Garfield spent two more months in eastern Kentucky, months in which he demonstrated a political touch not always evident among Federal commanders. In one somewhat grandiose proclamation, he urged wayward citizens to return to their allegiance to the Union. At the same time, he sought to avoid antagonizing the local populace and appeared to recognize that Kentucky was a state to be wooed rather than made subject to occupation. "If citizens have suffered from any outrages by the soldiers under my command," he announced, "I invite them to make known their complaints to me and their wrongs shall be redressed and the offenders punished." [8] Back in Columbus, Garfield's friends urged an already-sympathetic governor that Garfield's triumph entitled him to promotion, and on March 19 Governor Dennison signed his commission as a brigadier general, with the new rank dating from January 10.

On March 23, Garfield's brigade was ordered to join Buell's army at Louisville. By the time it had arrived, however, the Army of the Ohio had already decamped and was moving southward toward what would prove to be a timely rendezvous with Grant at Shiloh. When Garfield, having been directed to leave his brigade behind, finally caught up with Buell, he was assigned to command the Twentieth Brigade of General Thomas J. Wood's division. Garfield's command reached the bloody battlefield at Shiloh only as the third day's fighting died away. It was among several units sent in pursuit of the fleeing Confederates, but like much of Buell's command it was footsore from the long march, and its pursuit was ineffectual.

Garfield was appalled by what he saw of the battlefield. To his wife he wrote, "The horrible sights I have witnessed on this field, I can never describe. No blaze of glory that flashed around the magnificent triumphs of war can ever atone for the unwritten and unutterable horrors of the scene of carnage." Heretofore, Garfield had seen little to disturb his romantic concept of war; henceforth there would be little romance in it for Garfield. In the aftermath to Shiloh, he took a hearty dislike to General Wood ("a very narrow, impetuous, proslavery man . . . quite destitute of fine or manly feelings"), and was shocked in general by the seeming indifference of professional army officers to the evils of slavery. As General Halleck directed his glacial pursuit of Beauregard's retreating army, Garfield grew indignant at the conduct of the campaign and caustic on the subject of West Pointers. In-

creasingly he came to view the war in political terms, particularly
with regard to the slavery issue:

> Before God I here second my conviction that the spirit of
> slavery is the soul of this rebellion, and the incarnate devil
> which must be cast out before we can trust in any peace as
> lasting and secure. It may be a part of God's plan to lengthen
> out this war till our whole army has been sufficiently outraged
> by the haughty tyranny of proslavery officers and the spirit of
> slavery and slaveholders . . . that they can bring back into
> civil life a healthy and vigorous sentiment that shall make it-
> self felt at the ballot box. . . . [9]

Garfield's outlook was not improved by his responsibilities in
camp. He was obliged to spend a large amount of time in the sad-
dle, an occupational hazard which increased his susceptibility to
the dysentery which was endemic to the Union camps but to
which Garfield proved especially vulnerable. A growing sense of
depression, attributable in large measure to his poor health and
frustration with Halleck's campaigning, coincided with letters
from home advising that he was being increasingly talked about
as a candidate for Congress. Garfield was available, and he did not
wait for the office to seek the man. "I cannot but feel an interest
in what you say in reference to Congress," he wrote to Rhodes.
"Please write to me more about it." [10]

Following the uncontested occupation of Corinth by Union
forces, Wood's division was posted some 30 miles east of the town
and put to work in repairing the railroad. The resulting drudgery, punctuated by recurring attacks of dysentery, sent Garfield's
morale to a new low and lent additional charm to the prospect of
a seat in Congress. Characteristically, he sought to rationalize his
personal ambitions in terms of the national welfare, musing in
one letter to Rhodes that if the war in the West were to consist
largely of garrison duty he could "much better serve the country
in some other capacity." But to some Campbellites in Hiram, especially those already suspicious of Garfield's "worldly" interests,
his interest in political advancement loomed as a character flaw.
One of his rivals for the Republican congressional nomination,
Oliver P. Brown, sought to make political capital with the obser-

vation that "Garfield has an interest everywhere . . . but in the Kingdom of Heaven." [11]

By the end of July, four months of intermittent dysentery had brought Garfield's weight down from over 190 pounds to about 170, and he felt justified in applying for a furlough. Before leaving the field, however, he took care of a financial matter which had been on his conscience for some time. He sent a check for $60 to Mark Hopkins, and in so doing repaid with interest Hopkins' $40 loan at the time of Garfield's graduation. "It was a great favor to me at that time," he wrote, "but it was only one of the many and greater favors for which I have to thank you." [12]

Garfield was convalescing in Hiram, following a painful trip home from Corinth, when he heard on September 9 that he had been nominated for Congress from the newly-formed Nineteenth District. The nomination did not come to the young brigadier without a struggle. The Nineteenth District was a new grouping of five counties, each with its own parochial loyalties. The district convention at Garrattsville had five names before it, including the incumbent representative for the former district, John Hutchins. Hutchins was strong in his home county of Warren, but support there was largely neutralized by his relative unpopularity in Ashtabula, a result of his having defeated a local favorite, Abolitionist Congressman Joshua Giddings, in 1858. When balloting began on September 5, Garfield and Hutchins led the field of five. One by one the weaker candidates dropped out, but not until the eighth ballot did Garfield top Hutchins by the narrow margin of 78 to 71. In the wartime Reserve, however, the Republican nomination was tantamount to election.

Garfield, typically, had mixed feelings about the convention's action, and he wrote to a friend that he would much prefer to remain in the field if the war were to continue for more than a year. Meanwhile he would have ample time for reflection, since under the system then prevailing a "lame duck" Congress would meet in the spring of 1863, and the first session of Garfield's Thirty-ninth Congress would not be convened until the December of that year. Meanwhile, he received orders from the War Department directing him to report to Washington.

On September 16, Garfield left for Washington following two months in Hiram which represented his first real leave in a year. Garfield was a sentimental man, and a devoted if sometimes thoughtless husband; he had gotten no farther than Pittsburgh, where he had first visited on the canal boat in 1848, when he felt the first pangs of homesickness. "Everything conspired to make the visit dear to me," he wrote to Crete of his homecoming. "Our little darling never put her arms around my neck and hugged and kissed me so lovingly as in the farewell embrace. You walked and talked with me till the train whistled, and you tossed a sweet kiss after the flying train. It was all as my fondest wishes could ask and it augurs good for the future." [13]

Once in Washington, however, Garfield was almost immediately ensnared in the Capital's political labyrinth. Secretary Chase had heard of his coming, and when he invited Garfield to stay at his house the younger man accepted with gratitude. "His daughter Kate is quite a belle here," Garfield wrote home. "They have a fine residence and live in splendid style. Mr. Chase seems to be the only member of the cabinet who stands up firmly with Stanton . . . for the vigorous prosecution of the war for freedom and the union's sake." [14]

Garfield spent most of his time seeking a combat command. His entree with Chase was a major asset, but wartime Washington was packed with fortune hunters in search of commissions and commissioned officers seeking commands. At various times Garfield was considered in connection with contemplated operations against the South Carolina and Florida coasts, but none of these expeditions ever materialized. Boredom made him increasingly susceptible to the political backbiting all around him, and as a member of Chase's entourage he inevitably was drawn into the Radical camp. On one occasion, the secretary gave his protégé a biased but not altogether inaccurate description of the War Department hierarchy:

[Chase] then proceeded to give me an analysis of the War Department. Spreading out his fore and middle fingers so as to form a letter V he said, "There (end of forefinger) is Stanton, full of propulsive energy, strong and sincere, but impatient of

delay and restraint and feeling at times completely disheart-
ened by the perplexities of his position. Hence fitful and lacks
balanced steadiness. There (end of middle finger) is Halleck;
with immense brain, clear, powerful intellect, full knowledge
of his work, only as a professional performance; no more heart
about it than the shoemaker who pegs away at a boot. Here
(junction of knuckles of the fore and middle fingers) is the
President with a great and noble heart, most anxious to do his
duty, but don't know how and has not the power and independence to shake off the shackles of West Point. If Lincoln's
heart, Halleck's head and Stanton's executive energy could be
united it would make a magnificent Sec. of War or
President." [15]

While he was serving in the field Garfield's ire had been reserved primarily for his more pompous colleagues and for those
who appeared insensitive to the issue of slavery. In Washington
the scope of his criticism broadened, and his earlier admiration
for Lincoln began to waver. There was, however, a positive side;
Chase was almost as much a financier as he was an intriguer, and
long evenings with the secretary gave Garfield his first insights
into the mysteries of government finance. Moreover, Garfield's
earnestness and quick intelligence made a considerable impression on his mentor. On September 25, Chase noted in his diary a
conversation with Garfield which suggests that the younger man
was not missing many tricks:

> Returning from Gen. Hooker's, as well as going, Gen. Gar-
> field gave me some interesting portions of his own experience.
> This fine officer was a laborer on a canal in his younger days.
> Inspired by a noble ambition, he had availed himself of all
> means to acquire knowledge; became a preacher of the
> Baptist [sic] Church; was made the president of a flourishing
> literary institution on the Reserve; was elected to the Ohio
> Senate, and took a conspicuous part as a Republican leader.
> On the breaking out of the war he became a colonel . . . [and]
> gained promotion rapidly.[16]

Many of Garfield's letters to his wife alluded during this period to their purchase, in the fall and winter of 1862, of a small
house in Hiram. In the year that followed Crete would supervise

numerous additions and alterations, with her husband a vicarious participant. But for the short term, Garfield's absence in Washington was something of a strain on their marriage. In early October, Lucretia wrote shyly to request "a little *gossip*. From your letters to others I learn that you and Miss Kate are taking dinners out, visiting camps etc., and I have a good deal of woman's curiosity to hear about some of these doings; and is Miss Kate a very charming, interesting young lady? I may be *jealous* if she is, since you have such a fashion of becoming enamoured with brilliant young ladies." Garfield, in his reply, was very much the man of the world. "She is a woman of good sense and pretty good culture," he wrote, "has a good form but not a pretty face, its beauty being marred by a nose slightly inclining to pug. She has probably more social influence and makes a better impression generally than any other Cabinet lady." [17]

A more tactful husband might have taken more notice of his wife's feeling of remoteness from the social whirl of Washington, and of her understandable misgivings concerning Garfield's affinity for brilliant women. Instead, Garfield compounded his errors of omission by casually informing Lucretia that he planned to extend a proposed trip to New York City in order to drop in on Rebecca Selleck in Lewisboro. He appears to have been startled by the tone of her reply. Writing on October 19, Lucretia recalled the doubts which had at times assailed her during their early years of marriage, and how they had seemed to vanish during his leave at Hiram. But when she read of his proposed visit to Lewisboro, "the old pain came back to my heart, and . . . I began to fear . . . [that you wished only] to deceive me. . . . Most solemnly and earnestly did I pray . . . for a just and generous heart and He who hears the young ravens when they cry heard and answered my prayer." Garfield, in replying, could not quite see what all the fuss was about, but offered reassurance:

> I was . . . sorry to know that you had been sad and had passed through a struggle on account of my visit to Rebecca. I hope you will not harbor the thought that I have practised any deception toward you in my late conversation. I hope you will see me as I am, conscious of being indeed a true man, and that I am true to my *whole* history. I had a very pleasant yet

sad visit with Rebecca; pleasant because I was glad to revisit the scenes of six years ago and was enabled to do so without having my horizon clouded . . . sad in this, that I found her just arisen from a bed of pain and suffering. . . . [18]

For all his misgivings about the Lincoln administration, Garfield was capable of recognizing an effective political stroke when he saw one. He wrote approvingly of the Emancipation Proclamation, noting in a letter home that "the President's proclamation gives great satisfaction among all strong and vigorous men." Nevertheless, he was slow in coming to appreciate the quality of leadership which Lincoln was providing. In one notable instance of his pen getting the better of his good sense, Garfield wrote in another letter that it was a strange moment in history "when a second rate Illinois lawyer is the instrument to utter words which shall form an epoch memorable in all future ages." [19] Garfield believed in moving from point A to point B by the most direct possible means. He never understood the importance of creating a climate of opinion which would sustain a certain course of action, and his inability to do so during his own brief presidency would prove to be a serious handicap.

Although he chafed at his inactivity, Garfield took advantage of his time in Washington to visit sights in and around the Capital. On one bright October day he joined the Chase family in a visit to the Bull Run battlefield, which he described in detail in a letter to Rhodes:

> We went on . . . across Bull Run to the limit of the late battle about five miles beyond Centerville, and General Schurz, who was in the engagement, gave us a fine description of the whole two days' work and the shameful and unnecessary retreat which followed. We saw hundreds of graves, or rather heaps of earth piled upon the bodies where they lay. Scores of heads, hands and feet were protruding, and so rapid had been the decomposition of 34 days that naked, eyeless skulls grinned at us as if the corpses had lifted their heads from their death beds to leer at us as we passed by. Shells and round shot lay scattered all over the field and broken muskets and dismantled gun carriages were very plenty. . . .
> I picked up a joint promissory note of $1,000, which

would probably be valuable to the heirs of some poor skeleton. *"Your loving wife till death"* was the conclusion of a letter which lay near the skeleton arm which reached through the side of its grave, and had doubtless one day not long ago clasped the loving wife, but now the *"till death"* has opened for him the portal of the world where "there is neither marrying nor giving in marriage." [20]

Since it was apparent that he would be in Washington for some time, Garfield left the Chase residence in mid-November in favor of a boardinghouse on Pennsylvania Avenue. He was by then a congressman-elect, for he carried the Nineteenth District easily with 13,288 votes to 6,763 for his Democratic opponent, running well ahead of the Republican ticket as a whole. In Washington, his period of enforced inactivity came to a close almost at the same time as he was named to the court-martial to try General Fitz-John Porter for disobedience of orders at the second Battle of Bull Run.

Porter, McClellan's friend, had become to the Radicals a symbol of the professional army officers who were unable or unwilling to wage all-out war against the Confederacy. Given his views on West Pointers, and his close association with McClellan's critics in Washington, Garfield probably should have disqualified himself from sitting on the court. Moreover, he was a close friend of the ill-starred Irvin McDowell, who had briefed him at great length on his side of the second Bull Run debacle which had led to his removal as well as Porter's. But General Porter, when given an opportunity to object to any member of the court, made no objection, and Garfield did nothing to disqualify himself. Garfield apparently did not believe in disassociating himself from tribunals on grounds of bias so long as he was on the side of the angels. At the same time as the Porter trial, it appeared for a while that Garfield might be asked to sit also on a court of inquiry looking into the conduct of General McDowell in the same campaign. Far from disqualifying himself, Garfield cautioned Crete to take care that his notes on McDowell's briefing not be given unnecessary exposure.[21]

Time slipped by, and one after another Garfield's prospective field commands failed to materialize. Disappointment and poor health brought on another spell of melancholy which led Garfield to give expression to his frustration in a letter to Harry Rhodes. Garfield lamented how he had been born to poverty and was obliged "to begin the work of exhuming my manhood from the drift and rubbish which every chance had thrown upon me." It was his wife, with whom Rhodes shared the letter, who exhorted Garfield out of his self-pity with a statement of her own religious faith. "It is with me a positive certainty," she wrote, "that whatever be the circumstances *beyond our control* which surround us they are the best. . . . I believe, Jamie, if you will question yourself as to the time when you have developed most rapidly . . . you will find it was not when you were *helped* in any way but when you stood all alone." [22]

The Porter trial lasted from late November until early the following year, when on January 10 Porter was pronounced guilty and cashiered from the army. There is no reason to believe that Garfield's bias influenced the outcome, which was probably preordained considering the climate of opinion in wartime Washington. For Porter the court's verdict began a fight of two decades which, in the end, would bring vindication and restoration to duty status. For Garfield it meant release from Washington and a return to the field. On January 14, 1863, he was ordered to report to General William S. Rosecrans, commander of the newly organized Army of the Cumberland.

Chapter Six

GENERAL
GARFIELD

———— ◆ ————

When Garfield reported to the Army of the Cumberland in January 1863, Union fortunes were at a nadir. In the East, the Army of the Potomac confronted its foe across the Rappahannock as "Fighting Joe" Hooker sought to restore its effectiveness following the disaster at Fredericksburg. In Kentucky Buell's failure to move energetically in the direction of eastern Tennessee had proved to be his downfall, and had brought about his replacement by the hard-driving William S. Rosecrans. Only in the West were there portents—not easily read in that winter of 1862–63— of a brighter tomorrow. Although Grant had combined his own army with those of Sherman and McClernand above Vicksburg, it was not yet apparent that one of the war's decisive campaigns was about to begin.

In the end, the year 1863 would bring a bloody stalemate in the East and in much of the West, and federal forces would achieve their most significant victories along the Mississippi. For much of the year, however, it was Rosecrans' Army of the Cumberland which held out the greatest promise. "Old Rosey" had played a key role in securing West Virginia for the Union in the first year of the war, and his friends boasted that he was the only Northern commander who could claim to have outgeneraled Robert E. Lee. Rosecrans won new laurels in October 1862, when his troops repulsed a Confederate attempt to recapture Corinth. After assuming his new command, which he reorganized as the Army of the Cumberland, Rosecrans delighted the powers in Washington with an advance into eastern Tennessee. Rosecrans had suffered more than 13,000 casualties in a drawn battle with Bragg's army at Stone River, but in sharp contrast with the war in the East it was the Confederates, not the federals, who subsequently pulled back to lick their wounds.

Rosecrans combined aggressiveness and strategic sense to a degree rarely encounted in Union commanders. An Ohioan in his early forties, he had taught at West Point before leaving the army for a fling at business. He had returned as a captain of engineers in 1861, but his association with McClellan's successes in West Virginia marked him for speedy advancement. Rosecrans was a devout Catholic, a hard fighter, and opposed in principle to anything smacking of politics in the army. His shortcomings were those of temperament. He was sufficiently excitable under stress so that there were occasions on which he had abused certain of his officers. "Old Rosey," however, was no martinet. Whitelaw Reid characterized him as "easy of access, utterly destitute of pretense, and thoroughly democratic in his ways. . . . In the field he was capable of immense labor; he seemed never to grow weary, and never to need sleep. Few officers have been more popular with their commands, or have inspired more confidence in the rank and file." [1] However, his seemingly boundless energy and his conviviality were, to a degree, deceptive. Unable to pace himself in the field and possibly lacking confidence in his staff, Rosecrans operated in a state of nervous fatigue which would contribute to eventual disaster.

When Garfield reported to the Army of the Cumberland at Murfreesboro, Tennessee, he and Rosecrans hit it off on first sight. "He is the most Spanish looking man I know of," Garfield wrote to Crete, "and although he swears fiercely . . . he is a Jesuit of the highest style of Roman piety. He carries a cross attached to his watch dial, and as he drew his watch out of his side-pants his rosary, a dirty-looking string of friars beads, came out with it." [2] As the army recuperated from Stone River, there was time for relaxed conversations, and Garfield came to delight in discussions of theology with a Catholic protagonist. His association with Rosecrans led Garfield to question some of his earlier prejudices concerning West Pointers. He wrote to Chase of Rosecrans, "I . . . am glad to tell you that I believe in him, that he is sound to the bone on the great questions of the war, and the way it should be conducted. . . . If the country and the government will stand by him I feel sure he will justify their highest expectations." [3]

If Rosecrans' staff feared that Garfield came as a spy from Washington, the new arrival soon won them over. Garfield the soldier was ambitious and impatient, but he worked hard, had a ready laugh, and enjoyed the companionship of the field. Rosecrans had under his wing, as Frederick Williams has noted, "a highly intelligent, efficient, hard-working man (of) courage, initiative and vitality. . . . He also had an ambitious congressman-elect with definite ideas of how the war should be fought, with powerful connections in Washington, and with every intention of participating in bold strikes against the enemy." [4] Garfield hoped to be offered a division, and in a letter home he indicated that Rosecrans had promised him one. In the end, however, Garfield acceded to a request that he become the army's chief of staff, a post which had been vacant since Stone River. As he mulled the offer, Garfield looked at all sides. Although Rosecrans had described the post in glowing terms, Garfield wanted martial glory, and there was some question as to whether much glory was to be had in a staff post. Moreover, he must have realized that Rosecrans' relations with the War Department were strained at best, and that too close an association with "Old Rosey" could be a liability. In the end Garfield overcame his doubts and accepted Rosecrans' offer, though not without misgivings. "By taking that position," he wrote to Rhodes, "I should make a large investment in General Rosecrans, and will it be wise to risk so much stock in that market?" Garfield was very much on the make, but he was also a very frank correspondent.

By June 1863, the Army of the Cumberland consisted of

some 50,000 men, divided into corps commanded by McCook, Crittenden, and the redoubtable George H. Thomas. Of this total, 40,000 were infantry, 6,800 cavalry and 3,100 artillery. As chief of staff, Garfield's primary responsibility was to draft and to assure delivery of the commanding officer's orders to his disparate and often scattered command. This required considerable judgment, for the army's reliance on despatch riders, only occasionally abetted by telegraph lines, made it necessary for orders to allow the recipient as much discretion as circumstances permitted. There was a great deal of work and not much glamour. A contemporary description of Garfield described how "in a corner by the window, seated at a small pine desk—a sort of packing-box, perched on a long-legged stool . . . was a . . . sinewy-built man with regular, massive features . . . [hair] slightly tinged with gray, and a high, broad forehead, rising into a ridge over the eyes, as if it had been thrown up by a plow. There was something singularly engaging in his open, expressive face, and his whole appearance indicated, as the phrase goes, 'great reserve power.' " [5]

Garfield was also responsible for a variety of miscellaneous chores, one of which was the curbing of smuggling. Illegal trade across the Union and Confederate lines was endemic in wartime Tennessee, and incidents in which officers accepted bribes were by no means infrequent. Garfield inherited responsibility for a rudimentary military police system, which he sought to strengthen and even to use as an intelligence-gathering apparatus. He placed at its head an Ohioan who would become a life-long friend, David G. Swaim. The record of Swaim's Bureau of Military Information was not impressive regarding combat intelligence, but it was probably effective in cutting down on the volume of smuggling in Union-occupied territory.

Garfield's almost Quixotic thirst for military glory took account of others as well as himself and not infrequently appeared in the form of devices to improve morale in the ranks. In February he proposed to Rosecrans the creation of a "roll of honor" made up of officers and soldiers who had performed special acts of heroism. Rosecrans concurred, and in the end took as great an interest in the project as Garfield himself.

Southeast of Rosecrans' army, at Tullahoma, was the headquarters of the acerbic Braxton Bragg, whose Confederate army was almost equal to the Army of the Cumberland in size, and whose cavalry was superior in both quality and quantity. Rosecrans was no McClellan, but he had seen enough of what Bedford Forrest, Joe Wheeler, and other of Bragg's cavalrymen could do to his communications to grow apprehensive. Not until late June did he get his army underway, and even then he did so less from conviction than out of realization that no cavalry reinforcements would be forthcoming. Initially, at least, Garfield supported Rosecrans' course. In April he wrote to Chase describing the army's preparations, adding in explanation that "it is useless to advance into the rebel territory, unless we are prepared to hold the ground we win in battle." Writing to his friend Fuller, Garfield had some thoughts on the war which might have been read with profit by a number of federal commanders:

> In European wars, if you capture the chief city of a nation, you have substantially captured the nation. . . . Not so in this war. The rebels have no city the capture of which will overthrow their power. If we take Richmond, the rebel government can be put on wheels and trundled away into the interior with all its archives in two days. Hence our real objective point is not any place or district, but the rebel army wherever we find it.[6]

As April turned into May Garfield continued to respect Rosecrans' reasons for delay, but his patience was wearing thin. There was also concern in Washington, not only because of Rosecrans' inaction per se but because Lincoln feared that his failure to advance might enable the enemy to concentrate on Grant at Vicksburg. Rosecrans professed to be ready, but when Stanton detached troops from Burnside (on whom Rosecrans was counting to protect his left flank), Rosecrans insisted on a reassessment. On June 8 he sent a note to his corps and division commanders, inviting their views as to the wisdom of an advance. All seventeen polled, including Thomas, opposed an immediate advance, in part because a majority could find no evidence to support the War Department's contention that Johnston was being strengthened at Bragg's expense.

Rosecrans' motives for the poll are unclear, and there is reason to suspect that some of his generals told their commander what they thought he wanted to hear. Garfield, however, wanted none of this. He had not been included in the poll, which was limited to the troop commanders. Garfield was so vexed at the army's continued inaction, however, that he sent Rosecrans a long memorandum which he closed with a listing of nine arguments for an immediate advance:

> 1st. Bragg's army is now weaker than it has been since the Battle of Stone River . . . while our army has reached its maximum strength. . . .
> 2nd. Whatever be the result at Vicksburg, the determination of its fate will give large reinforcements to Bragg. . . .
> 3rd. No man can predict with certainty the result of any battle. . . . [but] I refuse to entertain a doubt that this army which in January last defeated Bragg's superior numbers, cannot overwhelm his present greatly inferior forces.
> 4th. A retreat would greatly increase both the desire and the opportunity for [Confederate desertions] and would very materially reduce his physical and moral strength.
> 5th. . . . . The defeat of Bragg would be in the highest degree disasterous [sic] to the rebellion.
> 6th. The turbulent aspect of politics in the loyal states [e.g., resistance to the Conscription Act] renders a decisive blow against the enemy . . . of the highest importance. . . .
> 7th. The Government and the War Department believe that this army ought to move against the enemy. . . .
> 8th. Our true objective point is the rebel army, whose last reserves are substantially in the field. . . .
> 9th. Your mobile force can now be concentrated in twenty-four hours and your cavalry . . . is greatly superior in efficiency and morale.[7]

Garfield could be quite assertive at times, and one of Rosecrans' division commanders, General David Stanley, spoke of his desiring "a little cheap glory." Nevertheless, one is compelled to admire Garfield's willingness to take on his commanding officer even after the latter's course had been endorsed by every other general in the command. Moreover, the Garfield memorandum was a thoughtful document which allowed fully for both military and political factors. Two of his points, numbers 2 and 9, may with the advantage of hindsight be regarded as not altogether persuasive. But the memorandum remains a thoughtful as well as a daring document, coming as it did from a thirty-two-year-old schoolteacher.

Garfield's frustration at the army's inaction coincided with the rise of Copperhead sentiment in the North, particularly in Ohio. The young brigadier shared with Lincoln a ruthlessness toward those who created dissention behind the lines; he took pleasure at having escorted the Copperhead congressman, Clement Vallandigham, to temporary exile in the Confederate lines. Thus when Garfield heard from Hinsdale of increasing peace sentiment at the Eclectic, he responded with one of his angriest letters:

> Tell all those copperhead students for me that, were I there in charge of the school, I would not only dishonorably dismiss them from the school, but, if they remained in the place and persisted in their cowardly treason, I would apply to General Burnside to enforce General Order No. 38 in their cases. They entirely mistake and misapprehend the character of the times if they suppose that the same license can now be used as in the days of peace. It is a grievous and shameful wrong to the memory of all our brave boys who are dying in front of Vicksburg and suffering everywhere for the country, to have these misguided ones at home permitted to spew out their silly treason at Hiram.[8]

By late June Rosecrans was ready. Garfield noted in his diary on the 22nd, that he had drafted, presumably in accordance with Rosecrans' directions, plans for a "grand movement in echelon, beginning on the right as a feint while it is the main purpose to throw the weight of our army upon Manchester & thence to Tullahoma before Bragg can get there." [9] Aside from all the delays, Rosecrans' Tullahoma campaign showed a sure hand. Avoiding a frontal move against Bragg's hilltop entrenchments, Rosecrans swung his army to the east, outflanking the two Confederate corps of Polk and Hardee and forcing them to withdraw to Tullahoma itself. The march was made in some of the heaviest rains of the war; Rosecrans later recalled that it took Crittenden's corps four days to cover one 21-mile stretch. The slowness of the Union advance permitted Bragg to withdraw in good order, and Garfield was among those who felt that the rains had cost the army its chance for a decisive blow. Bragg arrived at Tullahoma full of fight, but yielded to his subordinates' view that the place was indefensible, and on June 30 began a retreat southward to Chattanooga. On the same July 4 that saw the defeat of Lee's army at Gettysburg and the surrender of Vicksburg to Grant, Rosecrans was able to report the clearing of Confederate forces out of eastern Tennessee.

Rosencrans halted in Tullahoma while he argued unsuccessfully with the War Department for a joint offensive against Bragg in which Grant's army would support the Army of the Cumberland on its right flank. This sensible suggestion was vetoed by Halleck, however, while Garfield chafed at the time lost in this sterile exchange. On July 27, Garfield poured out his despair and frustration in a letter to his friend Chase:

> I have for a long time wanted to write to you, not only to acknowledge your last kind letter, but also to say some things confidentially on the movements in this department; but I have refrained hitherto, lest I do injustice to a good man, and say to you things which were better left unsaid. . . .
> I cannot conceal from you the fact that I have been greatly tried and dissatisfied with the slow progress that we have made in this department since the battle of Stone River. I will say in the outset that it would be in the highest degree unjust to say that the one hundred and sixty-two days which elapsed between the battle of Stone River and the next advance of this army were spent in idleness or trifling. During that period was performed the enormous and highly important labor which made the Army of the Cumberland what it is, in many respects by far the best the country has ever known. But for many weeks prior to our late movement, I could not but feel that there was not that live and earnest determination to fling the great weight of this army into the scale and make its power felt in crushing the shell of this rebellion.

Garfield then went into a detailed discussion of the importance of a movement which could have prevented the detaching of troops from Bragg's force to assist Confederate forces at Vicksburg. Alluding to his memorandum to Rosecrans, Garfield contended that "the seventeen dissenting generals were compelled to confess that, if the movement had been made ten days earlier, while the weather was still propitious, the army of Bragg would, in all human probability, no longer exist." He went on:

> I have since then urged with all the earnestness I possess a rapid advance, while Bragg's army was shattered and under cover, and before Johnston and he could effect a junction. Thus far the general has been singularly disinclined to grasp the situation with a strong hand and make the advantage his own. I write this with more sorrow than I can tell you, for I love every bone in his body, and next to my desire to see the rebellion blasted, is my desire to see him blessed. But even the breath of my love is not sufficient to cover this almost fatal delay. . . .
> If the War Department has not always been just, it has certainly been very indulgent to this Army. But I feel that the time has now come when it should allow no plea to keep this Army back from the most vigorous activity.[10]

Not long after Garfield's death, the vindictive Charles A. Dana—by then the influential editor of the *New York Sun*—would publicize this letter as an example of Garfield's betrayal of his commanding officer's trust. Even during Garfield's lifetime there were periodic rumors that correspondence between him and Chase had been instrumental in bringing about Rosecrans' dismissal. Without question, a letter such as Garfield's of July 27 shows lack of judgment, if only because of the compromising position in which it places the writer. But it is impossible to read into this emotional outpouring any selfish motive on the part of the writer. Garfield himself seems uncertain as to what he wishes to accomplish; after sounding as if the situation required Rosecrans' removal, he ended with an implicit plea for continued pressure on Rosecrans from Washington.

By mid-August, the army was on the move again. On September 10 it occupied Chattanooga, as Bragg pulled back to await reinforcements. Operating on extended supply lines, and no longer in touch with his adversary, Rosecrans grew anxious. His army had become badly dispersed as it searched for passes through the mountains, and it was vulnerable to a concentrated counter by Bragg. But days passed, and no attack came. The truth was that Bragg was himself confused by the topography. "A mountain is like the wall of a house full of ratholes," he complained. "The rat lies hidden at his hole, ready to pop out when no one is watching. Who can tell what lies hidden behind that wall?" [11]

When Rosecrans belatedly realized that his enemy was no longer in retreat he sought to reassemble his three corps in some wooded country 12 miles south of Chattanooga at Chickamauga Creek. A road through Rossville Gap provided a communication and supply line to the North, and when Bragg attacked on September 19, Rosecrans was ready for him. The result was a day of fierce fighting reminiscent of Stone River. The close of the first day saw both armies still on the field, although some ground had been given up on the Union left. In concentrating his main effort on the Union left, however, Bragg had picked on George H. Thomas, perhaps the best defensive fighter in the Union armies.

When fighting resumed the next day, Bragg chose to try his luck elsewhere. Just before noon, James Longstreet—borrowed in this emergency from the Army of Northern Virginia—sent half of Bragg's army against the Union right. Had the attack come an hour earlier, it would have encountered a strong defensive line; coming when it did, fate took a hand. General Thomas J. Wood, to whom Garfield had taken a dislike the year before, was one of Rosecrans' more capable division commanders. But having recently been excoriated by Rosecrans for slowness in carrying out orders, Wood did not stop to question an order from Rosecrans, issued at about eleven o'clock, directing him to "close up on Reynolds as fast as possible." In dictating the order to an aide, Rosecrans had been under the impression that Reynolds was immediately to Wood's left. In actual fact there was a division between them, and to carry out the order Wood was obliged to take his division out of line. This he proceeded to do, even in the face of clear evidence that a Confederate attack was impending.

The result was a debacle which brought an end to Rosecrans' career and almost destroyed his army. Longstreet's blow fell on the area just vacated by Wood, splitting the Union army and routing its right and center. An interested spectator was Garfield's later nemesis, Charles A. Dana, attached to headquarters as an emissary of Secretary Stanton. Dana, who had been napping, awakened before noon to the "most infernal noise" he had ever heard:

> He sat up, and the first thing he saw was General Rosecrans crossing himself. 'Hello!' he said to himself, 'if the general is crossing himself, we are in a desperate situation.' As he leaped into the saddle, Dana saw 'lines break and melt away like leaves before the wind.' Then headquarters disappeared. . . . 'The whole right of the army apparently had been routed.' [12]

Rosecrans attempted to rally his men, but it was no use. He and his staff were swept to the rear in a torrent of fugitives, horses, and wagons. Rosecrans, according to Garfield, "rode silently along, abstracted, as if he neither saw nor heard." Stunned and disconsolate, Rosecrans and his staff retreated up the Dry Valley road toward Rossville. They made occasional attempts to assess the situation behind them, but it was impossible to separate fact from rumor, and most information which reached Rosecrans indicated that the collapse of his army was complete. But there was still firing from the direction of Thomas's lines, and at one point Rosecrans and Garfield both dismounted and put their ears to the ground in an attempt to determine whether they were hearing the regular volleys which would indicate organized resistance or only scattered firing. There was no identifying the noise, and Rosecrans' immediate preoccupation was with the safety of his wagon trains. When Garfield volunteered to go to Thomas and ascertain the situation on the left, Rosecrans assented, in Garfield's account, "listlessly and mechanically." Rosecrans continued on to Chattanooga and obscurity; Garfield kept his presence of mind, and made a dashing inspection on his commanding officer's behalf which would become part of the Garfield legend.

Notwithstanding the campaign biographies of a later year, Garfield's ride was not to be compared with Pickett's charge. Only once in the course of traversing the Lafayette Turnpike did Garfield and his three companions come under fairly heavy fire. But when they finally reached Thomas, he and his escort were able to provide the corps commander with his first authoritative account of the disaster on the right and Rosecrans' subsequent movements. By 3:45, Garfield was able to send a despatch to Rose-crans which included a clear-headed appraisal of the situation ("I hope General Thomas will be able to hold on here until night and will not need to fall back farther than Rossville"). At Snod-grass Hill, he was an eager observer of Thomas's repulse of a Con-federate force which marshaled almost twice his own numbers. By evening he was almost euphoric, writing to Rosecrans, "Gen-eral Thomas has fought a most terrific battle and has damaged the enemy badly. . . . Our men not only held their ground, but at many points drove the enemy splendidly." When that evening Thomas elected to fall back to Rossville, Garfield was pained. In a postwar letter to Rosecrans he commented, "Gordon Granger will tell you that both he and I strenuously urged Thomas not to retire on Rossville, but that he had already given the order. I did not understand that your order to him was peremptory but only discretionary and both Granger and I were exceedingly anxious to have the army remain on the ground it had so valorously held during the day." [13]

As Rosecrans prepared his report on the battle, other post mortems were taking place in Washington. Although Lincoln ad-mired Rosecrans' aggressiveness, Stanton had been sharpening his knife for Rosecrans for some time. Not only was the secretary put out by "Old Rosey's" sharp tongue, but Dana's reports put Rose-crans in a poor light compared to Grant. While Garfield debated whether he should stay in the army or assume his seat in Con-gress, Lincoln agreed to the replacement of Rosecrans by Thomas. The decision was influenced to a considerable extent by Dana, who quoted Garfield and Wood as among those critical of Rosecrans.

"Old Rosey" received the bad news on October 19, four days after Garfield had said his farewells and left for Washington. In taking leave of Garfield, Rosecrans was his gracious self; the gen-eral order which announced Garfield's departure noted that "his high intelligence, spotless integrity, business capacity, and thor-ough acquaintance with the wants of the army will render his services, if possible, more valuable to the country in Congress than with us." Still unaware of his own fate, Rosecrans asked his erstwhile chief of staff to brief Stanton on the army's needs.

Thomas, fearing for Rosecrans' future, bluntly told Garfield, "You know the injustice of all these attacks on Rosecrans. Make it your business to set these matters right." Garfield's reply is lost to posterity, but his subsequent behavior suggests that he had found Rosecrans wanting, and did not regard it as incompatible with their friendship to say so. According to a newsman, Henry Villard, who visited Rosecrans' headquarters,

> Garfield took me freely into his confidence. He told me how fully convinced he was that his chief was making a mortal mistake in going to Chattanooga, how he tried to dissuade him from it, and how relieved he himself was to be permitted to join Thomas. While he did not say so directly, it could be inferred that his faith in Rosecrans' military qualifications was shaken, if not lost, and that he was not sorry to part official company with him. His changed opinion naturally made his position very embarrassing to him.[14]

Stanton was at Louisville when Garfield left for Washington, and in the course of a brief layover Garfield was called into the presence. It appears likely that Garfield spoke to Stanton much as he had to Villard, and that the secretary subsequently telegraphed to Washington that Garfield's account "more than confirm [s] the worst that has reached us as to the conduct of the commanding General and the great credit that is due Thomas." Garfield himself told Rosecrans that he had defended him to Stanton, and the latter's telegram may well have reflected Stanton's well-known bias against Rosecrans. But whatever the real explanation, the incident reflects no credit on Garfield, whose professions of loyalty to Rosecrans so contrasted with his appraisals of his late commander's behavior in the field. There was a ruthlessness to the young Garfield which would in time disappear. He regarded Rosecrans as a friend and mentor, but "Old Rosey" had failed to produce in time of crisis, and Garfield was not prepared to alter his account, not even for George H. Thomas. Here, as in certain later episodes, Garfield was curiously insensitive to the construction which others might place on his behavior. But he acted not from guile, but rather from the opposite, an excess of naïveté.

Garfield's departure from Chattanooga marked the end of his

military career. Like so many of his contemporaries, North and South, the war was the most important single event of his lifetime, and the experiences which it brought were never to be forgotten. For Garfield, the title of "general" was the source of the greatest pride, and the title which he preferred even after being elected president. For some time after leaving the Army of the Cumberland he contemplated a return to the field, for General Thomas had indicated that he was prepared to offer him a division. In the end, however, it was Lincoln himself who laid Garfield's martial ambitions to rest. Montgomery Blair has described the interview in which Garfield told the president that he was undecided as to whether he should leave the army for the House of Representatives:

> He was not inclined to leave the Army; he had become thoroughly identified with the Army of the Cumberland, and believed that as a commander of troops he would be a success. Mr. Lincoln replied that the Administration wanted a soldier from the field, who knew the wants of the armies from practical knowledge, and he hoped that the General would not hesitate about accepting his election; and as to commanding troops, they had more generals around loose than they knew what to do with.[15]

One suspects that Lincoln did not take Garfield's military pretensions too seriously and was interested primarily in securing one more dependable vote in the House. Curiously, even Garfield's friendly biographers have tended to gloss over his military service, stressing his ardor and bravery but conceding his inexperience and limited knowledge of the science of war. Actually, in the space of two years the Ohioan had demonstrated remarkable capacity both as a troop commander and as a strategist. Whatever his good fortune in the little Middle Creek campaign, he had demonstrated that he could get the best out of volunteer soldiers in the face of highly adverse weather conditions. Had he remained with the Army of the Cumberland, he would almost certainly have justified Thomas's confidence as a division commander and might even have qualified for higher command by the war's end.

As Rosecrans' chief of staff, however, Garfield was a mixed blessing. On one hand, his grasp of the war's fundamentals was ahead of that of many of his superiors. He recognized the need to maintain pressure on the Confederacy from all points. Although he conceded at times that the Army of the Cumberland should be equipped to hold the ground it might gain in battle, he would return in his letters to the paramount importance of destroying Confederate armies as opposed to occupying enemy territory. As chief of staff he kept the paper moving and, as noted earlier, he was not afraid to make his voice heard even against the collective wisdom of Rosecrans' combat commanders.

In tactical situations, however, Garfield's judgment was less sound. There is no evidence that he ever tempered the rashness which led him to divide his small force before Middle Creek. However commendable such élan, it was a liability in a chief of staff to Rosecrans, who was himself prone to impetuousness in tactical situations. Probably the ideal chief of staff would have been someone of the temperament of "Pap" Thomas; in any case, it was certainly not Garfield, who had waited so long for an advance that he could think of little else. For Garfield it was always "On to Richmond."

Garfield arrived in Washington on October 29, and was immediately pressed into service by Chase to address an emancipation meeting in Baltimore. Several similar speaking appearances followed, but Garfield returned to Washington in early November for interviews with Lincoln and Halleck concerning conditions in the Army of the Cumberland. He continued to harbor doubts regarding the wisdom of resigning his commission, particularly when he received a promotion to major general of volunteers, with the new rank dating from the Battle of Chickamauga. His dreams of military glory, however, were dissipated not only by Lincoln's preference that he enter Congress but by tragedy at home.

Garfield returned to Hiram in early November to pass the time before the opening of Congress and to see his new baby. Lucretia herself was still convalescing from the birth of their first son Harry—named after Harry Rhodes—when three-year-old

Trot came down with the "lung fever" to which her mother was so susceptible. For a time it was believed that she might recover, but by the last of November all hope was gone. On December 1 the grief stricken Garfield wrote to Harmon Austin, "Our darling Trot died at 7 o'clock this evening. We bury her day after tomorrow morning at 10½ o'clock. . . . Only such as you can know how desolate our hearts are tonight. Will you write me?" [16]

Scarcely had the services for Trot been held when little Harry came down with the same symptoms. Garfield delayed his return to Washington, and once more he and Crete hovered anxiously at bedside. Finally the fever broke, and Garfield felt that he could safely leave for the Capital. To a friend the shaken father wrote, "Our little boy was nearly well when I left home, though I thought for a day or two that I should have to drain the last drop in the bitter cup of sorrow by losing him also." [17] With a heavy heart Garfield settled into a boarding house on Pennsylvania Avenue, feeling more alone than ever before.

Chapter Seven

WASHINGTON

———◆———

Normally, the opening of a new session of Congress caused quite a stir in Washington. Rooming houses received their biennial coats of paint, and bars began a brisk traffic in political rumors. But 1863 was hardly a normal year, and the prospective opening of the Thirty-eighth Congress was buried in the back pages of the local press. Only a day before the session opened did the *Washington Star* provide an up-to-date list of the congressional delegations. For residents of the District of Columbia, the most relevant occurrence that winter was the inauguration of a link between the Potomac River and the Georgetown aqueduct; the ceremonies in connection with this welcome event largely upstaged the preliminary sessions of the war Congress. (The *Star* noted that while it had been tacitly agreed that excursioners to the aqueduct should drink Potomac water in honor of the occasion, certain of them "claimed exception from the rule.") [1]

The nation's capital was physically little changed from the overgrown town which had greeted Abraham Lincoln as president-elect nearly three years before. Money had been spent on public buildings even during the war, but the scattering of ambitious landmarks seemed only to accentuate the air of impermanence which permeated the wartime Capital. The Capitol building itself, with its ubiquitous scaffolding and yet-incomplete dome, seemed symbolic of the nation's still unfulfilled destiny. Inside, new congressmen gazed with awe at the Hall of Representatives, newly redecorated in red and gold. Visitors outside paused to stare at the statue of Washington, in which the Father of his Country, seated in full Roman regalia, looked askance at the construction debris on the Capitol grounds.

The city of Washington no longer housed the large number of troops which had camped on its doorstep in the first year of the war, and much of its life was business as usual. A personal ad in the *Star* offered $50 to "any person who will secure a situation for a lady in the Treasury Department." One Daniel Conner advised the owner of "the red cow that was sold at the Center Market last July" that he might reclaim his runaway beast upon payment of charges. But not everything was the same as before the war. The *Star* estimated, for instance, that the number of prostitutes in the city had increased tenfold to about 5,000 during the war, exclusive of those in Georgetown and Alexandria.

Overshadowed by war and the new aqueduct, the Thirty-eighth Congress convened on December 5. The Republicans quickly demonstrated their numerical superiority, electing Schuyler Colfax of Indiana as Speaker over his Democratic rival S. S. "Sunset" Cox. There were quite a number of new faces in this, the first Congress elected in wartime. From Pennsylvania came two champions of protection, William D. "Pigiron" Kelley and a future Speaker, Samuel J. Randall. Maine sent to Washington the most famous Republican of the Gilded Age, James G. Blaine. The new House comprised 102 Republicans, including what the *New York Tribune Almanac* called "unconditional unionists." Opposed to them were 75 Democrats and 9 border-state representatives who tended to vote with the Democrats. In the Senate, the administration majority was more impressive; there it could count on 36 votes against only 9 Democrats and 5 "conditional unionists." As for Garfield, he was doubtless flattered by the attention paid to his views on military affairs, and by the allocation of a seat on the Military Affairs Committee, chaired by a fellow Ohioan, Robert Schenck.

An authority on draw poker, Schenck was in some respects a typical legislator of the day. Although Schenck, like Garfield, was new to this Congress, he had a considerable background as a legislator and politician. A militant Whig in the 1840s, he had served four terms in Congress before accepting a diplomatic post under Fillmore. He had commanded a brigade at the first Battle of Bull Run, and at the second Bull Run had incurred a wound which left one wrist permanently crippled. Schenck was very much the bluff soldier; he shared Garfield's views concerning the prosecution of the war and was critical of Lincoln's handling of matters relating to slavery.

Garfield found his legislative work a welcome distraction, but it was some time before he could adjust to the loss of his daughter. The sight of Secretary Stanton's children at play awakened all the old pangs:

> How constantly the image of our precious lost one leaps into my memory and heart! I took dinner with Secretary Stanton today and his little ones were there to haunt me with contrasts between them and Trot. Her brightness so outshines theirs that I almost wondered [that] anyone could love them and not worship her. . . . Precious little darling, I wonder if she can know how her pap loves her and longs for her! [2]

Even in the best of circumstances, Garfield's hunger for companionship made him ill-suited to the often lonely life of a congressional boarding house. Now the bond of grief which united him and his wife led Garfield to question the restless ambition which had led him first to the field and then to Congress, at the expense of his home life. "Sometimes I think," he wrote home in February, "that I get far less leisure than any other mortal and have far less of the enjoyments of life. It is a fearful price to pay for a little publicity—to be obliged to throw away all the dear pleasures of home and family just at a time when enjoyment has the keenest relish." [3]

Garfield brought to Congress the same hard-nosed, somewhat brash views on the conduct of the war which had enlivened his year with Rosecrans. In an early speech in Congress he acknowledged that he had initially viewed the war in terms of the Union, but added that his attitude had changed:

I remember to have said to a friend when I entered the army, 'You hate slavery; so do I, but I hate disunion more. Let us drop the slavery question and fight to sustain the union.' . . . I started out with that position, taken in good faith, as did thousands of others of all parties, but the army soon found . . . the black phantom would meet it everywhere, in the camp, in the bivouac, in the battlefield. . . . The practical truth forced itself upon the mind of every soldier that behind the rebel army of soldiers the black army of laborers was feeding and sustaining the rebellion and there could be no victory until its main support was taken away.[4]

Party lines were not tightly drawn during the war years. In part this was a result of the administration's campaign to secure support from war Democrats, but it also reflected the reluctance of frontier-oriented legislators to accept the dictates of party leaders when momentous issues were at stake. Garfield, who as a college student had enjoyed defending "unpopular truth against popular error," made no effort to achieve a reputation for party regularity. In early January he spoke against an administration proposal to extend the provision for draft substitutes, a bill which Senator Henry Lane called "class legislation in favor of the rich and against the poor." Congressman Schenck introduced a substitute bill which would have abolished bounties and permitted a draftee to obtain a substitute only if the substitute were a blood relative. The Schenck bill was defeated, however, for the administration needed money as well as men, and the provision for substitutes had already brought in some $12,000,000 in revenue.

In a similar display of independence, Garfield was one of a handful of Republicans who voted against a bill to restore the rank of lieutenant general, and a companion resolution endorsing Grant for the place. Speaking on the bill, he argued that Congress should defer action until after the war since "the greatest race for the prizes of war is not yet ended." In February, when a resolution was introduced to thank Thomas for his stand at Chickamauga, Rosecrans complained to Garfield of the slight implied by the absence of any reference to himself as Thomas's commander. Garfield moved an amendment to insert the name of Rosecrans, but his efforts came to naught when the Senate failed to act on the bill as amended.

For all his militancy concerning the war, Garfield was still less radical than a significant section of his constituency—a point which was underscored in connection with his vote on a measure to assure equal pay for Negro soldiers. In December, Stanton had belatedly asked Congress for legislation to equalize the pay of white and colored soldiers. Thad Stevens introduced such a bill, only to see its provision for retroactive pay come under attack in the Senate. The bill as reported from committee provided equal pay retroactive to the date of enlistment for those who had been free men at the time of their enlistment, but retroactive pay only to the beginning of 1864 for all others. Garfield favored the Stevens bill, but endorsed the compromise as the best terms obtainable. His vote brought a number of protest letters from his constituents, and Garfield felt obliged to spell out his concept of his role as a congressman:

> I believe a representative should get all the light on every matter of public importance that his position enables him to and then speak and vote in such a manner as will, in his judgment, enhance the best interests of his constituents and the whole country. If the constituency, in reviewing the action of their representative, find him deficient in ability, judgment or integrity they have always the remedy of choosing another in his place. But while he is in office his course should be guided by his own judgments, based upon the suggestions of his constituents and all other attainable information. On no other grounds could I have accepted the office I now hold. . . .[5]

Garfield's return to Washington saw him still very much under the influence of Salmon P. Chase. When the new congressman voted against the Grant resolution, it was Chase who admonished him, urging him to take care before voting against the majority of his party. And as 1863 turned into 1864, Garfield found himself increasingly in sympathy with the views of the Chase faction on matters involving the prosecution of the war and reconstruction.

Garfield's inclination toward the Radicals, however, had a broader basis than his respect for the secretary of the treasury. It was a product also of his own antislavery predelictions, the sentiment of his district, and a belief not limited to congressmen that it was Congress, and not the Executive, which most accurately reflected the aspirations of the people and which should take the initiative in key matters of policy. No one directly challenged the constitutional doctrine of the separation of powers among three branches of government. There was, however, considerable difference of opinion as to exactly what measures could be promulgated by Executive decree and which were the legitimate purview of Congress. As late as 1895 Garfield's Ohio contemporary, John Sherman, would write, "The executive department of a republic like ours should be subordinate to the legislative department. The President should obey and enforce the laws, leaving to the people the duty of correcting any errors committed by their representatives in Congress." [6]

Thus it was to a restless and sensitive Congress that Lincoln, on December 8, 1863, first outlined his own program for reconstruction. Lincoln's plan, as outlined in his proclamation, envisioned a general amnesty for all who would pledge future loyalty to the United States, an amnesty from which only the top rank of Confederate officialdom would be exempted. The oath required acceptance of the government's wartime enactments regarding slavery, including the Thirteenth Amendment which abolished it, but Lincoln's plan did not otherwise come to grips with the thorny question of the future status of the Negro.

Radical Republicans were angered by the mildness of the presidential program, and their pique gave rise to a short-lived move to supplant Lincoln with Chase at the 1864 Republican convention. The Chase boom simmered quietly through the holidays and on February 20 emerged in the form of the Pomeroy Circular. Issued in the name of Chase's senatorial ally, Samuel P. Pomeroy, the statement proclaimed that the country required a change in leadership, and cited Chase as one who would see the war through to a successful conclusion.

But Chase's backers had badly misjudged the extent of dissatisfaction with Lincoln, and the Pomeroy Circular backfired. Moderate Republicans everywhere came to the president's defense and the Republican National Committee endorsed his renomination with only one dissenting vote. It is interesting that Garfield, although an admirer of Chase, was astute enough to see the impossibility of his replacing Lincoln. "It seems clear to me," he wrote to a constituent on February 25, "that the people desire the reelection of Mr. Lincoln and I believe any movement in any other direction will not only be a failure but will tend to disturb and embarrass the unity of the friends of the Union. . . . The administration is not all I could wish but it would be a national calamity to alienate the radical element from Mr. Lincoln and leave him to the support of the Blair and Thurlow Weed school of politicians." [7]

It is interesting to see Garfield, even at this early date, playing the conciliatory role within his party with which he would be increasingly associated in later years. But his emotions were still highly volatile, and when Frank Blair made a rare appearance on the floor of Congress to attack Chase's management of the Treasury Department, Garfield was no longer the dispassionate political strategist. He wrote indignantly to Rhodes that "the President is bound hand and foot by the Blairs and they are dragging him and the country down the chasm." As time went on, such letters would get him into difficulty with his constituents, who were considerably less critical than Garfield in their appraisal of the president.

In July 1864, the Radicals voted through their own scenario for reconstruction in the form of the Wade-Davis bill. In direct contradiction to Lincoln, the framers of the bill assumed that by seceding the Confederate states had forfeited their former prerogatives and as a result were nothing more than conquered provinces. Where Lincoln envisaged the re-establishment of state governments by 10 per cent of the loyal voters, the Wade-Davis bill stipulated that only after 50 per cent of the whites of voting age took such an oath could a legal government be re-established. Moreover, the category of ex-Confederate officeholders who were proscribed from voting or holding office was considerably expanded.

Considering the passions which the war had aroused, the Wade-Davis bill was not a particularly extreme measure. To secure the votes necessary to pass it, the bill's radical sponsors had omitted any mention of Negro suffrage, a cause near to their hearts. Because it had been framed with some care, there was great anguish among the Radicals when Lincoln killed the bill with a pocket veto. Its two sponsors issued a blistering rejoinder, warning the president not to usurp the power of Congress over the issue of reconstruction. By the time Congress adjourned and Garfield had returned to Hiram to seek renomination, his district was alive with rumors that Garfield not only sympathized with this Wade-Davis manifesto but had assisted in drafting it.

The stage was set for one of the Ohioan's oratorical triumphs. Invited by the local convention to explain his stand on the manifesto, Garfield marched onto the stage to deny that he had played any role in connection with it. Nevertheless, he told the pro-administration audience, Lincoln was not his "first choice" for the presidency. Garfield went on to say that "I hold it to be my privilege under the Constitution and as a man to criticize any acts of the President of the United States. . . . If . . . you are unwilling to grant me my freedom of opinion to the highest degree I have no longer a desire to represent you." [8]

Garfield was renominated by acclamation, and rode to victory on the flood of pro-administration ballots which followed the capture of Atlanta and Sheridan's campaign in the Shenandoah Valley. When statewide elections held in October in Ohio and Indiana showed a trend to the Republicans, Garfield was elated; to a friend in the Forty-second Ohio he wrote, "The election news so far as received is glorious—God Grant it may be the death knell of the Rebellion." [9] He himself won re-election by a total of 18,086 to 6315, a majority even greater than in 1862, in a campaign which was not without occasional light moments. Garfield himself told the story of how, in the course of a speech at Ashtabula, he chronicled the Union's latest military successes. "Gentlemen," he declaimed, "we have taken Atlanta, we have taken Savannah, we have taken Charleston, and we are about to capture Petersburg and Richmond. What remains for us to take?" A member of the audience broke up the meeting with his shout, "Let's take a drink!" [10]

Vindicated at the polls, Garfield returned to Washington to resume his dual role of supporter and critic to the administration. Although the most prominent Republicans in the House were still Thad Stevens and Speaker Colfax, one effect of the elections had been to increase the reputations and the self-esteem of younger Radicals such as Blaine, Garfield, and John Sherman. In the militant atmosphere of the new session, Garfield continued to demand total victory. When Lincoln traveled to Hampton Roads to meet with the Confederate commissioners, Garfield was amazed. "Our odd President is doing that odd thing," he wrote to General Irvin McDowell, "gone to Fortress Monroe to meet Stephens, Hunter and Campbell, whom both armies cheered as they came through. . . . We [are] engaged in a war more completely political in its causes, character and results than any other on record, and which no generalship is adequate to unless it be well mingled with a wise and comprehensive statesmanship." [11] But when Booth fired his fatal shot, Garfield felt the loss keenly. He had gone to New York on some financial matters, and only heard of the assassination on the morning of April 16. Perhaps recollection of his criticism of Lincoln reinforced the sense of loss; on the 17th he wrote to Crete, "My heart is so broken with our great national loss that I can hardly think or write or speak. . . . The day is nearly gone and I have as yet done nothing. I am sick at heart and feel it to be almost like a sacrilege to talk of money or business now." [12]

His trip to New York was the occasion for one of the few apocryphal incidents of Garfield's otherwise well-documented career. As related in various campaign biographies, Garfield was in lower Manhattan on the morning of the 16th, just as the full import of what had occurred in Washington was beginning to register on the crowds who milled in the streets. An account of what followed was allegedly contributed by "a distinguished public man, who was an eyewitness of the exciting scene":

> I shall never forget the first time I saw General Garfield. It was the morning after President Lincoln's assassination. The country was excited to its utmost tension, and New York city seemed ready for the scenes of the French revolution. . . .
> Fifty thousand people crowded around the Exchange Building, cramming and jamming the streets, and wedged in [as] tight as men could stand together. With a few to whom a special favor was extended, I went over from Brooklyn at nine A.M. and . . . found my way to the reception room for the

speakers in the front of the Exchange Building. . . .

By this time the wave of popular indignation had swelled to its crest. Two men lay bleeding on one of the side streets, the one dead, the other next to dying; . . . They had said a moment before that "Lincoln ought to have been shot long ago!" They were not allowed to say it again. . . .

'Vengeance' was the cry. On the right, suddenly, the shout rose . . . 'the *World!*' 'The office of the *World!*' . . . and the movement of perhaps eight thousand or ten thousand turning their faces in the direction of that building began to be executed. It was a critical moment. . . . Just then, at that juncture, a man stepped forward with a small flag in his hand, and beckoned to the crowd. . . . Taking advantage of the hesitation of the crowd, whose steps had been arrested a moment, a right arm was lifted skyward, and a voice, clear and steady, loud and distinct, spoke out, 'Fellow-citizens! Clouds and darkness are round about Him! His pavilion is dark waters and thick clouds of the skies! Justice and judgment are the establishment of His throne! Mercy and truth shall go before His face! Fellow-citizens! God reigns, and the Government at Washington still lives!'

The effect was tremendous. The crowd stood riveted to the ground with awe, gazing at the motionless orator, and thinking of God and the security of the Government at that hour. . . . What might have happened had the surging and maddened crowd been let loose, none can tell. The man for the crisis was on the spot, more potent than Napoleon's guns at Paris. I inquired what was his name. The answer came in a low whisper, 'It is General Garfield, of Ohio.' [13]

Lincoln's successor, the mercurial and tactless Andrew Johnson, proceeded to put into effect during the congressional recess of 1865 a reconstruction plan modeled after that of Lincoln. In 1864, three Southern states, Louisiana, Arkansas, and Tennessee, had been reorganized in accordance with Lincoln's 10-per-cent formula. Johnson "recognized" these three states, and undertook to apply the same formula to the eight remaining states of the former Confederacy. Like his predecessor, Johnson chose to take the legal view that the seceding states had never in fact left the Union and, like Lincoln, he was prepared to offer a broad amnesty. But as a concession to the Radicals, the newly admitted states were required to abolish slavery and repudiate their war debts, two provisions which had been absent from the earlier Wade-Davis bill.

Once again, the question of Negro suffrage appeared to have been swept under the rug. Johnson was the sworn enemy of the Southern aristocracy; he was, however, no friend of the Negro. Garfield was not yet prepared to join the erstwhile Abolitionists in demanding the immediate enfranchisement of the freedmen, but he took a position not far removed. Speaking on the Fourth of July at Ravenna, Ohio, he conceded that there was justifiable apprehension at the prospect of granting the franchise to "the great mass of ignorant and degraded blacks, so lately slaves."

> I am fully persuaded that some degree of intelligence and culture should be required as a qualification of suffrage, but let it apply to all alike. Let us not commit ourselves to the senseless and absurd dogma that the color of the skin shall be the basis of suffrage, the talisman of liberty. . . . If an educational test cannot be established, let suffrage be extended to all men of proper age regardless of color.[14]

As the new session of Congress assembled in December, John Greenleaf Whittier published in the *Nation* an "Ode to the Thirty-Ninth Congress":

> Make all men peers before the law,
> Take hands from off the negro's throat,
> Give black and white an equal vote.[15]

Moderate Republicans, however, were convinced that Northern public opinion was not yet prepared to give the ballot to the Negro. Moreover, many persons sympathetic to the Negro, including Garfield, had not yet given up hopes of co-operation with President Johnson. In a meeting with Johnson following the opening of Congress, Garfield had what he called a "full and free" exchange of views with the president:

> I gave him the views of the earnest men, North, as I understand them, and we tried to look over the whole field of difficulties before us. . . . Some foolish men among us are all the while bristling up for fight and seem to be anxious to make a rupture with Johnson. I think we should assume that he is

with us, treat him kindly, without suspicion, and go on in a firm, calmly considered course, leaving him to make the breach with the party if any is made. I doubt if he would do it under any such circumstances.[16]

In February, Garfield made a speech on the floor in which he reiterated his acceptance of the Lincolnian thesis that the Confederate states had not in a legal sense left the Union. But with a verbal dexterity which reflected his bias toward the Radicals, he went on to contend that the Confederate states "by their own act of treason and rebellion . . . had forfeited all of their rights in the Union," without releasing themselves from their obligations. "It rests with the people of the Republic to enforce the performance of these obligations and, so soon as the national safety will permit, restore [the Southern states] to their rights." [17]

In terms of his own future, Garfield decided prior to the Thirty-ninth Congress to seek a new committee assignment. In part, his attitude was a logical outgrowth of the war's end, for the Military Affairs Committee had little with which to concern itself in peacetime beyond the Regular Army budget. Nevertheless, he was pleasantly surprised to learn that he had been assigned by Speaker Colfax to the prestigious Committee on Ways and Means, which had primary responsibility for revenue measures. Financial legislation had interested Garfield ever since his period as Chase's house guest in the fall of 1862, and now he reported exuberantly a statement attributed to Secretary of the Treasury McCulloch that Garfield "had read the history of finance more thoroughly than any other Member of Congress."

By the time Congress adjourned in July, the breach between Johnson and the Radicals had widened, and the president had determined to make his reconstruction policy the main issue in the elections. Garfield stopped by Williamstown on his way back to Hiram, but his enjoyment of the college commencement was marred by his reflections on the forthcoming political bloodletting. He reached home on August 3, in time for the district convention at Warren which renominated him by acclamation. Although Garfield considered himself one of the more independent spirits of the House, his support for the bulk of the Radical reconstruction program had in fact given him better rapport with his constituents than he had enjoyed for some time. There was never any doubt about his own district, but Garfield was sufficiently in demand as a speaker that the campaign ended by being one of his most strenuous. He was on the road almost constantly from late August until election day, traveling the length and breadth of Ohio, with occasional engagements in Michigan, Indiana, and Illinois.

> Sept 18 Went to Seville—Rain, rain, rain. Spoke with Gov. Cox & Sam. Galloway in Fair Building. Evening spoke two hours at Ashland. Took train for Dayton.
>
> Sept 19 Reached Urbana—Bridges in front & flank swept away by flood. Went to Columbus—dined with Gen. Comly. Cars to Xenia where I arrived 10 P.M.
>
> Sept 20 Spoke on Court House steps. Shellabarger followed me. Spoke again short time to a delegation from Cedarville—Rain, Rain, Rain!!! Took cars evening for north, reached Columbus 10 P.M. and at 2 A.M took Cleveland train.[18]

Garfield maintained his hold on the Nineteenth District, almost matching his 3 to 1 ratio of two years before. It was becoming apparent that his was a "safe" Republican district, and this knowledge would permit him a degree of independence in the House to which all congressmen aspired but which comparatively few could afford. Over-all, the elections repudiated Andrew Johnson and assured Radical ascendancy in the new Congress as in the old. Any prospect which the president may have had of gaining support for his program had been jeopardized by the Black Codes, legislation enacted in most Southern states with a view toward keeping the Negro in a status as close to slavery as circumstances permitted. When ten states of the old Confederacy failed to ratify the Fourteenth Amendment, which prohibited the states from abridging civil rights or denying due process of law, the stage was set for a Radical sweep leading up to the final confrontation between Congress and the Executive. As one Radical exulted, "the House of Representatives can send a dozen members off to a picnic, and yet leave a majority large enough to pass a radical measure over the President's veto." [19]

Meanwhile, Northern liberals who were loathe to see the

readmission of Southern states without explicit guarantees on Negro suffrage took comfort from the South's unwillingness to accept the political realities growing out of Appomattox. The summer of 1866 had seen racial violence in Memphis and New Orleans, yet a majority of Northerners would probably have overlooked such developments had the South been more forthcoming in regard to the Fourteenth Amendment. The *New York Times* editorialized, "There is not one thing so much dreaded today by Wendell Phillips, Sumner, Boutwell, Stevens, and the rest of that school, as the acceptance of the [Fourteenth] Amendment by the Southern States—followed, as they know it would be . . . by the admission of the Southern members into Congress." [20] Such action might indeed have meant an end to the Republican majority.

One obvious effect of the congressional elections had been to knock Johnson's own reconstruction program out of the running. Henceforth, as a result of its own recalcitrance, the South could expect nothing better than terms similar to the old Wade-Davis bill. Indeed, the more militant Radicals were demanding guaranteed voting rights for the Negro. It was in this atmosphere that certain of the Radicals began to call for the president's impeachment. Wendell Phillips, for one, insisted that it was necessary to go a step beyond the defeat of Johnson's policy, and that the author of that policy must himself be removed from office. When, on March 2, the president vetoed a bill providing for the indefinite military occupation of the South, Congress passed it over his veto amid fresh clamor for Johnson's impeachment.

Garfield had voted for the first reconstruction bill, and he was one of only a handful of congressmen who had gone on record in 1865 as favoring Negro suffrage. Nevertheless, he had not yet embraced the Radical program *in toto;* in a letter on January 1, 1867, he wrote to Hinsdale, "I feel that if the Southern states should adopt the constitutional amendment within a reasonable time, we are morally bound to admit them to representation. If they reject it, then I am in favor of striking for impartial suffrage, though I see that such a course is beset with grave dangers." As for impeachment proceedings, he continued to hold back, no longer out of any belief that there could be any real co-operation between the president and Congress but out of concern for the repercussions which would attend any such step. In contrast to many of his colleagues, Garfield took a responsible and for the most part moderate view of the key issues of reconstruction. But he lived in an era of passionate oratory, and once on the floor of Congress he was sometimes carried away by the sound of his own voice. The ink was scarcely dry on his letter to Hinsdale when Garfield, on February 8, told the House that the Fourteenth Amendment asked "nothing for vengeance but everything for liberty and safety."

> I here affirm that so magnanimous, so merciful a proposition has never been submitted by a sovereignty to rebels since the day when God offered forgiveness to the fallen sons of men. . . . [The Southern states] have deliberated; they have acted. The last one of the sinful ten has at last with contempt and scorn, flung back into our teeth the magnanimous offer of a generous nation. It is now our turn to act. They would not cooperate with us in rebuilding what they destroyed. We must remove the rubbish and rebuild from the bottom.[21]

Garfield took for granted that the initiative for such rebuilding lay with Congress. Five days after this speech was made he voted routinely for a bill sponsored by George Julian and Thad Stevens which provided for the indefinite military administration of the unreconstructed South. When President Johnson sought to soften the military governments established by the Julian-Stevens bill by appointing military commanders sympathetic to the South, Garfield was incensed. One such district commander was Major General Winfield Scott Hancock, a brilliant corps commander with the Army of the Potomac whose strict constructionist outlook on political matters put him very much in the president's corner in matters concerning reconstruction. As military commander for Louisiana and Texas during much of 1867, Hancock gave wide latitude to local courts and kept the Army very much in the background. He was taking his orders from the president, and was not legally bound to exercise all the powers granted him. To Garfield, however, Hancock's actions were nothing less than sabotage; in a speech on January 17, 1868, he insisted

It is not for [Hancock] to search the defunct laws of Louisiana and Texas for a guide to his conduct. It is for him to execute the laws which he was sent there to administer. . . . With such a combination against us, does anyone suppose that we can take one step backward; much less that we will permit an officer of our army to fling back in our faces his contempt of our law, and tell us what policy shall be adopted? [22]

This was fairly strong medicine to be used against one of the heroes of Gettysburg, and Garfield later apologized to Hancock for the personal tone he had employed, little realizing that he and his adversary would in time be rival candidates for president of the United States. It is a commentary on the passions of the time that the normally fair-minded Garfield could allow himself to be so carried away.

The end of the session left Garfield badly fatigued, and prompted him to carry out a long-planned visit to Europe with Crete. Leaving New York on July 13 aboard the *City of London,* the Garfields arrived in Liverpool on the 26th. For the studious congressman, Europe was a succession of delights. To be sure, the Elgin marbles were a disappointment ("they are more decayed and fragmentary than I had expected") but he was fascinated by the workings of Parliament. His timing was excellent, for the House of Commons was debating a reform bill, and the debate was sharp:

> Gladstone rises and opens the debate on the opposition side in an adroit speech of eight minutes. Evidently reserving himself for a fuller assault later in the Evening. He is the ablest English speaker I have heard & the best. Disraeli shows great tact in determining how far to persist & when to yield. [23]

From London the Garfields visited Scotland, traveling for a time in the company of the Blaines and the Lot Morrills. From Scotland they crossed the North Sea, traveled across Germany and France, and reached their ultimate destination, Rome. They returned in November, barely in time for the new session of Congress but greatly refreshed in outlook. Garfield wrote wistfully of his summer, "I find that my short trip has made me desire to go again even more than I did at first." [24]

As pressure for impeachment mounted, Garfield remained doubtful. In December 1867, he voted against a resolution urging Johnson's impeachment. However, after the president had defied the Tenure of Office Act by his dismissal of Secretary Stanton, a new impeachment resolution was put forward and this time it had Garfield's support. As the trial itself began, Garfield watched the drama with the keen interest of a professional speechmaker, but his diary does not reflect any special sensitivity on his part to the constitutionl issues involved. He continued to harbor misgivings concerning the proceedings, not on constitutional grounds but out of concern that Johnson would be succeeded by Ben Wade, the president of the Senate. Wade was an Ohio neighbor of Garfield's, but the two were not close.

Notwithstanding his misgivings about Wade, when the impeachment trial fell one vote short of conviction Garfield was angry and disappointed. Like some of the Radicals, he felt that Chief Justice Chase had favored the defense, and the trial marked the end of their close association. Garfield wrote to Rhodes, "The conduct of Mr. Chase during the trial . . . has been outrageous. . . . I have no doubt that he is trying to break the Republican party and make himself president." [25]

Garfield was never comfortable concerning the issues involved in reconstruction, and his vacillation on the question of impeachment reflected his disturbed state of mind. On the impeachment issue as in the Porter court-martial, however, Garfield tended to be swayed by other than the legal facts of evidence. He did not try to put himself in the president's position, and although he was not a prime mover in connection with the attempted impeachment neither does he appear to have reflected on its significance in constitutional terms. Johnson, like Porter, was guilty of obstructing policies which Garfield and the Republican party favored.

Chapter Eight

THE
CONGRESSMAN

As the 1860s turned into the 70s, Garfield of Ohio came to be regarded as a respected member of the lower House. His studious habits stood him in good stead, for then as now the House was a complicated maze, and effectiveness came only with a thorough knowledge of the House rules. At the same time, his basic conviviality enabled him to make friends on both sides of the aisle. But the going was never easy, and the atmosphere was one of every man for himself.

The old Hall of Representatives, now a repository for statues, was a regular stop for visitors to the nation's Capital. Because there were no congressional offices, congressmen were obliged to conduct all business from their desks on the floor. As a result, the atmosphere was that of a not-too-exclusive men's club. Within the hall ventilation was poor and the acoustics worse. Congressmen either dozed, wrote letters, or lounged about during the speeches of their colleagues; page boys circulated among them with autograph albums, and the tips from visitors thus obtained helped send many a page boy to college. Smoking on the floor was forbidden—there were cloak rooms for that—and members were expected to wear coats. The chewing of tobacco, however, was endemic, and despite the presence of cuspidors the dark red carpeting was pocked with brown stains.

Partially because of his raucous behavior on the floor, the nineteenth-century congressman enjoyed no special status in the eyes of the public. One newspaperman writing in the 1870s likened speaking before the House to "trying to address the people in . . . Broadway omnibuses from the curbstone in front of the Astor House." [1] When Henry Adams had occasion to urge a cabinet officer to employ tact with certain congressmen, the secretary replied with some heat, "You can't use tact with a congressman! A congressman is a hog! You must take a stick and hit him on the snout!" [2] Garfield took a more positive view, and tended to see his working environment as a special challenge. "There is no harder place in the world," he wrote, " [in which] to make a reputation . . . than . . . the American House of Representatives. Less ability and tact will win fame in the Senate. Of all the distinguished men now in that body, there are not five, not educated in this House, who if transferred to it, would ever again be heard of." [3]

Garfield may have been prejudiced; certainly few congressmen passed up an opportunity to move to the less challenging environment of the Senate. Nevertheless, other descriptions of the House suggest that Garfield's appraisal may be a valid one. In any case, both houses of Congress tended to take an aggressive posture in their dealings with the Executive. Having done little more than chafe at the powers exercised by Lincoln during the Civil War, Congress saw the period of reconstruction as one in which to re-establish itself as a coequal branch of government, if not perhaps a bit more than equal. With the election of Blaine as Speaker in 1869, the House entered a more assertive period in terms of its relations with both the White House and the Senate. The seniority system was not yet operative in the House, and the Speaker enjoyed almost absolute control over committee assignments. Blaine—the first in a line of powerful Speakers—enforced a degree of dicipline among his Republican colleagues through a combination of charm and the adroit manipulation of committee assignments.

Although Garfield adjusted quickly to the House routine, he tended to talk too much. An admiring biographer conceded that "the House wearied a little of his polished periods and began to think of him as too fond of talking." [4] Nevertheless, he was credited by many with being among the more diligent as well as among the more erudite members of the House. When he decided to speak on a subject, he generally turned the address into a major research project. As one reviews Garfield's addresses on weighty subjects such as "The Age of Statistics," "Revenues and Public Expenditures," and "To Strengthen the Public Credit," one can hardly avoid concluding that, however dull, these orations represented considerable scholarship on the part of the speaker.

Along with his interest in finance, Garfield had the frontiersman's faith in the efficacy of universal education. Scholarship had meant a great deal to him, and he became its champion in a forum which tended to view intellectuals with disdain. Garfield was a regent of the Smithsonian Institution, at that time the country's foremost scientific society, and in 1869 he attempted unsuccessfully to secure a government subsidy which would have helped in meeting the Smithsonian's operating expenses.

Second only to Garfield's scholarly interests, and in many respects more pertinent, was his fascination with the machinery of government. At a time when the average congressman viewed government operations almost entirely in terms of patronage and the pork barrel, Garfield was a one-man Hoover commission. In the face of the indifference or hostility of a large number of his colleagues, the Ohioan set about implementing his conviction that the national census-taking should be more than a head count and should attempt to gather economic and social statistics for the whole country. After a lengthy critique of past censuses, which had been administered by politically appointed U. S. marshals, Garfield recommended in 1869 that a Census Bureau be established under an appropriate cabinet department. The bill which he drafted managed to get through the House, but died in the Senate; the affair is of interest primarily as a reflection of Garfield's interest in the administrative side of government. It was a curious interest for a romantic such as Garfield, who preferred to think in terms of great issues such as slavery and the Union. But the Ohioan was observant enough, and interested enough, to find much in the day-to-day operations of Congress that was susceptible of improvement.

The framing of legislation was heady wine, even when the Senate proved obdurate. Such activity, however, was only a small part of a congressman's duties in Garfield's day. Much of his time was consumed in running errands for constituents; over a two-month period during 1870, for instance, he had requests to search for a missing letter, to secure favorable action on a pension claim, to obtain approval for a patent extension, to determine whether a "baggage man" had been fairly appointed, and to secure a pass on the Pacific railroad. Garfield attempted to accommodate most such requests, but his staff consisted of only a single male secretary and the demands on his time were onerous. After spending half of one day running errands in various government departments he wrote in his diary, "I do not know that I have ever been more weary of this type of vicarious suffering than I am tonight. The great crowd of people that come upon me for one thing or another draw heavily upon my vital forces and go far toward exhausting . . . [me].[5]

Some of the demands of his constituents could be finessed, and Garfield was one of the first congressmen to make his appointments to West Point and Annapolis on the basis of a competitive exam. Unlike his friend Blaine, who made maximum use of the patronage available to him to develop a passionately devoted following, Garfield found the endless jockeying for postmasterships the ultimate in drudgery. For all his complaints, however, he was capable of finding intellectual stimulus in much of the legislative process. Writing in his diary in 1873, he described a typical day:

The same old story. Letters in the morning; Committee at half-past ten; House at twelve. Went nearly through the estimates for the PO Dept. After the morning hour took up the Legislative App. Bill. Pushed it steadily until one-quarter before five. Made good progress. . . . Had a brisk debate as usual on the Bureau of Education.[6]

The House of Representatives of the post-Civil War era represented a considerably more promising arena for an ambitious congressman than it would in the late twentieth century. Not only was it a quarter the size of the House today but, in the absence of a rigid seniority system, a member could aspire to committee assignments consistent with his interests and aptitudes. Garfield's reputation grew, in part as a result of his own efforts in committee and on the floor and in part because of the limited intellectual stature of the majority of his colleagues. But even he was stymied in one of his prime objectives, that of securing the chairmanship of the Committee on Ways and Means. Although Garfield was on good terms with both Republican Speakers, Colfax and Blaine, the closest he came to his committee goal was a single term on the Ways and Means Committee. Finally, in 1871, he was named chairman of the Committee on Appropriations, and thus was able to continue his interest in financial legislation from a post second only to the chairmanship of Ways and Means.

An ethical concept of public life today which was unheard of in Garfield's day is that which we call conflict of interest. Whatever its merits, the idea that a public servant must disengage himself from all obligations which might conflict with his official duties is a relative newcomer to the American political scene. George Washington speculated in public lands, and Abraham Lincoln kept up his law practice while in Congress. Somewhat in the manner of state legislatures today, election to Congress was regarded by a lawyer as a means of enlarging his reputation and bringing in a few more cases. The fact that Congress was in recess from July until December encouraged and often required a congressman to pursue some form of outside income.

Garfield's second term as congressman coincided with a wave of speculation in oil lands, and for much of 1865 the ostensible legislator was searching for capital with which to purchase oil land in the area of his Middle Creek campaign of three years before. For the most part, however, Garfield's moonlighting took the form of a part-time law practice. He had been admitted to the Ohio bar in 1861, under the system then in vogue whereby an aspiring lawyer merely read up on Blackstone and presented himself for examination. But when war came, Garfield quickly put aside any thought of law practice.

The circumstances under which Garfield subsequently represented his first client were curious to the point of being bizarre. During his first term in Washington, the Military Affairs Committee had been directed to inquire into instances when individuals had been detained, usually on orders from the War Department, without the protection afforded by peacetime legal procedures. Although it was Thad Stevens who had actually proposed the resolution in question, Garfield had supported it, and the resulting investigation had led to a sweeping clearance of military prisons which called Garfield to the attention of one of the great constitutional lawyers of the day, Jeremiah Sullivan Black.

Black had served four years in Buchanan's cabinet, first as attorney general and then, briefly, as secretary of state. Although a strong believer in states' rights, he had urged the arming of federal installations in the South and was an outspoken Unionist. Like Garfield, he enjoyed championing unpopular causes; in general, however, he was about as improbable a companion for the Ohio congressman as one could imagine. Not only was he a states' rights Democrat, more than twenty years Garfield's senior, but his only indirect association with Garfield had been when the latter had included Black's son Chauncey among a group of Hiram students expelled for misconduct in 1853.

Garfield and Chauncey Black re-established social relations in wartime Washington, however, and through Chauncey the freshman congressman came to know the elder Black. By 1865 they were sufficiently fast friends that they even contemplated forming a law partnership. It was at this time that Black undertook to handle before the Supreme Court a celebrated civil rights case involving one Lambdin P. Milligan. Milligan was an Indiana Copperhead who had been arrested in 1864, tried for conspiracy by a military court, and sentenced to be hanged—a decision which Garfield, at that time, might well have applauded. There were various stays of execution, however, and with the close of the war Milligan was able to challenge the competence of the military tribunal which had tried him by applying for a writ of habeas corpus. The case reached the Supreme Court at a time when military tribunals were in bad odor, in part because of doubts regarding the trial of the Lincoln conspirators. As Black searched for lawyers to assist in the Milligan case, he was attracted to Garfield, not only because of their friendship but because of the Ohioan's Republican political credentials, his opposition in Congress to arbitrary arrests, and his demonstrated capacity as an orator.

The upshot of this was that Garfield, who had never argued a case in court, assisted in reversing Milligan's conviction in one of the landmarks of American constitutional law, *ex parte* Milligan. In a decision announced in December 1866, the Supreme Court agreed unanimously that the military tribunal in question had no jurisdiction over Milligan as long as the civil courts were available and functioning. In some autobiographical notes prepared for his 1880 election campaign, Garfield noted that his role in the *ex parte* Milligan case "gave me immediately a standing in the Supreme Court of the United States and began to bring me in cases." [7]

Garfield had the requisites of a successful lawyer as well as the temperament of a college professor, and for much of his career would be tempted by the prospect of switching to one of these professions. For all his grumbling over the lot of a congressman, however, he was fitting rather neatly into his niche on Capitol Hill. Since his first unhappy term of bachelor boarding he had taken to bringing his family with him to Washington. This in turn had involved a choice between more boarding house living or the renting of a house, and in 1869 Garfield determined to build a home of his own. Aided by a loan from his Army of the Cumberland comrade, David Swaim, he purchased a lot on the corner of Thirteenth and I Streets and was able to build a comfortable brick house on it for a total of about $10,000.

The house itself was squarish, and furnished in the heavy Victorian style of the day. On entering the visitor found the parlor on his left, complete with an upright piano, a slate mantle, and a pair of three-foot Chinese vases. To the right of the entrance was a sitting room, while beyond it was a large and ornately papered dining room. Above, on the second floor, was Garfield's study; there visitors marveled at the walls lined with books and with the file boxes of memoranda on specialized aspects of government finance.

Part of the charm of Washington for the Garfields was that they had developed in the Capital a new circle of friends who complemented nicely the Hiram group centering on Hinsdale and Rhodes. Unlike many "successful" men, however, Garfield rarely outgrew a friendship, and though he and Crete came to be on good terms with the families of Jerry Black, James G. Blaine, Robert Ingersoll, and John Hay, among many, there was no trend away from their old friends at Hiram where they continued to spend much of the year. For all his intellectual interests, Garfield's tastes were simple and his values were the solid virtues of the American Midwest. According to one chronicler,

> His home-life was that of the plain New England farmer element from which he sprang . . . taking little note of the fancies of fashion. He liked substantial furniture, good engravings, a big cane-seated chair, an open fire, a simple meal, a wide brimmed felt hat and easy-fitting clothes. . . . His memory for anecdotes was almost as good as Lincoln's, but he remembered best such as he got in his reading of biography and history and were applicable to some intellectual theme he was discussing, rather than the merely quaint and humorous.[8]

In Congress, Garfield took a pragmatic approach to the financial issues of the day, and gradually built up a modest following of his own. On matters affecting reconstruction, however, party lines became tightly drawn, and Garfield voted consistently with his Republican colleagues, particularly since it became apparent that restoration of home rule in the South was to be the cornerstone of the Democratic party. On two other controversial issues of the day, the "greenback" question and the tariff, party discipline was lax and local interests were often paramount. In both instances the solid support which Garfield enjoyed in the Nineteenth District enabled him largely to follow the dictates of his research.

The great currency issue centered upon whether and/or how to retire the paper money, greenbacks, which the government had issued beginning in 1862 to finance the war. The pros and cons of their issuance had been hotly debated, with critics pointing out that increased currency in circulation would raise prices and thereby increase the cost of financing the war. Others saw the issuance of fiat money as a breach of faith which would have the effect of driving "specie"—i.e., gold-backed currency—out of circulation. The exigencies of wartime finance momentarily overcame all opposition, however, and during the war the government issued some $450,000,000 in greenbacks. Nevertheless, as early as December 1865 the House resolved, by a 144 to 6 vote, in favor of the early resumption of specie payment. The issue continued to simmer in the postwar years, with debtor classes in the North and West emerging as champions of inflation.

Basically, the question of hard versus soft money was a class issue which would pit debtor and creditor against one another for the remainder of the nineteenth century. Farmers welcomed the greenbacks from the outset, while they were made palatable to Wall Street by the fact that many government bonds specified repayment in specie.[9] Ohio was a primary battleground in the war of the currencies, with soft-money forces more often in the ascendancy than not. In the winter of 1866–67, Garfield's disgust at the failure of the Southern states to ratify the Fourteenth Amendment was equaled by his concern over delays in the resumption of specie payments. To Hinsdale he wrote,

> In reference to finance, I believe that the great remedy for our ills is an early return to specie payments, which can only be effected by the contraction of our paper currency. There is a huge clamor against both and in favor of expansion. . . . There is passion enough in the country to run a steam engine in every village, and a spirit of proscription which keeps pace with the passion. My own course is chosen, and it is quite probable that it will throw me out of public life.[10]

Even as he wrote this Garfield was working closely with Secretary of the Treasury McCulloch to secure passage of a bill which would permit the secretary to exchange the government's floating debt for long-term bonds, and similarly to exchange bonds for greenbacks. It was characteristic of Garfield that he viewed the bill entirely in terms of its economic logic, and with little regard for either its social implications or for the political realities involved in its passage. Garfield's colleagues had no intention of making such a sweeping concession of power to Andy Johnson's secretary of the treasury, and in the end a ceiling was placed on the number of greenbacks which could be retired in any month.

Just as it had tended to split on civil-rights issues during the war, the Ohio delegation found itself sharply divided on the financial issues of the postwar decade. At the beginning of the Fortieth Congress Garfield found himself in opposition to his old committee chairman, Schenck, who had introduced a bill to prohibit the retiring of any more greenbacks under the House resolution of 1865. Garfield attempted to have the new resolution recommitted, but inflation was in the air and Schenck's resolution was adopted by a vote of 127 to 32. Garfield took pride in his own consistency and wrote to Hinsdale, "I am glad to have the opportunity of standing up against a rabble of men who hasten to make weathercocks of themselves." [11]

For several years neither the advocates of inflation nor the forces for hard money was able to secure a breakthrough, and the proportion of greenbacks in circulation remained little changed. Following the financial panic of 1873, however, there were new demands for inflation. Twice during the first session of 1874 Garfield delivered extended addresses on the perils of fiat money, and while it is doubtful that he made many converts among his congressional colleagues, the speeches reinforced his image as a Westerner with an essentially Eastern outlook. After recalling the unusual circumstances in which the greenback experiment had first been launched, Garfield insisted that the demands of wartime financing were no longer present, and that the nation's economy demanded a sound dollar:

> The trouble with our greenback dollar is this: it has two distinct functions, one a purchasing power, and the other a debt-paying power. As a debt-paying power, it is equal to one hundred cents; that is, to pay an old debt. A greenback dollar will, by law, discharge one hundred cents of debt. But no law can give it purchasing power in the general market of the world, unless it represents a known standard of coin value.[12]

In currency matters, unlike most others, Garfield was resistant to compromise except as a last resort. Concerning the tariff, which was emerging as a subject of importance to the industries which had sprung up in the war years, Garfield was a protectionist, but with little of the zeal which he brought to monetary issues. In a speech in 1866, he took a position on the tariff which would change comparatively little over the years:

> I hold that a properly adjusted competition between home and foreign products is the best gauge to regulate international trade. Duties should be so high that our manufacturers can fairly compete with the foreign product, but not so high as to enable them to drive out the foreign article, enjoy a monopoly of the trade, and regulate the price as they please. This is my doctrine of protection. If Congress pursues this line of policy steadily, we shall, year by year, approach more nearly to the basis of free trade, because we shall be more nearly able to compete with other nations on equal terms. I am for a protection that leads to ultimate free trade. I am for that free trade which can only be achieved through a reasonable protection.[13]

Garfield was by no means insensitive to the interests of his constituents in tariff matters, and over the years he would press for tariff schedules which would offer generous protection to Ohio's burgeoning steel industry. Moreover, he had little criticism for lobbying as such, and was rather insensitive to the extent to which Congress was becoming a sounding board for the country's great corporations. He was critical, however, of overly enthusiastic lobbying by special interest groups—activity which was never more apparent than when tariff schedules came up for revision. He deplored the unrealistic demands of tariff lobbyists who, in his view, were playing into the hands of the free traders. He spelled out his views at some length in a letter to a constituent, written in 1871 in the wake of an especially hard winter. Noting that the entire tariff system was under fire because of excessive rates on household necessities such as coal, he warned that high rates might well prove counterproductive. "If I do not entirely mistake the signs of the times," he wrote, "the high tariff men will be very glad to stand on my ground before a year is passed. The great danger now is that the reaction against the tariff will go too far, just as the high tariff men . . . went too far in pushing duties up." [14]

It is difficult to say whether Garfield's views and votes as expressed in Congress embodied a recognizable political philosophy. His views on the tariff were consistent with his belief in a truly competitive market place. As early as 1865, he had supported a measure to prevent any state from creating a railroad monopoly within its borders, calling the bill "a plain declaration of the right of Congress to regulate commerce." His attitude on the tariff, together with his preoccupation with sound currency, type him as a fiscal conservative, though of the pragmatic rather than the doctrinaire variety.

By present-day standards, Garfield was very much an advocate of the trickle-down theory of economic progress, whereby one facilitates the growth of business productivity on the assumption that all will eventually benefit. When Grant contemplated a program of public works to alleviate the hard times which had followed the 1873 depression, Garfield would have none of it, writing to Hinsdale,

> We had something of a struggle to keep him [i.e., Grant] from drifting into that foolish notion that it was necessary to make large appropriations on public works to give employment to laborers. But the Secretary of the Treasury and I united our forces in dissuading him from the scheme, insisting that the true remedy for the finances at present was economy and retrenchment, until business restored itself.[15]

The charge has been made, not without some basis, that congressmen in the Gilded Age were little more than errand boys for the new commercial interests. Few legislators, however, saw anything subversive in a close relationship with the commercial interests in their districts. For the most part they were in some awe of the material advances which they saw all about them, and this was as true of Garfield as of any. Speaking in 1874 on "The Railroad Problem," he made it fairly clear that he did not regard railroads as a "problem" but as one of the major blessings of his generation. "The American people have done much for the locomotive," he observed, "and it has done much for them." He saw the influence of railroads in political as well as economic terms, noting that "the railroad has not only brought our people and their industries together, but it has carried civilization into the wilderness, has built up States and Territories, which but for its power would have remained deserts for a century to come." [16] There was much truth in this, and Garfield's remarks reflected his faith in scientific progress. Unfortunately, by 1874 he was somewhat defensive on the subject of railroads.

Chapter Nine

PRESIDENT GRANT

———————◆———————

Commenting on the politics of the Gilded Age, Professor George Mayer has observed that "the election of Grant closed a chapter in the history of the Republican Party. The heroic days of its youth were gone, the burning issues settled, and the goals of its founders fulfilled. Leaders who had been willing to risk denunciation, ridicule, and social ostracism for their principles settled down to what they hoped would be a long twilight of respectability." [1]

In point of fact, this sought-after tranquility was never quite achieved, for as so often happens the resolution of one great political issue merely laid the groundwork for new ones. The decade following the Civil War found the South perversely unwilling to accept the political results of the war as they affected the Negro —a fact which leading Republicans, who hoped to make the freedman the cornerstone of their party in the South, found highly unsettling. The Republican party found itself in the anomalous position of having participated in a successful war only to emerge in scarcely better shape than it had been for the election of 1860.

In 1868, the American electorate added a new laurel to those of the hero of Appomattox with the election of Ulysses S. Grant as president. Once Grant had decided that he was a Republican —a determination which was disconcertingly long in coming— his nomination and election were regarded as assured. Subsequently, it came as a shock to many Republicans when Grant and Colfax, running against a weak Democratic ticket headed by a former governor of New York, Horatio Seymour, carried less than 54 per cent of the popular vote. Although the G.O.P. carried the electoral college by a large majority, Seymour's popular vote was a potent reminder that the Democrats were still a more "national" party than their rivals, who had yet to develop an effective organization in the South.

Such political eddies went largely unnoticed in the Western Reserve. Garfield had a brief scare when it appeared that his vocal Ashtabula neighbor, Senator Ben Wade, might choose to run for Congress following the expiration of his Senate term. Notwithstanding his poor opinion of Wade's capabilities, Garfield felt that the situation called for some gesture on his part, and indicated to Wade that he was prepared to stand down in the Nineteenth District if Wade chose to run for Congress. Fortunately for Garfield the older man was not interested, and Garfield was easily renominated and elected.

Although there were few people in public life who could claim that they "knew" President Grant, Garfield shared the hopes of many for the victorious general whose slogan was "Let us have peace." Disillusionment was not long in coming. Garfield shared the surprise of Republican party leaders when Grant failed to consult with congressional leaders and named a cabinet dominated by wealthy business executives. Congressional Republicans were not long in showing their pique. The Senate not only failed to confirm Grant's initial choice for secretary of the treasury, but refused to approve a House bill which would have repealed the contentious Tenure of Office Act. Garfield was one of those who voted against repeal; there was something wrong, in his view, with casting aside so precipitously the legislation which had been the legal basis for the impeachment proceedings against

Grant's immediate predecessor.

Grant's naïveté was nowhere more apparent than in regard to patronage issues, and one of the first legislators to be embarrassed on this score was Garfield. Shortly after Grant's inauguration, Garfield had solicited the views of leading citizens in his district and had accepted their recommendation of an individual to be postmaster for the town of Ravenna. Much to Garfield's chagrin, he then discovered that Grant had already filled the post. Garfield sought an interview with the president over this violation of standard practice, and found him not only contrite but willing to withdraw his own nomination. Garfield chose not to press the matter, but as one who was himself a stickler for proprieties the incident colored his view of the administration and its *modus operandi*. Garfield was not dependent on patronage for the good will of his district, which was just as well, since the president considered himself an Ohioan and was prone to regard Ohio appointments as his personal prerogative.[2]

The elevation of Blaine to Speaker of the House brought a reshuffling of House committee assignments. Although Garfield had continued to hope for the chairmanship of the Committee on Ways and Means, this choice assignment went to the veteran congressman from Massachusetts, Henry L. Dawes. Later, Garfield would complain in his diary that it was his failure to take a stronger stand in favor of the protective tariff which had cost him the chairmanship. He felt that he had been badly treated by Blaine, and wrote to Hinsdale, "I have no doubt that I should have had the Ways and Means but for the fact that I have positive opinions and have frankly and squarely expressed them." [3] Garfield may in fact have been penalized on the strength of a feeling that he was "less sound" on the tariff than some of his colleagues. But Dawes was an able legislator and senior in service to Garfield; one suspects that, in attributing his setback to his forthright convictions, Garfield was indulging in a bit of rationalization.

In charging Blaine with having bowed to the tariff lobby, Garfield was voicing reservations which he had felt from the outset about the man from Maine. It was not that they did not have a great deal in common. Each came from a poor background, and they tended to hold similar views on such issues as monetary policy and reconstruction. They enjoyed good company and excelled at the give and take of debate on the House floor. But there were also significant differences. Garfield had a convivial outlook, and a reputation as a good worker had given him a certain stature among his colleagues. But he was a relative unknown in comparison to Blaine, who had been a marked man from the first time he had entered the Hall. "His tall, erect figure, his face . . . with its prominent, intelligent nose, its fine dark eyes and flashing smile, marked him out as much from the crowd of new statesmen as did his formidable gifts for public debate. . . . His readiness of thought, his personal 'magnetism,' his delightful sense of humor, soon gathered about him countless friends, admirers, [and] followers to whom for a long time Blaine embodied nothing short of genius." [4]

Whereas Garfield thought in terms of issues, Blaine understood what people wanted. He was not by choice a manipulator, but his gift for organization and his infallible memory for names and faces led him as surely to the party headquarters as Garfield's instincts led him to the Library of Congress. In his strategic position as Speaker, Blaine worked closely with representatives of the great manufacturing interests, and sought to demonstrate that the Republican party was their ally. Garfield was scarcely less zealous on behalf of American manufacturers, but thought not in terms of political alliances but of the perfectability of man.

For different reasons, neither Blaine nor Garfield was sensitive to the ethical pitfalls inherent in public service at a time when the floor of Congress was all but taken over by representatives of iron foundries and railroads. "A clamorous, competing crowd of flashy men . . . now besieged the Capitol in force, buttonholing the politicians everywhere, plying them with liquor, cigars, and money." [5] Blaine, whose vision of the future had himself at the head of a Republican party dedicated to the needs of American business, peddled in his spare time the bonds of the Little Rock and Arkansas Railroad. Garfield and a few others supported the immense grants of land to the railroads (the Northern Pacific alone received some 47 million acres of Western land) out of a romantic conviction that railroads were the harbinger of national prosperity. But many legislators were openly or covertly in the employ of competing railroads, and no one in Congress seemed anxious to call them to account.

Garfield's indifference to this situation is curious, for his own outlook bordered on the puritanical and one of his first chores under the Grant administration had been to investigate one of the more publicized financial scandals of the 70s. Shortly after Grant's inauguration, two of Wall Street's more notorious tycoons, Jay Gould and Jim Fisk, set into motion a plan designed to "corner" the available gold supply and to realize enormous profits at the expense of traders who were obliged to pay their European creditors in gold. The only immediate obstacle to this scheme was the U. S. Treasury Department, which by selling government gold could keep the gold price down. To head off this possibility, Gould and Fisk assiduously cultivated the president and members of his family. In conversations with Grant, Gould emphasized that the immediate beneficiary of any gold shortage would be the American farmer, whose greenbacks would increase in value.

Convinced that Grant would not interfere, Gould and Fisk began to buy gold, and by September 24 their purchases had driven the price of gold to an all-time high. In so doing, they drove to the wall a large number of reputable bankers whose commitments required them to continue purchases of gold. In the end, Grant was persuaded by the banking community of the necessity of government gold sales; the market price for gold then dropped as precipitously as it had risen, though not before Gould and Fisk had unloaded their own gold at a tremendous profit.

These were the facts that came to light after Garfield, as chairman of the Committee on Currency and Banking, was empowered by a House resolution to conduct an inquiry into the "black Friday" gold panic. Garfield attacked the problem with his usual energy, seemingly oblivious to the potential political ramifications of his investigation. After a series of interviews in New York, he wrote that "the abysses of wickedness which are opening before us in the investigation are among the most remarkable things I have met." In its report, much of which was written by Garfield, the committee made no attempt to gloss over the reliance of the plotters on their connections with Grant. But the report identified Gould as "the guilty plotter of all these criminal proceedings," and failed to establish any link between the conspirators and Grant himself. The president was a highly suspicious individual, and the gold investigation might easily have been the occasion for a breach between him and Garfield. As it happened, however, the White House seemed relieved that the committee report was not even more damaging. Garfield wrote in June 1870 that "the President expresses himself under a good many obligations to me for the management of the Gold Panic investigation." [6]

Nevertheless, Garfield grew increasingly critical of the administration. Among Grant's initial cabinet choices, the nomination of Garfield's old friend Jacob Cox as secretary of the interior had been particularly well-received. In the fall of 1870, however, the president chose to listen to Cox's detractors in a dispute over a land claim, and the straightforward Cox had no choice but to submit his resignation. Garfield's desire to maintain good relations with the administration did not keep him from excoriating Cox's critics from the floor of Congress; to Cox himself he wrote that "the worst fears of the country are realized in reference to your resignation. It is a clear case of surrender on the part of the President to the political vermin which infest the government." [7]

Of less immediate concern to Garfield, although even more ominous in terms of Republican party unity, was the breach between Grant and Sumner over the issue of Santo Domingo. From the time he first took office, Grant was attracted by the prospect of annexing the island, which had been abandoned by Spain in 1865, as a special preserve for freedmen. There, in Grant's simplistic view, the American Negro could have his own civilization, separate from the mainland but still part of the United States. Bypassing his own Department of State, Grant sent his personal secretary, Orville Babcock, on a tour of the island. Babcock met with the reigning warlord, one Buenaventura Baez, and returned to Washington with a treaty of annexation in his pocket. Grant duly submitted the treaty to the Senate for ratification, only to encounter the unbending opposition of the haughty chairman of the Committee on Foreign Relations, Charles Sumner.

Strongly influenced by Sumner's opposition, the committee

reported adversely on annexation in March 1870, and Sumner began a series of speeches on the floor in which he castigated the administration in highly personal terms. Not content with questioning the wisdom of adding 300,000 Negroes to the population, Sumner chastised the presidential secretaries and portrayed the president as the tool of corrupt adventurers. In January 1871, the House concurred in a Senate resolution which urged a vote on whether to establish a committee to investigate the desirability of annexation. Subsequently, however, Garfield helped to pass an amendment which noted explicitly that the resolution did not commit Congress to a policy of annexation. In the end Sumner was able to block ratification of the treaty, but only at the cost of his committee chairmanship, for the Senate caucus was convened at Grant's request and removed the Massachusetts senator from his position.

Whatever its other shortcomings, the Grant administration throughout its two terms sought means to enforce the constitutional amendments which had been designed to protect the Negro. The same postwar letdown which brought about a lowering of ethics in government, however, took its toll of the reformist zeal which had been so much in evidence before and during the war. The most dramatic challenge—the abolition of slavery—was an accomplished fact. Similarly, passage of the Fourteenth and Fifteenth Amendments had gone a long way toward meeting the legal needs of the emancipated Negro. As for enforcement, however, most Northerners had gone to war to save the Union, not the black man; interest in the ultimate fate of the freedmen was limited largely to reformers who had long supported the Negro's cause and to Republican politicians who saw in Negro votes the basis for a two-party system in the conquered South. Arrayed against this curious alliance were the erstwhile rulers of the South, whose campaign of passive resistance against federal enforcement of Negro rights would prove to be one of the most spontaneous and effective on record.

During Grant's two terms, the key issue of reconstruction centered on when and on what terms home rule would be returned to the South. The administration gave it a real try, but was handicapped by inertia in the North, the dubious motives of some of its own stalwarts, and the fact that the newly freed Negro was rarely in a position to contribute greatly on his own behalf. Finally, as one author has noted, "It became expedient for political and business interests in the North to conciliate the South, and the price on which the South was united in demanding was an end to the enforcement of Negro rights." [8] Reconstruction under Grant consisted largely of enforcing military rule while encouraging adoption and enforcement of the Fifteenth Amendment which conferred the vote on the black man. Two Force Acts, passed in May 1870 and February 1871, authorized the president to employ the Army to assure compliance with the Fifteenth Amendment, and provided for fines and imprisonment in cases of the intimidation of voters. A third Force Act, aimed at the Ku Klux Klan, prescribed heavy penalties on persons "who shall conspire together, or go in disguise . . . for the purpose . . . of depriving any person or any class of persons of . . . equal privileges or immunities under the laws."

Garfield found himself increasingly perplexed by the problem of reconstruction. He spoke only infrequently on issues relating to it, but even as he sought to concentrate on financial legislation he and his colleagues were reminded that the social issues of the war were still very much with them. Garfield attempted to deal with each question as it arose, and in the form in which it arose. Thus he routinely supported the first two Force Acts, only to balk at the third on the grounds that the power which it granted the president to suspend habeas corpus and to proclaim martial law was extreme. "In so far as this section punishes persons who . . . shall deny or refuse to others the equal protection of the laws, I give it my cheerful support," said Garfield, "but when we provide by Congressional enactment to punish a mere violation of a state law we pass the line of constitutional authority." [9] Garfield's legal turn of mind made it difficult for him to achieve a consistent voting record, but it was obvious that he had not forgotten the lessons of *ex parte* Milligan. In any case, the Force Acts were only partially successful. Public opinion in the North became restive following repeated instances in which federal troops were obliged to intervene on behalf of the

Negro. Republican hopes for a power base in the Old Confederacy gradually waned; in one instance, after the governor of Mississippi had requested protection from Negro voters, a delegation from Ohio called on President Grant to warn him that if he sent troops to Mississippi the Republicans would lose Ohio.[10]

The combination of maladministration in Washington and impasse in the South had seriously eroded Grant's once-immense prestige before his first term was half over. As early as March 1871, Garfield wrote to a constituent that "political affairs look very dark at the present time. The administration has been losing ground rapidly, and . . . some of our best men begin to despair of Grant's reelection." [11] The fall from grace by the enigmatic hero of Appomattox was in fact well under way. By early 1871, it was evident that the president's rupture with Sumner had underscored ideological differences within the party and in so doing had precipitated a major rift. While Sumner and Charles Francis Adams deplored the decadence of republics, others rallied to the anti-Grant standard. Lyman Trumbull left the regular fold, denouncing patronage abuses in the New York Customs House. Carl Schurz continued his demands for reform of the civil service. Although the Grant name retained its magic in much of the country, the president's alienation from the country's opinion makers was dramatized by the defection of key newspapers from the regular Republican ranks. Editors Horace Greeley and Whitelaw Reid of the *New York Tribune,* Samuel Bowles of the *Springfield Republican,* Murat Halstead of the *Cincinnati Commercial,* and Joseph Medill of the *Chicago Tribune* were among the dissidents who ultimately bolted the party to hold their own convention in Cincinnati. Although the Liberal Republicans were a disparate group, there was a predominance of the low-tariff men and administrative reformers with whom Garfield had considerable in common. Several of the prime movers, including Reid and Halstead, were among his personal friends. There is no question that the discouraged Garfield found the Liberal Republicans a real temptation; in February 1872, he wrote to Cox that he was prepared to join the reformers if the movement continued to gain ground.[12]

The Liberal Republican movement appeared sufficiently ominous to Grant that the president attempted briefly to cut the ground out from under them on the civil service issue. In the spring of 1871, Congress had authorized the president to prescribe "rules and regulations for the admission of persons into the civil service" and to appoint an advisory board which would look into the questions of the qualifications necessary for government service. Grant himself approved this humble beginning, and appointed the editor of *Harper's Weekly*, George William Curtis, to head the commission. The president sent a special message to Congress in December in which he requested funds and authorization to put the commission into operation, empowering it to make recommendations concerning the classification of government positions and means to eliminate the dunning of officeholders by the party in power. Garfield was among those who had strongly supported this step, observing in support of the original bill that "I am exceedingly glad that we are able at last to give, for the first time in the history of this Government, a legislative expression in favor of civil service reform."

Had the reform issue caught on with the public, there is little doubt that much could have been done in an election year with such a clear-cut issue. But the reformers of the Gilded Age were essentially upper-class idealists like Curtis, and their disdain for the legislative process in Washington was heartily reciprocated by the hostility of the average congressman toward "reform" legislation and its advocates. Grant had never really checked out his civil service proposals with the Senate cabal on which he was dependent for support, and a triumvirate comprising Senators Cameron of Pennsylvania, Morton of Indiana, and Conkling of New York set about sabotaging the bill with undisguised glee. The Senate's most outspoken Liberal, Carl Schurz, came in for a torrent of abuse. Conkling insinuated at one point that the German-born Schurz had been in contact with foreign spies, and offered a resolution under which "any Senator who has acted in collusion with foreign agents" might be liable to fine or imprisonment! [13]

Garfield was not a special champion of civil service reform, and he did not play a prominent role in connection with the civil service bill. He was obliged to involve himself the following year, however, when the Appropriations Committee of which he was chairman all but refused to recommend funds for the Civil Service Commission. Although the Senate had voted the princely sum of $50,000 for the project, Garfield could not persuade his committee to match even this small sum. Stung by the rebuff, he spoke on the floor in favor of the Senate figure, arguing that "it is due to the President, it is due to ourselves . . . that a fair trial shall be made of the attempt at reform." In the end, an appropriation of $25,000 was arrived at. But the president made no further effort on behalf of the commission, and in the end it languished and died.

In May 1872, a rather disorganized convention of Republicans opposed to Grant nominated Horace Greeley for president and B. Gratz Brown of Missouri for vice president. This ticket gained the reluctant endorsement of the Democrats, who desired to present a united front against Grant, but nationally it was the subject of a good deal of ridicule. Greeley's baby face and side whiskers, topped by a white plug hat, gave him the aspect of an absent-minded country doctor. With the dissidents having effectively read themselves out of the party, the regular Republicans went through the motions of renominating Grant, this time with Senator Henry Wilson as his running-mate.

The 1872 campaign saw Garfield go through his customary election year metamorphosis. In July he was truly disgusted with Grant; he noted in his diary, "I dread the opening of the campaign. It promises to be full of bitterness and of all that is low and uncomfortable in politics." He made no effort to feign enthusiasm for the national ticket, and in his correspondence placed himself among those who were supporting Grant only because of the absence of a viable alternative:

> In favoring Greeley, I presume that you find some drawbacks. I do in preferring Grant. If Grant is elected we can at least hope that the changes in public affairs will be for the better rather than the worse. If Greeley wins, I don't believe he can resist the pressure from rebelism and reactionary copperhead-ism which I fear will swallow him and all such good men as you and other Republicans who go with the new movement.[14]

As the campaign progressed, however, Garfield's combative instinct was once again aroused. His own re-election was assured, particularly since redistricting had taken out of his district the one county, Mahoning, in which he had never run strongly. But he stumped the state for much of the summer and fall, excoriating rebel brigadiers and contrasting the past services of Grant and Greeley. Election day, however, found him again in a philosophical mood. "To many men this campaign has been a choice of two evils," he wrote in his diary, "and in some respects it has been so to me. The faults of the Republican Party are many and serious, but compared with the combinations against them, even their faults are virtues." [15]

Notwithstanding his misgivings, Garfield's decision to stick with his party in 1872 was crucial to his subsequent advancement. It is doubtful, his letter to Cox notwithstanding, whether Garfield would ever have followed the Liberal Republicans into a coalition with the despised, soft-money Democrats. But had he done so he would certainly have gone the way of Sumner and Trumbull, with a few mourners but with no visible political future. In playing it safe in 1872, Garfield entered a new political phase. Heretofore he had thought of himself as an independent Republican who followed the dictates of his conscience, even though the number of instances when he actually voted against the majority of his party was comparatively small. In the future he would become even more closely identified with Republican policies, and less prone to diverge from the main stream of the party. Having bit the bullet in 1872, he was well on his way to becoming a party regular.

Chapter Ten

THE ASHES
OF DISGRACE

———————◆◆———————

On May 10, 1969, the United States celebrated with speech and ceremony the centennial of the completion, at Promontory, Utah, of the first transcontinental railroad. Even as viewed from the twentieth century, the Pacific railroad, as it was known in Garfield's day, was recognizable as a remarkable technological achievement. There was also a greater awareness in 1969 than there had been before of the role played in the completion of the railroad by those handmaidens of progress, avarice and greed. For the fact was that the developers of the Pacific railroad were not so much builders as they were gluttons at the public trough.

The transcontinental railroad was physically a joint enterprise of the Union Pacific, which worked out of Omaha, and the Central Pacific, which laid its track eastward from California. In corporate terms the key role was that of the Credit Mobilier of America, a construction company which had been chartered in 1864 by the president of Union Pacific, Thomas Durant. The Credit Mobilier contracted with the Union Pacific to build the railroad, an arrangement which enabled the Credit Mobilier to milk the Union Pacific of its assets. These were considerable, inasmuch as Congress in its generosity had provided the Union Pacific with some $50,000,000—almost double the eventual building costs. The attitude in Washington was perhaps best expressed by Senator Henry Wilson, who observed in a burst of enthusiasm, "I give no grudging vote in giving away either money or land. I would spend $100,000,000 to build the road and would do it most cheerfully, and think I had done a great thing for my country. What are $75,000,000 or $100,000,000 in opening a railroad . . . that shall connect the people of the Atlantic and the Pacific. . . . Nothing!" [1]

By the time the Fortieth Congress convened in December 1867, however, the air was full of rumors of fraud in connection with the Pacific railroad. Because both the Union Pacific and the Central Pacific were paid a subsidy based on the miles of track laid, the work was often shoddy and there were even times when track was put down on top of ice and snow. When Congress convened, Representative Oakes Ames of Massachusetts, one of the directors of Credit Mobilier, undertook to distribute 160 shares of the company's stock among key legislators on the Hill. As Ames wrote to his brother, in a philosophical vein, "There is no difficulty in getting men to look after their own property."

Ames was primarily a businessman; his father had been manager of a shovel factory in Eaton, Massachusetts, an enterprise which had become even more profitable under the management of his two sons. Oakes Ames had gone to Congress as a Republican during the war, but he had little aptitude for statesmanship. He and Garfield appear to have had only casual contacts, but one of these was to have far-reaching consequences, for Garfield's return from Europe in the fall of 1867 put him in Washington at just the time when Ames was peddling his shares in Credit Mobilier. The Ohioan would appear to have been an unlikely candidate for solicitation. Not only was he then only a two-term congressman and in no position of special influence, but he was almost as enthusiastic about railroad building as Henry Wilson. Nevertheless, Ames offered his Ohio colleague ten shares of stock at $100 per share, which was about half of their value at that time. Garfield was understandably tempted; since he had been abroad he had heard none of the whispers concerning the company. Before he could come to a decision, however, he was warned against the purchase by Jerry Black, who filled him on the stories concerning the company. Reluctantly, according to his later testimony, Garfield told Ames that he would not accept the profferred stock.

Notwithstanding the rumors regarding Credit Mobilier, it was not until five years later that the story broke. The whole matter became public knowledge in the fall of 1872 when a disgruntled Credit Mobilier stockholder named McComb advised Charles A. Dana of the *Sun* about Ames' stock-distributing activities. The story was a journalistic windfall by any standard; for the petulant Dana, who in the years since Chickamauga had developed an almost pathological dislike for Garfield, the fact that Garfield's was one of sixteen names on McComb's list was an added fillip. The formal expose came during the 1872 election campaign under a heading, "THE KING OF FRAUDS: How the Credit Mobilier Bought its Way into Congress." [2] Considering its subsequent impact, there was at first comparatively little reaction to the *Sun's* story, which had to compete for attention with the election campaign, the death of General Meade, and a fire which burned out 65 acres of Boston.

Garfield had been in Montana when the story first broke. On arriving in Washington he met with two newsmen, Piatt of *The Capitol* and Boynton of the *Cincinnati Commercial,* whom he authorized to deny that he had subscribed for or received any Credit Mobilier stock. As he compared notes with his congressional colleagues, however, he became aware of the seriousness of his predicament. Several of the accused congressmen had without question accepted stock, and were prepared to rationalize but not to deny it. Another disturbing element was his friend Judge Black. Black knew all about Credit Mobilier, for he was representing McComb in a suit against the company. Black's recollection of his and Garfield's conversation about the company, however, was at variance with Garfield's denials to the Washington newsmen. Referring to a conversation between them, Black wrote that "the following are the points of it according to my recollection:

1. You regarded O. A. as a perfectly upright man. . . .
2. He offered you some stock in Cred. Mob., offered to sell it at par. . . .
3. You declined at first to take it . . . because you had not the money . . . and then he offered and urged you to take it on credit which you did.
4. When you made the contract you . . . had no reason to believe that the Cred. Mob. had any connection with the Un. Pac. RR Co. or anything else which Cong. could by any possibility be called on to legislate.
5. At a subsequent time, when you proposed to adjust your indebtedness for the stock, Mr. A. put you off . . .
6. At a still later time he showed you an acc't in wh. you were charged with the price of the stock at par, and credited with the dividends rec'd by him for you. This left a balance in yr. favor wh. he then paid." [3]

This would have been a perfectly plausible explanation on Garfield's part; the only trouble is that this is not what he had told the press or would tell the committee. Meanwhile, sensitive to the political implications of the affair, Garfield called on Blaine to urge a full investigation of the *Sun's* charges. Garfield recommended further that he and Blaine, two of the congressmen on McComb's list, jointly introduce the resolution. This was done, and the final session of the Forty-second Congress saw the creation of two committees, one for each house, to determine whether any legislator had given or received a bribe in connection with the construction of the Pacific railroad.

The discredited Congress returned, ironically, to newly refurbished working quarters. In the House, the corridors had been painted a fashionable "French gray." The committee rooms had been similarly redecorated; that of the Appropriations Committee, "tastefully finished in imitation of Greek arabesque," was pronounced by visitors to be one of the most comfortable rooms in the building.[4]

In this setting of physical elegance sixteen legislators began to explain their dealings with the Credit Mobilier. The House investigating committee, chaired by Representative Luke Poland of Vermont, drew a variety of testimony from its witnesses. Bingham of Ohio made no secret of having bought stock from Ames; he only wished he had subscribed for "ten times more." Pennsylvania's "Pigiron" Kelley admitted to having bought shares, noting that "it was just like buying a flock of sheep." Until Vice President Colfax attempted to deny all, and succeeded only in entangling himself in a mesh of contradictions, it appeared that the Poland Committee might have little to investigate.

Garfield himself appeared puzzled as to how his name had appeared on Ames' list, and he may have suspected an attempt by Dana to discredit him. In consultation with the key witness, he asked if Ames did not recall his having refused the stock. Thus prodded, Ames conceded that he was uncertain, and indicated as much in his testimony before the committee. According to Ames' first testimony, he had "agreed" to get ten shares for Garfield, and to hold them until he could pay for them, but the Ohioan had never paid for the stock or taken possession of it.

> Q. He never paid any money on that stock nor received any money from it?
> A. Not on account of it.
> Q. He received no dividends?
> A. No sir; I think not. He says he did not. My own recollection is not very clear.
> Q. So that, as you understand it, Mr. Garfield never parted with any money nor received any money on that transaction?
> A. No, sir; he had some money from me once, some three or four hundred dollars, and called it a loan. He says that is all he ever received from me and that he considered it a loan. . . .
> Q. Did you understand it so?
> A. Yes, I am willing to so understand it. I do not recall paying him any dividend, and have forgotten that I paid him any money.[5]

That so-called loan was to prove troublesome. When Garfield himself took the stand on January 14 he attempted to set forth the circumstances of the loan, testifying that "Mr. Ames never gave nor offered to give any stock as a gift. I once asked and obtained from him and afterwards repaid to him, a loan of $300; that amount is the only valuable thing I ever received from or delivered to him. . . . I had been to Europe the fall before and was in debt and borrowed several sums of money at different times and from different persons." [6] Jerry Black was in the chamber as counsel for another witness, and Garfield must have tensed as his friend asked permission to put a question to him. But Black was a friendly interrogator, and made no allusion to his recollection that Garfield had in fact purchased some stock from Ames on credit. He appeared to be trying to elicit from Garfield a statement that Black had warned him against the stock—a statement which would have lent credence to Garfield's denial of having owned any. But Garfield did not rise to Black's lead, and gave only noncommittal replies.

Notwithstanding the untimely coincidence of the "loan" from Ames, the matter might have been laid to rest had Ames not grown apprehensive on his own behalf. Not only was he under heavy pressure from the Poland Committee, but the Credit Mobilier directors were said to be wondering to whom, if not to Garfield and others, Ames had given the stock with which he was provided. Ames had as his counsel Congressman Ben Butler, an old antagonist of Garfield's, who sought to portray his client as the only honest man at the hearing. In part to account for the "missing" stock, Ames began to change his story, and indeed to indicate that he regarded his loan to Garfield, the exact amount of which turned out to be $329, as an advance on stock dividends which he would receive.

Although Ames had turned into a hostile witness, the case was never more than one of his word against Garfield's. Ames was unable to explain why his colleague had received no stock certificate, why he had not received regular dividends, or why he was not carried as a stockholder on the books of the company. But Garfield made a serious tactical error in failing to refute this new testimony before the committee. His letters indicate that he felt silence to be the best policy ("The only course for me to take for the present is to bear in silence whatever is cast upon me until the investigation is concluded; then I shall speak"). As a result, the investigation dragged on to its conclusion without any further testimony from Garfield.[7]

The Poland Committee delivered its report on February 18. It found no evidence of bribery, but recommended expulsion in the cases of Ames and one Democrat, Brooks of New York. The committee did not regard itself as competent to take action against Colfax, but the vice president's contradictory testimony in effect brought an end to his political career. The report dealt only in passing with Garfield, but it was highly damaging in that the committee accepted Ames' version of the dealings between them. According to the committee, Garfield "agreed to take ten shares of Credit Mobilier stock, but did not pay for the same." Garfield's failure to challenge Ames' later testimony was an error of the first magnitude, for the committee's report as released in effect charged him with perjury. Considering that Ames had proved for the most part a co-operative witness, whose charges had been explicitly challenged only by Garfield, the committee appears to have been predisposed to accept his version in the absence of a more vigorous defense by the Ohioan.

Garfield's initial reaction to the Poland Committee report was one of bewilderment. Referring in one letter to Ames' testimony he wrote, "He has produced no scrap of writing from me in evidence whatever, that I ever purchased the stock, no draft bearing my name or initials and though the committee find that there was nothing in my case deserving of censure, yet they have followed his statement of it in making up the summary of the case." [8] Representative Poland, when queried about the report during Garfield's presidential campaign, maintained that if his fellow-Republican had put the facts on record more effectively the committee's report would have read quite differently. But no one disputed the editorial writer of the *New York Times,* who wrote of the Poland Committee report, "Of the members referred to Messrs. Kelley and Garfield present the most distressing figure. . . . The only possible comment on their cases is that had they taken a perfectly upright course in the matter and refused to have anything to do with the stock no occasion for contradictions could have arisen." [9]

The upshot was that Garfield found himself in a situation such as he had never experienced before, that of defending his reputation against a charge which could mean the end of his political career. But the Credit Mobilier was only the beginning of Garfield's time of troubles, and no sooner had Congress ad-

journed in March 1873 that the Ohioan found himself embroiled
in a new controversy. In the last week of February, Ben Butler
had taken the lead in attaching a rider to the General Appropriations Bill which would provide for an increase of congressional
salaries from $5,000 to $7,500 per year. Although Garfield shared
the general view that an increase in salaries was overdue, he opposed the rider as proposed by Butler on the grounds that any salary increase should be part of a general salary bill which would
consider all branches of the government. Nevertheless, the House
approved the Butler amendment by a vote of 93 to 71, including
a provision which would make the pay raise retroactive to include
the Congress just ending.

In the final days of the session, the Appropriations Bill was
one of a number in which differences between the Senate and
House versions had to be worked out in conference. Ordinarily,
the House conferees would have been drawn from Garfield's committee; because the entire membership of the Appropriations
Committee had opposed the salary rider, however, Blaine chose
Butler and Samuel Randall to accompany Garfield as House conferees. On March 2, the joint committee held a day-long session
in which it reviewed some 65 points of difference in the House
and Senate versions of the Appropriations Bill. Once again Garfield attempted to remove the retroactive feature of the salary
rider, only to be voted down. His suggestion that the increase be
retroactive for one year instead of two was similarly defeated
within the bipartisan committee. Summarizing the day's proceedings in his diary, Garfield predicted, "This will make great trouble and I am in doubt [as to] what I should do. If I sign the report I shoulder a part of the responsibility of the increase of
salaries." [10]

A politician with a greater flair for the dramatic might have
disassociated himself from what he recognized as an unwise bill
with some ringing declaration that would endear him to his constituents. A more cautious legislator, already facing one political
crisis, might have managed more discreetly to avoid any identification with what would be called the great "salary grab." Garfield, for no better reason than his proprietory interest in seeing
the Appropriations Bill go through, finally voted for it in com-

mittee and again on the floor. Considering that he had done no more than to bow to the inevitable, it is paradoxical that his vote for the "salary grab" brought him more abuse than had the Poland Committee report. To the honest farmers of the Western Reserve, a congressman who voted himself an extra $5,000 in salary was guilty of nothing short of stealing. From Cleveland, where he was trying a law suit, Garfield wrote to his wife, "To my surprise I find that just now there is more agitation in regard to my vote on the increase of salaries than there is in regard to Credit Mobilier. . . . I shall try to meet manfully whatever comes to my lot; but it is hard to bear the small talk of little carpers who know nothing of the case." [11]

To Garfield's political rivals in the Nineteenth District, the congressman who had regularly rung up 3 to 1 ratios in his successful election campaigns at last appeared vulnerable. In three of the district's five counties, Republican conventions met and passed resolutions of censure, calling on Garfield to resign. There can be no question that Garfield, who craved approbation, was deeply hurt. To W. C. Howells, father of the novelist and an editor in the Reserve, Garfield wrote, "The action of the Ashtabula Convention hurts me more than I am willing to tell anybody but you. Were I to consult my own feelings I would instantly withdraw from a service that brings such fruit as the result of ten years of the best and most faithful service I have been able to give." [12] On the urging of friends, however, he set about defending himself against the charges arising from both Credit Mobilier and the "salary grab."

Prompted by Hinsdale, Howells, and other friends, Garfield issued a *Letter to the Republican Voters of the Nineteenth District* in which he set forth his side of both stories. Although he did not comment on the fact, Garfield was extremely fortunate that his difficulties had come too late to influence his re-election in 1872 and in time to permit him to mend his fences prior to 1874. In any case, Garfield's explanations of his role in these *causes célèbres* were skillfully put. He pointed out the inconsistency in the Poland Committee's acquitting him of wrong doing, yet then going on to endorse Ames' version of the dealings between them. He deplored the handling of the salary rider, yet was able to point out that his predecessor, Joshua Giddings, had in 1856 benefitted from a similar retroactive increase without being called "a thief and a robber." Garfield had been politically astute enough to return to the Treasury the back pay which Congress had voted itself, and his testimony that he had not personally profited from the "salary grab" did much to strengthen his case.[13]

Since the beginning of the Credit Mobilier investigation Garfield had passed through several stages of doubt and self-recrimination. His first reaction to Ames' revelations had been perplexity at the charges and embarrassment that he could have had any financial dealings with Ames. His reaction to the uproar over the salary amendment was different; not only was Garfield convinced that he had acted sensibly in voting as he had, but his faith in representative democracy was shaken by the discovery of how fickle was the electorate of even his own district. Here Garfield was unable to see the forest for the trees. Convinced of his own rectitude and that of most of his colleagues, he underestimated the popular indignation over the successive scandals of the Grant Era.

This difficult period brought out in Garfield two seemingly diverse qualities: a tendency toward self-pity, which is evident in many of his diary entries, and a fierce determination not to go down without a fight. Thus by May he had completed a 28-page pamphlet entitled *Review of the Transactions of the Credit Mobilier Company* in which he pointed out quite dispassionately the discrepancies between the testimony of Ames and the conclusions which the Poland Committee had seen fit to draw from it. Seven thousand copies of the pamphlet were printed and distributed, some of them to newspaper editors outside the Nineteenth District. It closed on a defiant note:

> If there be a citizen of the United States who is willing to believe that for $329, I have bartered away my good name, and to falsehood have added perjury, these pages are not addressed to him. If there be one who thinks that any part of my public life has been gauged on so low a level as these charges would place it, I do not address him—I address those who are willing to believe that it is possible for a man to serve the pub-

lic without personal dishonor. . . . and I confidently appeal to
the public records for a vindication of my conduct.[14]

Notwithstanding such rebuttals, many Ohioans regarded
Garfield as politically dead. There was a gubernatorial election in
1873 but in contrast to previous years, when Garfield was much
sought after as a speaker, there was now no need for his services.
Garfield watched from his front porch in Hiram as the Republican candidate for governor, handicapped by the severe depression
which was closing businesses all over the country, went down to a
close defeat. Garfield did make a few trips to different towns in
his district, however, and took comfort from the assurances of his
supporters that in 1874 things would be different.

Writing in his diary at the year's end, Garfield reflected on
the changes in his own personality:

> I am less introspective than formerly. . . . [but] the old
> view of my early years has gone. Then I thought how I looked
> forward to the time when I should have achieved something
> worthy of remembrance. . . . I have not achieved much but I
> have climbed to the heights where the wind blows furiously
> and cold. . . . The year 1873 has, like myself, suffered some
> hard knocks and abuses and passes away into oblivion scarred
> and bruised and not greatly regretted.[15]

The end of the year was not a total loss, however, for the opening
of the Forty-third Congress brought a glimmer of encouragement.
Although the newspapers had been full of rumors of what would
befall those committee chairmen who had been named in connection with the Credit Mobilier, Garfield found support from an
unexpected quarter when his colleagues on the Ohio delegation
presented a petition to Speaker Blaine asking that he be retained
as chairman of the Appropriations Committee. In the end Blaine
concurred, and in addition appointed Garfield a member of the
powerful Rules Committee. The Ohioan was not reflective
enough to ponder the significance of his reinstatement in the face
of what he himself recognized as a serious indiscretion on his own
part. He was touched by the action of his Ohio colleagues, however, and gratified that Blaine had not attempted to please the reformers at his own expense.

By the spring of 1874 the worst appeared to be past, and Garfield's correspondence took on a brighter tone. "I am glad to hear that the people of the Nineteenth District are gradually recovering from the political tempest by which they were tossed last Fall," he wrote to one constituent. "I know that I have done them more efficient service this Winter than at any other time since I have been in public life." [16] But he was not yet out of the woods; in fact, he was to be subjected to a final embarrassment before his crucial campaign for re-election. A year before, Garfield had been asked by a fellow member of the Ohio delegation, Richard C. Parsons, if he could take over from Parsons a commitment to represent the De Golyer-McLelland Construction Company in its bid for a $700,000 contract being let by the District of Columbia Board of Public Works for the construction of sidewalks. When after an assiduous lobbying campaign the De Golyer firm was awarded the contract, Parsons shared his handsome $16,000 contingency fee with Garfield.

This $5,000 windfall would have gone unnoticed as one more legal fee had not an investigation revealed that the De Golyer company had spent some $72,000 in lobbying for the dubious wooden pavement which it succeeded in foisting off on the District of Columbia. Garfield's role had been a relatively innocuous one, for the unit price to be paid had already been set; nevertheless, he had allowed the use of his names and services by a less-than-reputable organization, and the whole affair underscored the pitfalls of congressional moonlighting. Yet when the *Chicago Tribune* raised questions as to why Garfield had received such a handsome fee for such small service, the Ohioan was incensed. To Hinsdale he wrote,

> In regard to the pavement case, I propose to stand on my rights as an American citizen. . . . There is nothing either of law or morals to prohibit a member of Congress from practicing his profession and so far as I hear, every member of the Committee of Investigation says that I did what I have a plain right to do. . . . The only unpleasant thing about it is that the same company that employed Parsons as their lawyer also employed lobbyists to help get the contract.[17]

THE ASHES OF DISGRACE

The end of the session in June found Garfield suffering from fatigue and tempted by the possibility of another voyage to Europe. His political survival was not yet assured, however, and he returned to Hiram to do battle. In his solidly Republican district the fight would be for the G.O.P. nomination, and although Garfield's stock was not at its usual high there were signs that his opponents were having difficulty in uniting behind one candidate. Although Garfield himself spent the first part of the summer at Hiram, he kept in close touch with friends and political liaison men. When the District convention met at Painesville on August 13, he was renominated with 100 votes out of 134 cast. The convention vote was only a formality, for the delegates had been committed in advance in county primaries. As early as August 10 Garfield was writing his thank-yous, telling his old friend Harmon Austin, for instance,

> I have not time now to express the very deep and almost painful sense of gratitude I owe to you for the power of your friendship and the great wisdom and ability with which you have managed the contest. For more than a year you have carried me in your heart and thought almost hourly, as few men have carried a friend.[18]

There was clear light at the end of the tunnel, although Garfield and his friends did not relax their vigilance. One imponderable was the appearance of an independent Republican, H. R. Hurlburt, as a third candidate in addition to Garfield and his Democratic opponent, Wood. Another was the appearance in the District of copies of a special edition of the *New York Sun* which summarized all of Garfield's malfeasances and which represented a major effort by Charles A. Dana to put an end to Garfield's political career. As he traveled through his district in the Ohio autumn, Garfield sought more than ever to gauge the temper of his constituents. Though his blood was up, Garfield's speeches were a solid, reasoned defense of his work in Washington and of his role in connection with Credit Mobilier and the salary amendment. "I have had a hard and exhausting campaign," he wrote to a friend in October, "but I shall beat the rascals who have been opposing me." [19]

149

And beat them he did, although Garfield's own total of 12,-591 votes was sharply down from the more than 19,000 which he had polled two years before. Hurlburt appeared to have drawn support from Democrats as well as Republicans; although he received only 3,400 votes, many of these may have been Democratic, for Wood's total of 6,245 was down 2,000 from the Democratic vote of 1872. Although a large number of Republican voters stayed at home, comparatively few voted with the opposition.

Garfield himself was satisfied. In response to one congratulatory message he wrote, "In view of the general deluge that has swept over the party, and in view of the bitter and malignant assaults made upon me, I feel that I came out better than could have been expected." Such was the democratic faith of the past century that Garfield's victory came to symbolize more than political survival; in some quarters it was tantamount to moral vindication. No less a scholar than James F. Rhodes, author of the multi-volumed *History of the United States,* has observed with some awe, "It is indisputable that he won his case before very intelligent juries. His district was celebrated . . . for its intelligent and high-minded people. . . . To these he argued his case and received a vindication." [20]

By the time Garfield was a candidate for president, many would have forgotten the Credit Mobilier and the "salary grab," to say nothing of the De Golyer pavement affair. The Democrats would attempt to use these issues to his detriment, but without notable success. For in the tradition of the Horatio Alger format, Garfield's vindication by the voters of his district constituted a spiritual cleansing by the democratic process. *Vox populi, vox Dei.*

Even with the perspective of nearly a century it is not easy to resolve the conflicting testimony of Garfield and Ames. In gaining his victory at the polls, Garfield in effect ran against the Poland Committee report, charging with some basis that the committee was not justified in accepting Ames' story as it had. The real facts, however, are not easily ascertained. Apart from any deliberate falsification which may have occurred, both Garfield and Ames were attempting to recall conversations which had taken place five years earlier. Although Garfield's diary entries occasionally show signs of having been written for future historians, his indignation in those relating to Credit Mobilier is unfeigned.

The most damaging critic in terms of Garfield's testimony is not Oakes Ames, who died only weeks after Congress voted that he should be censured but not expelled. Rather, it is Garfield's good friend Jerry Black. Black was not getting any younger, and his memory, too, could play tricks; but the Judge had a clear recollection that Garfield had once spoken to him about having purchased some Credit Mobilier stock. . . .

Chapter Eleven

A DISPUTED
ELECTION

———◆———

Although he might have been excused for thinking so, Garfield did not have a monopoly on trouble in the years 1873 and 1874. In the former year the country was hit by the most severe business depression it had yet experienced. Rather appropriately, it was a distrust of railroad construction schemes on the part of the nation's banking houses that played a major role in bringing on the crash. As investors became wary of the once-popular railroad bonds, banks lost a major source of funds and had to draw on their own assets in order to raise cash.

When farm crops came onto the market in September there was still greater pressure for the banks to provide funds with which to purchase the harvest. With luck, the banks might have survived the pinch by borrowing in Europe; in 1873, unfortunately, Europe was itself in the throes of a banking crisis and no help was to be had from that quarter. In the United States, the collapse of the New York Warehouse and Security Company on September 8 triggered a rash of bank closings which eventually put more than 5,000 firms out of business. The iron and steel industry was particularly hard hit; by the end of the year more than a third of the nation's steel furnaces were shut down. There was a special shock on September 18 when the great house of Jay Cooke & Company closed its doors. Jay Cooke had been closely linked with the Grant administration and was a Republican financial backer of some years standing. His collapse lent political over-tones to the depression which ensued.

The banking crisis of 1873 ushered in a period of hard times which was to last for six years. Agricultural prices were particu-larly hard hit and many a farmer, unable to make his land pay, moved West and made the 70s the decade of the cowboy. Even as Congressman Garfield was remaining faithful to his hard-money views in the 1874 election campaign, farmers asked why there should be a decrease in the supply of money at the very time that farmers were most burdened with mortgages and unmarketable crop surpluses. The first voices of protest came to be heard. The Granger movement, inaugurated in the summer of 1873, in-veighed against railroads and Eastern monopolists.

In the election year that followed, Senator Oliver P. Morton of Indiana earned Garfield's scorn as he became a conspicuous convert to currency inflation in his campaign for re-election. Other Republicans, unable to embrace such a heresy, rallied be-hind a bill drawn up by John Sherman which was advertised as providing a "moderate" degree of inflation, even though in fact it increased the amount of money in circulation by only 5 per cent. Sherman's bill split Grant's cabinet and sorely perplexed the pres-ident, who had never completely lost his identification with the hardscrabble farmer. In the end, to the delight of Garfield and of the party's Eastern wing, Grant vetoed the bill.[1]

But rural unrest was only one of the problems plaguing the country in the mid-70s. As the states of the former Confederacy returned to the Union they also returned to their old Democratic allegiance, to the detriment of the Negro and to the distress of the Republican party. When Texas and Alabama were carried by the Democrats in 1873 and 1874 respectively, the G.O.P. had been ousted from all except five state houses in the deep South. Despite constitutional amendments and enforcement acts, the southern Negro had lost his political leverage and was increasingly dependent upon the good will of his former masters. For the Republicans, little had gone right south of the Mason-Dixon line. Their local organizations had proved unable to develop deep roots, partly because of the party's identification with the Negro, and partly because state organizations were all too often dominated by fly-by-night operators who had little interest in the party's long-range objectives. By way of contrast, the reviving Democrats never lost sight of their main objective, a return to self-rule and something closely approaching the ante-bellum social structure.

But as national parties, neither the Democrats nor the Republicans were in any condition to approach a presidential election with complacency. The Democrats, for all their unity of purpose in the South, found little in common with their Northern brethren, whose views on monetary matters were hardly different from those of the Republicans and made no allowance for the South's need for development capital. The Republicans, however, were hardly in better shape. The party was shaken by scandal, and had scarcely recovered from the split of 1872 which had led Garfield to wonder if it would ever win another election. Its hopes of gaining a political base in the South were all but gone. Perhaps most ominous of all, there was no heir apparent to Grant who, in his miscast role as head of the party, presided over the quarreling legions of Conkling and Blaine.

The Republicans were becoming accustomed to off-year election reverses, but the 1874 congressional elections nevertheless came as a shock. In the Midwest, dissident farmers entered into *ad hoc* coalitions with the Democrats, while in the East the Democrats benefited from crossovers by normally Republican voters who were fed up with Grant and his administration. Although the Senate remained Republican, the Democrats gained control of the House with 169 seats to 109 for the Republicans and 14 for various independents.[2] Merely by surviving the 1874 debacle, Garfield emerged as one of the leaders and proven vote-getters of his party.

Meanwhile, Garfield's family responsibilities had increased over the years. In 1865, Crete had given birth to a second son whom they had named James Rudolph. Two years later there was a daughter, Mary, whom they called Molly. Three more sons followed, at two-year intervals. One they named for Garfield's good friend General Irvin McDowell, another for his father Abram. Their last child, Edward, lived only two years. By the mid-70s, Garfield was more and more conscious of his obligations to his family and attracted to a career of full-time law which could make him financially independent. Even with Crete's improvements, the little house in Hiram was badly overcrowded.

With all the competing demands on his time, Garfield still found time to keep up his interest in education. He was a trustee and a regular financial supporter of the former Eclectic, whose name had been changed to Hiram College after the war. When Burke Hinsdale was appointed president in 1870, Garfield's connection with the college was as close as ever. When Garfield reluctantly concluded that his family had outgrown the house on the edge of the campus, he sold it to the Hinsdales.

Garfield's connection with Williams was somewhat less close, but he never lost his admiration for Mark Hopkins or his enchantment with the Berkshire Hills, and it was his connection with Williams that inspired Garfield's best-known aphorism in the field of education. Whereas Hiram College had prospered in the decade following the Civil War, in part because of the foundation laid by Garfield, Williams had fallen on somewhat harder times. Some members of the faculty and trustees felt that the college was suffering from its dependence on Hopkins, who by 1871 had been teaching at Williams for 35 years and who was approaching his seventieth birthday.

Garfield had corresponded sporadically with several members of the Williams faculty, and he had in 1871 exchanged several letters with John Bascom, the professor of rhetoric, concerning the college and its problems. Thus, when Garfield attended a closed meeting of Williams alumni in New York City on December 28, 1871, he probably had some intimation of what Bascom planned to say there; other alumni present, who included David Dudley Field, William Cullen Bryant, and a former governor of Massachusetts, Emory Washburn, obviously did not. Bascom, in a brief but angry speech, attacked the college trustees as too old and too conservative; he charged further that the faculty was both underpaid and lacking in the necessary facilities. Finally, he spoke the unspeakable and suggested that President Hopkins himself was a mixed blessing, in that he was a poor administrator and had permitted a situation to develop in which people felt that the college depended solely upon him.

Garfield respected Bascom and recognized the validity of much of what he said. But when Garfield was called on for a few remarks, the Mark Hopkins whom he remembered was the mentor who had invited him to Williams and who had lent him the money which had enabled him to graduate. In what amounted to a rebuttal to Bascom, Garfield insisted that the best policy for any college was to maintain a faculty which could lead and inspire; buildings and laboratories were of secondary importance. Since he spoke extemporaneously it is not possible to determine his exact words, but the phrase which passed into American folklore was Garfield's contention that "the ideal college is Mark Hopkins on one end of a log and a student on another." [3] Garfield spelled out his views at somewhat greater length in a letter to a fellow Williams alumnus the following month:

> I venture to suggest two things that ought to be kept steadily in view in all efforts to promote [Williams'] welfare. First, that it continue to be a College in the fullest and best meaning of that word and neither try to become a University nor try to adopt university plans; second, that the chief efforts made in its behalf shall be directed not so much to halls and buildings as to an increased endowment, for paying professors, for making tuition as nearly free as possible and for putting the cost of living within the reach of students whose means of support are most slender. So long as Williams College can offer salaries which will command and retain the very best teaching talent of the country, she will offer a far greater attraction to thoughtful and ambitious students than any splendor of her architecture or richness of her cabinets and libraries. [4]

In the U. S. Congress, no one exceeded Garfield in his devotion to education as an ideal. It is hardly surprising that he was much in demand as a commencement speaker and as a sponsor for legislative measures associated with education. But for all his enthusiasm Garfield's concept of education was a narrow one, one which was closely identified with study of science and the classics. He was for several years a trustee of Hampton Institute, a newly founded college for Negroes in Norfolk, Virginia, but he soon found himself out of sympathy with the emphasis on vocational education. "Very much manual labor," he wrote on one occasion to a member of the Hampton faculty, "is incompatible with a very high degree of mental cultivation." [5]

With the president's hand slack at the reins, the Grant administration moved into its final year discredited and in disarray. Garfield had been too concerned about his own political survival to worry unduly about the administration, but his outlook resembled that of another party strategist, William E. Chandler of New Hampshire, who had urged a house cleaning of the party which would get rid of some of its undesirables "without tearing too much up." Something like this appeared in prospect in 1874 when Grant, apparently attempting to bolster the hard-money wing of his cabinet, appointed Benjamin H. Bristow as secretary of the treasury. Bristow, a mustachioed veteran of Grant's Army of the West, was not only an able lawyer but something of a champion of civil service reform.

The only trouble was that Grant did not wish to reform the civil service or anything else if it involved inconveniencing his friends. When Treasury Department inspectors uncovered evidence of widespread frauds in the collection of the excise tax on whiskey, Grant was easily played upon by parties to the fraud, one of whom was his own private secretary, Orville Babcock. "Let no guilty man escape," the president told Bristow when confronted with the evidence against the "Whiskey Ring." But he gradually became convinced that Bristow was employing the tax investigation to further his presidential ambitions at the expense of the administration. In the end he fired Bristow, and provided a character deposition for the wily Babcock which assisted in securing his acquittal.

Scandal followed scandal. Garfield's old committee chairman, Robert Schenck, had enjoyed a tour as American minister to Great Britain, a political sinecure which permitted ample display of his poker expertise in the drawing rooms of London. In his spare time, however, Schenck had been hawking shares in Emma Mines, a rather dubious silver venture in the American West. When it became clear that Emma Mines were in for heavy sledding, Schenck unloaded his own shares just before the stock fell. Soon he was on his way back to Ohio, immune from prosecution because of his diplomatic status but no longer *persona grata* in the United Kingdom.[6]

Garfield was not a close friend of Secretary Bristow's, but they had known each other in the war and Bristow may have regarded the Ohioan as a kindred spirit. Bristow was in fact interested in the Republican presidential nomination, and in the course of sounding out Garfield concerning his candidacy he appears to have convinced Garfield that Grant was being pushed into running for a third term. Garfield had certified his "regularity" by supporting Grant in 1872, but he had no desire to do so again. To a constituent he wrote,

> We must throw off the third term nightmare before we can have any party success. The President declines to disclaim his candidacy. . . . There is but one course left for us in Ohio. We must in plain and unmistakable words . . . repudiate the doctrine of a third term. In the next place we must put forward an unexceptionable man for governor. I think we ought to take Hayes.[7]

In Congress, the transfer of control of the House to the Democrats had been costly to Garfield in terms of committee assignments. No longer was he chairman of the Appropriations Committee but a minority member of the Committee on Ways and Means. Nor was Garfield particularly impressed by the committee chairmen chosen by Speaker Samuel J. Randall. But he was genuinely relieved to find his own work load so much lighter. "In some respects I am pleased with the change," he wrote. "It will give me less work and I shall have more time to engage in a free fight on the floor." [8]

As Garfield prophesied, freedom from committee responsibilities would contribute to his emergence as a party spokesman. For the moment, however, Garfield enjoyed his freedom from responsibility, and a reporter for the Ashtabula *Sentinel* has left an engaging picture of Garfield the Congressional Scholar:

> Few public men in Washington keep up literary studies. General Garfield is one of the few. No one [is] more constant in attendance at the capitol than he . . . yet he keeps abreast of current literature, allowing no good book to escape him. When a long-winded . . . debate blows up in the House watch Garfield. He is an economist of time. Chatting and button-holing as he goes, he quietly glides out, passes through the rotunda and escapes into the serene realm of Mr. Spofford, where, amid all that amplitude of books, he regales himself in reading and in literary conversation. He and Mr. Spofford are close friends and whenever a box of new books arrives from Europe or New York a message gets to Mr. Garfield to that effect and he has the first peep.[9]

Ten years before, the strain that Garfield had undergone in connection with the Credit Mobilier and his subsequent campaign for re-election might have brought on a depression such as that which inspired his criticism of Rosecrans prior to Chickamauga. Success and a settled home life had mellowed Garfield, but in the early 70s he nevertheless contemplated leaving politics for the financial reasons noted earlier. But even the older, more mature Garfield had a streak of intellectual restlessness. He had served in Congress for more than ten years, and some of the old zest was gone. Moreover, Garfield may have had some idea that his voluntary retirement, after his triumphant re-election in 1874, would lay to rest any imputation that he was in politics to make his fortune.

For several years Garfield weighed two attractive offers involving full-time law practice. Jerry Black had made it clear that he would welcome Garfield as a partner in his law firm. This offer carried with it one major liability, however, for it entailed making his permanent home in Washington, which Garfield had no desire to do; having sold his old home to the Hinsdales, he was already looking for another home in the Reserve. More tempting to Garfield was an offer from a well-known Cleveland law firm, Burke and Eppes. He was strongly tempted to join them until his close involvement in the election of 1876 and its aftermath reminded him of how much politics was now in his blood.

In 1875, Garfield made his first and only trip to the Far West, although he had traveled as far as Montana three years before. Accompanied by an Army of the Cumberland comrade, General Edward McCook, Garfield left Chicago on April 24 and arrived in Oakland, California on the 30th. After two weeks of visiting in the bay area the party headed south to Los Angeles, but Garfield missed connections with General Rosecrans who was living in retirement there. They returned east by way of Yosemite and the boom towns Virginia City and Carson City. Garfield did not share Blaine's awe of millionaires, but he was nevertheless amazed at the wealth on display in the West. Writing to Crete from San Francisco, he reported that there were at least two hundred millionaires in the city:

> They did not make their money slowly by those small methods which make men narrow and penurious; but they did it partly by great boldness and enterprise, and partly by the lucky accidents which attend a mining country. Hence they are generous and broad-minded. I find it necessary to brace myself against the inclination to rebel against the fate that placed me in such a narrow groove in reference to business and property.[10]

Garfield's trip West renewed the temptations of a lucrative law practice, but once back in Washington he found his fellow Republicans reluctant to see him go. Friends reminded him of the general assumption that Blaine would soon be leaving the House, if not for the White House for the Senate; Blaine's departure would leave Garfield heir to his leadership. But it was the challenge of the forthcoming election campaign as much as any personal ambition that appears to have tipped the scales. On May 30 he wrote to a constituent, "Our leading Republicans here are greatly opposed to my withdrawing, and on some accounts I should be glad to devote myself to the great campaign of this Fall. I will not, however, in any way embarrass my friends in the Dist. by unreasonable delay [in reaching a decision]." [11]

Although most Republicans were relieved when Grant finally took himself out of the presidential race, the party remained

James A. Garfield as a "canal boy on the tow path."

A wartime engraving of Garfield as a major general.

The Garfield and Rudolph families at the Rudolph home in Hiram, Ohio. (Left to right, Mrs. Garfield, Sr., President Garfield, and, seated, top left, Mrs. Garfield.)

GARFIELD'S POLITICAL

DEATH WARRANT

HIS INFAMOUS LETTER,

**In which he declares himself adverse to the
Laboring Man's Interests, and in
favor of the Employers' Union,
advising them to employ
the Cheapest Labor
Available.**

Personal and Confidential.

HOUSE OF REPRESENTATIVES.
WASHINGTON, D. C., Jan. 23, 1880.

DEAR SIR:

Yours in relation to the Chinese problem came duly to hand.

I take it that the question of employees is only a question of private and corporate economy, and individuals or companies have the right to buy labor where they can get it cheapest.

We have a treaty with the Chinese Government which should be religiously kept until its provisions are abrogated by the action of the General Government, and I am not prepared to say that it should be abrogated until our great manufacturing interests are conserved in the matter of labor.

Very truly yours,

J. A. GARFIELD.

H. L. MOREY,
Employers' Union, Lynn, Mass.

Photo-engraved fac-simile of THE ENVELOPE.

The cover of a Democratic campaign pamphlet which attempted to exploit the Morey letter.

Garfield delivering the inaugural address which had kept him up most of the previous night.

A contemporary newspaper engraving of the Garfield inaugural ball.

A contemporary print of the assassination. Actually, Garfield was wearing a light grey suit and Guiteau a dark one. In addition, the waiting
room was almost deserted at the moment of the shooting.

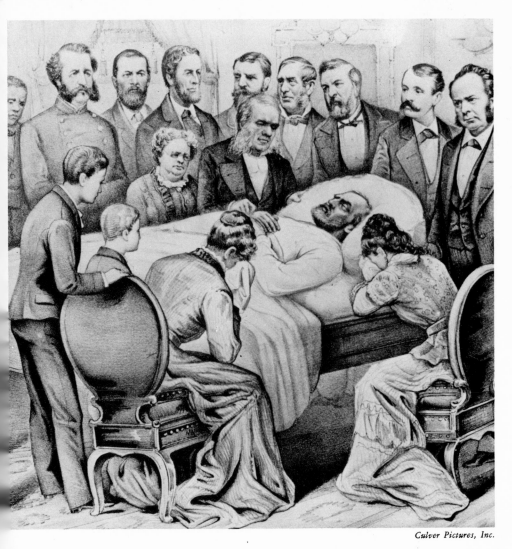

A Currier & Ives print of the death of President Garfield.

THE LAST BULLETIN.

. . .

ELBERON, N. J.,
SEPT. 19, 1881, 11.30 P. M.

The President died at 10.35. After the bulletin was issued at half-past five this evening the President continued in much the same condition as during the afternoon, the pulse varying from 102 to 106, with rather increased force and volume. After taking nourishment he fell into a quiet sleep about thirty-five minutes before his death, and while asleep his pulse rose to 120, and was somewhat more feeble. At ten minutes after ten o'clock he awoke, complaining of severe pain over the region of the heart, and almost immediately became unconscious, and ceased to breathe at 10.35.

D. W. BLISS.
FRANK H. HAMILTON.
D. HAYES AGNEW.

An early broadside announcing the president's death.

splintered and demoralized. The Senate cabal which had backed
Grant was never able to unite on a successor, with the result that
it appeared for a time that the nomination might go to the hard-
driving Blaine almost by default. But, as Professor George Mayer
has observed, Blaine's stock fluctuated wildly during the pre-convention period. Desperately searching for an issue which would
enable the Republicans to regain the political initiative, Blaine
delivered a speech in the House on January 10 in which he
moved to exclude Jefferson Davis from the provisions of an amnesty bill then before the House. Calling Davis "the author . . .
guiltily and willfully of the gigantic murders and crimes at Andersonville," Blaine protested on behalf of the widows and or-
phans of the North any "crowning with the honors of American
citizenship the man that organized that murder." [12]

It is a commentary both on Blaine's own prospects and on
those of his party that he felt obliged to resort to such demagog-
uery. But Blaine's speech had exactly the effect that he desired in
that it provoked a wrathful response from an ex-Confederate, Ben
Hill of Georgia. After Hill had heatedly defended both Davis and
the South's treatment of prisoners in general, Garfield, apparently
on his own initiative, took the floor to rebut Hill. On January 12
Garfield spoke for nearly two hours in support of Blaine's main
contention: that Davis had taken no action to ameliorate conditions in Southern prisons, even when informed of them. Unlike
Blaine, however, Garfield indulged in no blatant waving of the
bloody shirt, and in fact spoke more in sorrow than in anger. It
was just as partisan a speech as Blaine's, but its moderate tone put
its author in much the better light. Garfield's mail following the
speech was so favorable that he found himself both pleased and
annoyed. "For four years," he grumbled to Hinsdale, "I have
been . . . doing a very large amount of important and valuable
work. . . . I replied to Hill in a speech on which I laid out only
four or five hours work yet if I am to judge from the responses
which came to me . . . I have made more reputation and directed
the attention of the country to myself more than in all the financial work I have done." [13]

For all his invocations of Andersonville, by summer Blaine
was in deep trouble over his old stock dealings. Only by subter-

fuge had he managed to recover from a bookkeeper named James
Mulligan some incriminating letters which he had written on behalf of the Little Rock and Fort Smith Railroad. Once the existence of the letters was common knowledge, however, Blaine determined on a characteristically bold stroke. He took the floor on
June 5 and, after denying that the House committee which was
looking into lobbying activities on the Hill had any right to see
them, proceeded to read selectively from the Mulligan letters, in-
terspersing professions of wounded innocence. Blaine's maneuvers
in the pre-convention period perplexed even Garfield. The
Ohioan was a connoisseur of fine speeches, and he noted in his
diary that the effect of Blaine's speech was "dramatic and elec-
tric." But he retained a realistic prospective concerning his
friend's candidacy, writing in his diary on June 8,

> In the evening I called on Blaine and talked with [him] in
> regard to some passages in the Mulligan letters which are
> being criticized. . . . I shall not be surprised if he is nomi-
> nated at Cincinnati, yet I feel some doubt about the effect of
> these letters on his success as a candidate. He certainly is not
> the highest type of reformer. Hardly a reformer at all. But I
> have no doubt he will give us an honest and brilliant adminis-
> tration.[14]

Blaine achieved his immediate objective when the Judiciary
Committee postponed any further hearings on his railroad dealings until after the convention had completed its business. But
the strain had been tremendous, and on June 11, the Sunday before the convention was to open in Cincinnati, Blaine collapsed
on the steps of the Congregational Church in Washington. For
two days he lay in critical condition while Garfield, who had followed his friend's fluctuating political fortunes as closely as he
had ever followed his own, wrote in his diary, "If he dies . . . it
will be the work of political assassins, as really as though he had
been stabbed." [15]

Although the Ohio delegation, with Garfield's full approval,
was backing Rutherford B. Hayes, Garfield assisted the ailing
Blaine in communicating with his lieutenants in Cincinnati on
various political matters. In the end Blaine recovered, even

though his political fortunes did not. Despite Ingersoll's oratorical fireworks, the convention shied away from the mercurial Blaine in favor of the solidly respectable dark horse, Rutherford B. Hayes. Garfield was sad for his friend Blaine, but regarded Hayes as eminently acceptable.

The Democrats sought to make political capital out of the furor over political corruption by nominating for president Governor Samuel J. Tilden of New York, who was widely credited with having broken the Tweed ring in New York City. The campaign which ensued was typical of the period in that it was extremely closely contested despite the absence of dramatic issues. The Democrats, notwithstanding the presence of Tilden on the ticket, appeared somewhat miscast as reformers. In the end, Hayes' main liability was probably not Grant's legacy of corruption but the business depression which continued to lay upon the land.

Garfield's main contribution to the Republican campaign was a speech in August in which he rebutted an able presentation on behalf of the Democrats by L. Q. C. Lamar of Mississippi. In a well-delivered bit of campaign oratory, Lamar had contended that the Republicans were oppressing the South; that they had corrupted the national government; and that they had failed to follow through on civil service reform. In his reply Garfield sought to finesse Lamar's second and third points, though he asserted at one point with respect to corruption that the Republican party "will punish its own rascals." He sought instead to focus on the entire question of reconstruction, and whether in fact the South had accepted the political results of the war as they affected the Negro. Whereas Blaine waved the bloody shirt and would deny amnesty to Jefferson Davis, Garfield asked rhetorically if the South was not welshing on commitments which it had undertaken when the states of the Old Confederacy were readmitted to the Union.

Delivered as they were at the height of a political campaign the speeches of both Lamar and Garfield were greeted with praise or scorn, depending on the politics of the commentator. As for Garfield, he was taken to task by none other than Jerry Black, who not only challenged the appropriateness of certain of the

Ohioan's historical allusions but zeroed in on Garfield's contention that the Republican party could be reformed from within. What, Black asked in a public letter, had the Republicans done after Credit Mobilier? Far from being punished, the accused had been "promoted, honored and advanced." This was hitting close to home, although Black did not attempt to suggest that he was thinking especially of Garfield. In fact, Charles A. Dana took Black to task for just this omission. "What I object to most," wrote Dana, "is the compliment you pay to this rapscallion [Garfield]. . . . In my judgment, nobody, except perhaps Schuyler Colfax, came worse than he out of the Credit Mobilier business." [16]

Garfield's own re-election campaign went smoothly in 1876, in part as a result of the publicity accorded his rebuttals to Hill and Lamar and in part because this time there was no threat of a Republican bolt. Nationally, however, the Republicans were in deep trouble. On election day Garfield noted in his diary, "I have voted at six Presidential elections but never at one [for] the results of which I feel so much doubt." Three days later he wrote angrily to Fuller, "It now appears that we were defeated by the combined power of rebellion, catholicism and whiskey, a trinity very hard to conquer. . . . We shall have a hard, uncomfortable struggle to save the fruits of the great war. . . . If we had saved the House it was almost certain that I should have been elected Speaker, but of course that has gone down in the general wreck." [17]

Like Garfield, most of the country assumed that Tilden had been elected. His popular majority was more than 250,000, and he had carried such key Northern states as New York, New Jersey, Connecticut, and Indiana. But as he scanned the returns one Republican official, John Reid of the *New York Times,* saw a gleam of hope. Republican state governments still existed in Florida, South Carolina, and Louisiana, and they exercised almost absolute control over the returning boards. A bit of quick arithmetic convinced Reid that if Tilden's apparent victory in these three states could be overturned the Republicans would elect Hayes with 185 votes to 184 for Tilden. On the morning of November 7, G.O.P. Secretary Zachariah Chandler sent a terse query to the three party chairmen, "Can you hold your state? Answer immediately." On the same afternoon Chandler blandly announced that Hayes had been elected.

Garfield was in Washington three days after the election when he received a telegram from President Grant, who was in Philadelphia, asking that he join a group of "visiting statesmen" who were being sent to the three disputed states to observe the counting of the votes. Garfield was not enthusiastic about the prospect; in his diary he noted piously that "we have only one duty, to ascertain who is elected and see that he is so declared." Nevertheless, on November 11 he started for New Orleans, to join there two other friends of Hayes, John Sherman and Stanley Matthews, on the most blatantly partisan mission of his political career.

Garfield assumed, probably correctly, that except for the widespread intimidation of Negro voters, Louisiana would have been carried by Hayes. In point of fact, however, election frauds could be found in many places, and the Democrats could claim with some justice that an inspection of some of the states carried by Hayes would yield interesting results. But of the four states in which returns were being challenged, three had been carried by Tilden, though in all of these it was a Republican returning board which would determine the validity of the votes. In the words of his official biographer, Garfield and his Republican associates "managed to arrange things with the Louisiana Returning Board in such [a manner] that the electoral vote of the state would be announced as cast for Hayes, but they achieved this in such a manner as to satisfy Garfield's constantly expressed desire for a perfectly legal procedure." [18] In the case of Louisiana, which the Democrats initially carried by some 6,000 votes, this meant employing a much broader interpretation of "intimidation" than had been necessary in Florida or South Carolina. Garfield's capacity for rationalization was never more apparent than during his stint in New Orleans as a "visiting statesman." Only a year before, a House committee had criticized certain actions of the Louisiana Returning Board, and Garfield himself had referred to them as "a graceless set of scamps." It was a measure of Garfield's growing identification with his party that could bring himself to participate in such a charade.

Nevertheless, Garfield and his companions were not complete hypocrites. Lew Wallace, the future novelist, was in New Orleans at the time of the election and volunteered in a letter to Hayes,

> It is terrible to see the extent to which all classes go in their determination to win. Conscience offers no restraint. Nothing is so common as the resort to perjury. . . . If we win, our methods are subject to impeachment for possible fraud. If the enemy wins, it is the same thing—doubt, suspicion, irritation go with the consequence whatever it may be.[19]

It was not hard for visitors with a built-in Republican bias to conclude that the methods employed by "the enemy" were completely incompatible with the democratic process, and that they justified any methods which might be employed to overturn them. John Sherman wrote to Hayes on November 23 that "We are now collecting the testimony as to the bulldozed parishes. The means adopted are almost incredible, but were fearfully effective upon an ignorant and superstitious people. That you would have received at a fair election a large majority in Louisiana, no honest man can question." [20]

By the end of November Garfield was back in Washington, and it was apparent that the three disputed states in the South, together with Oregon, would file two sets of returns. The election had resulted in a situation for which there were no constitutional precedents. The Constitution provided that "the President of the Senate shall, in the presence of the Senate and the House of Representatives, open all certificates and the votes shall then be counted." But counted by whom? As Garfield chose to interpret this clause, the votes should be counted by the presiding officer of the Senate, who in the absence of a vice president was President *pro tempore* Thomas W. Ferry, a Republican. The Democrats insisted that the votes should be counted in joint session (in which the Democrats would be in the majority) or that there be a verdict of "no election" and the issue turned over to the House. By early December tempers had reached a level not equaled since the Civil War, and there were wild rumors that General Winfield S.

Hancock, whose military district embraced much of the Atlantic seaboard, was preparing to move on Washington to install Tilden as president.

To Republican strategists such as Garfield, the immediate tactical objective was to get the Democrats to agree to having the votes counted by the Senate. Garfield was extremely sensitive to the divergent currents within the Democratic party, and in a letter to Hayes he expressed his belief that the Democrats had an Achilles' heel:

> Two forces are at work. The Democratic businessmen of the country are more anxious for quiet than for Tilden, and the leading Southern Democrats in Congress, especially those who were old Whigs, are saying that they have seen war enough and don't care to follow their Northern associates. . . . Just what sort of assurances the Southern members want is not quite so clear. . . . but it would be a great help if, in some discreet way, those Southern men who are dissatisfied with Tilden and his violent followers could know that the South was going to be treated with kind consideration by you.[21]

Garfield was not the only one of Hayes' advisors who wanted to open channels of communication to the opposition, but he was probably the most eloquent. Replying to Garfield's letter Hayes wrote, "Your views are so nearly the same as mine that I need not say a word." So Garfield set about ascertaining how many Democrats might be persuaded to go along with the Republican tactic of having the votes counted in the Senate, and what might be their asking price.

Although Garfield turned a deaf ear to loose talk about "another civil war," others did not. President Grant was uneasy about the whole business, and did not see how the Democrats could accept a vote presided over by Senator Ferry. Moreover, the Republicans themselves were not all that enthusiastic over Hayes; Conkling of New York, who knew little of Hayes and did not like what he saw, broke with his colleagues on the issue of how to count the vote. When Garfield realized that some compromise mechanism for the vote count was in the offing he could hardly conceal his disgust, writing to Hayes,

I have no words strong enough to describe my indignation at the fact and manner of the surrender which the Senate has made of our position. The danger of violent resistance to your inauguration has absolutely passed away. . . . Nothing in the world was necessary but for the Senate to support its presiding officer in following the early precedents. . . .

I don't believe that ½ of 1% of our party had any doubt of the justice and essential fairness of your Election, and of the President of the Senate to declare it. And now those Republicans who have borne the brunt of the campaign . . . see the certainty of an assumed result traded off for the uncertain chances of what a committee of one majority will do. . . . A compromise like this is singularly attractive to that type of men who think that the truth is always half way between God and the Devil.[22]

For all their wrath, the Democrats were more easily sold on the Electoral Commission than were their opponents. The Democrats were confident that the Commission could not sustain the Republican returns in all three Southern states under any terms of reference on which its members might agree. Notwithstanding the depth of feeling on both sides with respect to the election, no one anticipated the rigidity with which party lines would be adherred to on the Electoral Commission. So in the final days of January agreement was reached on a commission to comprise fifteen members, five from the Senate, five from the House, and five from the Supreme Court. The odd member from the Senate was to be a Republican, the odd member from the House a Democrat, and the first four justices, equally divided as to political affiliation, would choose the fifth justice among themselves. Decisions of the Commission were to be final unless overruled by both houses of Congress.

Garfield was not only opposed to the commission on political grounds but on constitutional grounds as well. On January 25 he spoke against it for more than an hour, insisting that under the Constitution the president of the Senate was clearly empowered to count the votes. Consequently, when the bill authorizing the commission was passed in the House by 191 to 86, Garfield was conspicuous among the "nays," and it came as something of a surprise when the Republican caucus elected him as one of the two

House Republicans to serve on the commission. Garfield himself was somewhat taken aback, particularly after Jeremiah Black reported to him that a number of Democrats thought that, having opposed the commission on constitutional grounds and having committed himself on the Louisiana question, Garfield should disqualify himself. Party loyalty won out, however, and Garfield agreed to serve, writing to Hinsdale that "the uniform practice of the courts is that Judges sit on the merits of the case who are of opinion that the Court has no jurisdiction." [23]

The Electoral Commission began its hearings on February 1, with all eyes on the "fifth judge," Justice Joseph P. Bradley. Originally it had been expected that Justice David Davis would be named to complete the commission, but when Davis declined his colleagues chose Bradley, a nominal Republican but a judge who enjoyed the respect of both parties. The first state taken up was Florida, where the pro-Hayes ballots of the Returning Board were challenged by pro-Tilden returns endorsed by the governor and the state supreme court. Garfield, among others, set forth the Republican constitutional argument that the commission could not look beyond the ballots as certified by the returning board "without going to the bottom of the poll." But as the separate opinions were delivered, and it became apparent that the commission was voting strictly along party lines, it was Bradley who held the center of the stage. His vote on February 9 in favor of the Hayes' electors set a pattern in which substantive decisions would invariably go to the Republicans by an 8 to 7 vote. The Democrats were livid with rage; the venerable Jeremiah Black, who was serving as one of the Democratic counsels, spoke for many when he said, "God damn them, they will beat us and elect Hayes, but we shall give them all the trouble we can." [24]

The circumstances varied somewhat from case to case, but Black was right. Both sides were able to marshal plausible briefs on behalf of the rival electors, but when it came to the crunch Bradley was invariably to be found with his fellow Republicans on the key votes. As for Garfield, his conversion from the ardent, independent-thinking congressman of the late 60s to the party wheel horse was complete.

But the Democrats were not finished yet. After the decision

on Louisiana a group of House Democrats, mainly from the North, decided to attempt a filibuster to delay the convening of a joint session to count the vote until after Hayes' March 4 inauguration day. Hayes' various agents, however, had made good use of the intervening months to whittle away the support for Tilden among Southern Democrats. By the time the Electoral Commission began its hearings the press was referring openly to an "understanding" by which Hayes, if elected, would not support the remaining carpetbag governments in the South. What had actually taken place was a good deal more complicated. With neither party wedded in any personal way to its colorless standard-bearer, Hayes' friends had succeeded in persuading influential Southerners that a Republican in the White House was a small price to pay for a withdrawal of federal troops, Northern capital investment, and a federal subsidy for the Texas and Pacific Railroad. And so the threat of a filibuster flickered and died.

Fittingly enough, Garfield was in at the symbolic climax of the events through which the Republicans had turned an apparent defeat into victory. The occasion in question was the so-called Wormley Conference, a meeting between friends of Hayes and certain Southern Democrats in the Wormley Hotel in Washington in which the two sides confirmed arrangements reached earlier in return for acceptance of Hayes' election by the South. The threat of a Democratic filibuster still hung over the House, and the task of Garfield, Stanley Matthews, and their colleagues on the evening of February 26 was to make such soothing noises as would prevent any resumption of the filibuster, and yet not make commitments which Hayes was not prepared to honor. According to a long entry in his diary, Garfield was concerned that the Democrats present, particularly Congressman Burke of Louisiana, would attempt to tie Hayes down to specifics:

> Burke drew me aside and read from a paper some propositions, among them that civil and political rights should be guaranteed to the negroes [by the state government of Louisiana], that there should be no political prosecution, that the Nichols legislature should elect at least one Republican senator, etc. This and Matthews' talk led me to believe that there had been former consultations and that a compact of some

kind was meditated. I spoke a few moments stating that nobody had any authority to speak for Governor Hayes beyond
his party platform and letter of acceptance, and it would be
neither honorable nor wise to do so, if any one had such authority; that those Southern Democrats who are resisting fili-
bustering are doing so on the ground of high public duty and
honor; and any bargain would make their motives far lower.

Nothing pained Garfield more than the appearance of a political
bargain, and the smoke-filled room at Wormley's was not for his
delicate nostrils. But he recognized that the situation called for
some assurances of a very general sort, and these he proceeded to
provide. As Garfield summarized his remarks,

> For myself I had no doubt that the new administration would
> deal generously with the South, and the whole nation would
> honor those Southern men who are resisting anarchy and thus
> are preventing civil war; but neither they nor we could afford
> to do anything that would be or appear to be a political bar-
> gain.[25]

So it was that Garfield played a key role in resolving one of
the most intense political crises which the country had yet experienced. It was, to be sure, a tarnished triumph. There would have
been no crisis at all except for the willingness of Garfield and his
fellow Republicans to go to almost any length in pursuit of a narrowly partisan goal. But throughout the exciting winter of
1876–77, the Ohioan displayed a sure hand in exploiting the
weaknesses of the opposition, and in so doing he placed the new
president very much in his debt.

Chapter Twelve

MINORITY
LEADER

There was an element of hypocrisy in some of the "understandings" which had paved the way for Hayes' inauguration. Prominent Republicans had obtained on his behalf solemn promises from Southern spokesmen that the rights of the Negroes would be respected even after a withdrawal of federal troops. But there was a certain fuzziness to many of these undertakings, as was demonstrated by the fact that as late as the Wormley Conference politicians on both sides were still trying to determine what had been agreed upon. There was also a tendency, particularly in the South, for Democratic spokesmen to make promises on which they could not deliver. When Hayes began the withdrawal of troops from South Carolina, Governor Wade Hampton signed a pledge to secure "to every citizen . . . black as well as white, full and equal protection in the enjoyment of all his rights under the Constitution of the United States." [1] This is not exactly the way it worked out in South Carolina or elsewhere, but it is not easy to point the finger. Hampton was an honorable man and a racial moderate; in any case, it was no longer feasible for the Republicans to prop up carpetbag governments in the South. If Hayes appeared to be placing more confidence in Southern assurances than the situation justified, it is also true that the president's bargaining position was not an especially strong one.

One of the lesser casualties of the Hayes-Tilden Compromise of 1877 was Garfield, who had played such a prominent role in its realization. When deals were in the air prior to the creation of the Electoral Commission, a number of Southern Democrats indicated that they were prepared to allow the Republicans to organize the House—which would have meant electing Garfield Speaker—in return for the package which included home rule, a Southerner in Hayes' cabinet, and the Texas and Pacific Railroad. There was always something ephemeral about the Speakership possibility, and Garfield himself maintained a healthy scepticism as to whether he, after having voted consistently with his fellow Republicans on the Electoral Commission, would be the recipient of Democratic votes for Speaker. But Hayes believed otherwise; he urged Garfield not to become a candidate for Sherman's Senate seat on the grounds that he would doubtless be elected Speaker.[2] Garfield acquiesced, but more from a feeling that he should defer to the president's wishes than from any confidence as to the outcome. In the end the Democrats elected their own Speaker, leaving Garfield to write to a constituent,

> I did not feel as though I ought to have been asked to make the sacrifice in regard to the Senatorship, but when the request was made I did not think it would be generous in me to refuse. I hope the people of Ohio will appreciate the motives that led to the sacrifice. It is perfectly clear that I could have been nominated.[3]

It might have been expected that Garfield, who had chafed under eight years of Grant's leadership, would have welcomed the accession to the White House of a politically experienced successor with whom he had been on good terms. In point of fact, however, Garfield became disillusioned with Hayes almost as rapidly as he had with Grant. President Grant at least had been a known quantity; Hayes was a stubborn man who, though he consulted within the party, was prone to follow his own erratic course. Even before the Hayes administration was under way Garfield was conscious of differences in style and temperament between the president and himself. He wrote in his diary in March that "intimate as I have been with Governor Hayes . . . I have not yet been able to regain that feeling of familiarity that I am sure he would be willing should continue between us." [4] There was a certain remoteness to Hayes, and Garfield generally preferred more gregarious company.

Garfield had private doubts about Hayes' wisdom in appointing an ex-Confederate, David Key, as postmaster general, although he probably recognized that the president was committed to such an appointment. What really upset Garfield were signs that the Democrats were reneging on an implicit promise to let bygones be bygones with respect to the Louisiana Returning Board. When the new Democratic state machine filed charges against the old Returning Board Garfield was angry, and his attitude was not improved by Hayes' conciliatory posture. "The policy of the President has turned out to be a giveaway," grumbled Garfield. "He has *nolled* suits [and] discontinued prosecution . . . while they have spent their time in whetting their knives for any Republican they could find." [5]

Whatever Hayes' failings, he came into office with clear-cut objectives. Having withdrawn the last of the federal troops from the South when he first came into office, he turned to the issue of civil service reform, writing in his own diary that "we must limit and narrow the area of patronage. . . . We must be relieved of congressional dictation as to appointments." [6] On April 23, the administration appointed a commission to investigate abuses in the New York Customs House, the primary producer of jobs for Conkling's New York machine. Two months later, after the commission had documented widespread incidence of bribery, forced contributions, and overstaffing, Hayes issued an Executive Order on the subject of ethics in the government service:

> No officers should be required or permitted to take part in the management of political organizations, caucuses, conventions, or electoral campaigns. . . . No assessments for political purposes on officers . . . should be allowed. This rule is applicable to every department of the civil service.[7]

Like most presidents undergoing their first experience with office-seekers, Hayes was a true convert to the cause of reform. There was also, however, a political motive in his attack on the Conkling organization. Republican machines elsewhere were as corrupt as those in New York if not more so; yet their leaders had not opposed Hayes' nomination, they had not failed to deliver their states in the election, and they had not broken with the Republican caucus over how the electoral votes were to be counted. Conkling not only embodied all of these liabilities but his state was one in which Hayes' secretary of state, William Evarts, had visions of developing a pro-administration organization. Thus the administration stood to gain doubly by attacking Conkling. Not only would it gain the approbation of reformers, but it could significantly weaken a hostile party faction which had opposed the administration at every turn.[8]

The upshot was that Hayes, acting on the report of the commission which had investigated the New York Customs House, moved to oust its two top officials, Collector Chester A. Arthur and the Naval Officer, Alonzo B. Cornell. Both refused to resign, and Conkling called a convention of New York Republicans which he succeeded in turning into an anti-administration rally. Throwing down the gauntlet, Conkling denounced the administration as dominated by hypocrites: "When Dr. Johnson defined patriotism as the last refuge of scoundrels, he was unconscious of the then undeveloped capabilities and uses of the word Reform." [9]

In the end Conkling chose to fight his battle on the grounds of senatorial courtesy, i.e., that the president was attempting to appoint individuals unacceptable to the senators from their state. Considering that Garfield would himself experience as president a confrontation with Conkling very much like that of Hayes, his reaction to the Hayes-Conkling imbroglio is of some interest. He was initially cool to Hayes' Executive Order, and contrasted its moralistic tone with Hayes' having continued the presidential practice of appointing favorites to office. Although Garfield was no admirer of Conkling, he regarded the president as having offended the New Yorker to no particular end. In the course of a call at the White House in March 1878, Garfield cautioned the president that if he wished to retain influence within the party he would have to move more slowly on the matter of civil service reform.[10]

Party unity was important to Garfield, and it was not to be sacrificed without cause. At about the same time as his warning to Hayes, Garfield quoted approvingly in his diary a statement by Jacob Cox that Hayes had "utterly failed to accomplish anything in the way of Civil Service reform and that he had pursued no system that could be defended by any class of politicians." [11] There was, to be sure, an element of sour grapes in Garfield's complaints, for he did not believe that the president was working as closely as he should with the Republican leadership in Congress. But Hayes' inability to retain the respect of an essentially well-disposed colleague such as Garfield suggests that the administration was in fact rather disorganized in the pursuit of its objectives. In the end, even the senators who upheld the administration against Conkling had misgivings about the Customs House affair. Dawes of Massachusetts, now moved to the Senate, observed that "civil service reform, holy and noble as it [is], must be postponed in order to resist the Solid South and the silver movement, and restore Harmony in the Party." [12]

As if the administration were not troubled enough with the problems of implementing the president's hopes for sectional reconciliation and administrative reform, the years 1877–78 saw another of the country's periodic flirtations with cheap money. Advocates of inflation were divided into two overlapping camps. One comprised the Greenbackers, who in 1878 elected the largest number of congressmen, fifteen, which they had yet sent to Washington. At the same time, the fact that silver was being mined in increasing quantities in the West gave rise to sentiment in favor of renewed coinage of silver as a means of increasing the amount of money in circulation. In November 1877, Representative "Silver Dick" Bland of Missouri introduced a bill which called for the free and unlimited coinage of silver at the rate of 412½ grains to the dollar. Although Garfield denounced the bill and voted against it, a slightly modified version, the Bland-Allison bill, was passed by a vote of 163 to 34. Garfield did not exaggerate in concluding that he stood "almost alone in the West" in opposing the bill.

Actually, Garfield was not as inflexible on silver coinage as his vote might indicate. He had been impressed with the growing demand for silver coinage, and at the Ohio Republican convention he had sought to work out a currency plank which would not be too much of a political liability in the odd-year gubernatorial elections. The plank of which he eventually approved called for the coinage of both gold and silver at an equitable but unspecified ratio. Writing to Hinsdale, Garfield conceded that this represented something of a modification of his previous views, but he noted that France had apparently been successful in keeping both metals in circulation. In closing, he confirmed that "I have become a probationary convert to bimetalism." [13]

Had Garfield wished to make a bit of political capital he could have gone with the crowd and either voted for or abstained on the Bland-Allison bill. Congressman William McKinley, who would later reach the White House following a dramatic election victory over free-silver advocate William Jennings Bryan, voted for the bill. But the ratio specified in the bill struck Garfield as inequitable, and financial matters were one area in which he was rarely disposed to compromise. Although Hayes vetoed the Bland-Allison bill it was quickly passed over his veto, with Garfield once more in the minority. Garfield was disgusted over the whole business; he saw Hayes as having dissipated in his quarrel with Conkling the support on the Hill which might have sustained his veto. He wrote in his diary that "the President was not only unable to influence a single vote but lost some in the House. He has pursued a suicidal policy toward Congress and is almost without a friend." [14]

As minority leader Garfield had few functional responsibilities but, as chief strategist for Republicans in the House he found himself much more in the limelight than in his earlier committee roles. For all his interest in the framing of legislation, he was not without aptitude for his opposition role. This was just as well, since the gulf between Hayes and his fellow Republicans in Congress was such that Garfield was obliged to use his powers of persuasion to the utmost on behalf of the administration. But he was agile in debate, and well-equipped to defend his party's program on the floor.

The combination of continuing hard times, silverite sentiment, and Northern reservations concerning Hayes' policy contributed to a Democratic sweep in the 1878 elections which gave them control of the Senate as well as the House; the isolation of the president was almost complete. He was hardly more popular on the Hill than Andrew Johnson had been, but unlike the Tennesseean Hayes could exercise his veto with some assurance that there were still enough Republican votes to uphold it. Notwithstanding this, few presidents have undergone more persistent harassment than President Hayes. In April 1879, for instance, the Democrats added to the Army appropriations bill a rider which would repeal federal elections laws designed to assure voting rights for the Negro. Garfield's opposition to the bill grew out of conviction as well as necessity, for he was opposed both to the substance of the rider and to the practice of using appropriations bills as vehicles for bills which could never be passed on their own merits. In this case he found Hayes of much the same mind, and the president vetoed the bill. Once again, House Republicans were able to sustain the veto.

One chapter out of the past which refused to stay closed was the celebrated court-martial of General Fitz-John Porter. Porter had persisted in attempting to clear his name of the stigma arising from his trial and dismissal in 1862. Although Grant had turned a deaf ear to his petitions, the availability of Confederate military records late in the Hayes administration led to the convening of a new military board under General John M. Schofield. The Schofield inquiry—one of several which preceded Porter's final vindication—acquitted Porter of all charges except unwise criticism of his superiors, and Democrats in Congress introduced a bill providing for Porter's reinstatement in the Army.

The political overtones to the case made it highly unlikely that Garfield would arrive at a decision different from that which he had reached in 1862, but as he had during the hearings of the Electoral Commission he went through the motions of reviewing all the evidence. He concluded that the Confederate records— which largely supported Porter's decision not to attack in accordance with his orders—were less relevant to the case than Porter's apparent hostility to his superior, General Pope.[15] Garfield did not live to see Porter's eventual reinstatement, but he found the findings of the Schofield board galling enough. Considering that he was a practicing lawyer, Garfield had a curious disdain for legal evidence. A trial, like an election, was a means to an end, and Garfield was not one to allow his view to be clouded by facts which did not support his prejudices.

Whereas the president had few friends even among his own party in the Senate, he had in Garfield a House minority leader who was closely attuned to sentiment on the Hill and who was prepared to work for the administration program out of loyalty if not out of admiration. In fact, Garfield's estimate of Hayes rose as the president succeeded in turning opposition attacks to his own advantage. The resumption of specie payments, under the aegis of Secretary of the Treasury Sherman, also had Garfield's warm approval. As early as July 1877 he was able to write to Hayes that the extra session just ended had united the G.O.P. "more than anything since 1868 and bids fair to give us 1880." [16]

Things were indeed looking up for the Republicans. The Democrats, notwithstanding their control of both Houses of Congress, had failed to come up with any program beyond sniping at Hayes. By 1879, too, there were signs that the long depression was nearing an end; a poor harvest in Europe combined with a bumper crop in the Midwest to produce a farm revival which acted as a shot in the arm for the entire economy. Railroad construction, which had languished for more than five years, was resumed on a large scale. Although the Hayes administration, acting on the laissez-faire economic dogma of the day, had done next to nothing to dampen the effects of the depression, the return of prosperity not surprisingly redounded to the advantage of the party in power. There was a surge of optimism in the land, a feeling that the reunited nation was once again on the road to prosperity.

The country had celebrated its centennial in 1876, and the passing of this milestone brought a brief flurry of examinations into the state of the Republic. Garfield was asked for an article on Congress for *Atlantic,* and his contribution appeared in the July 1877 issue under the title, "A Century of Congress." The timing of any such article was hardly ideal; the country had just survived the Hayes-Tilden election controversy, and memories of the Grant scandals were still fresh. But Garfield came up with a piece which avoided most of the pitfalls of centennial oratory and showed that he had come to some of the same conclusions as had the Founding Fathers:

> Now, more than ever before, the people are responsible for the character of their Congress. If that body be ignorant, reckless, and corrupt, it is because the people tolerate ignorance, recklessness, and corruption. If it be intelligent, brave, and pure, it is because the people demand these high qualities to represent them in the national legislature. . . .
> Congress must always be the exponent of the political character and culture of the people; and if the next centennial does not find us as a great nation, with a great and worthy Congress, it will be because those who represent the enterprise, the culture, and the morality of the nation do not aid in controlling the political forces which are employed to select the men who shall occupy the great places of trust and power.[17]

Although the Garfields were very much at home in Washington, the sale of their house in Hiram had left them somewhat at loose ends with respect to a home on the Reserve. To meet this situation Garfield purchased in 1877 a 160-acre tract of land at Mentor, some 25 miles east of Cleveland on the line of the Lake Shore and Michigan Southern Railroad. The bungalow that came with the land was far too small for the Garfields, however, and after a couple of years they began drawing up plans to replace it with something larger. The result was a two-and-a-half story frame dwelling well-suited to their needs. Behind the gingerbread, for instance, "Lawnfield" included a separate wing for Garfield's mother, who was still going strong in her late seventies and who alternated living with the Garfields and her daughter Mary Larabee in nearby Solon.

One of Garfield's friends and supporters in the Reserve was William Cooper Howells, editor of the Ashtabula *Sentinel* and father of the aspiring novelist who had been called upon by Garfield in Columbus many years before. By 1878 the younger Howells was a resident of Cambridge, Massachusetts, a successful novelist, and editor of the same *Atlantic* which had commissioned "A Century of Congress." In later years, Howells recalled an occasion when he and his father had spent a night with the Garfields at Lawnfield. Howells was telling his host of some of his Cambridge neighbors when Garfield stopped him. Walking along his property the congressman waved to his neighbors. "Come over here," he called, "he's telling about Holmes and Longfellow and Lowell and Whittier." Howells was flattered and impressed. "I went on," he wrote to Mark Twain, "while the whippoorwills whirred and whistled round, and the hours drew toward midnight." [18]

Garfield had no false dignity, and one of his charms was that he had not altogether lost the emotive enthusiasm of his youth. He was something of a paradox, combining as he did both a love of physical activity which made him one of the most robust politicians of his day, and a love of books which gave him a reputation for erudition far beyond that of all but a few of his colleagues. Garfield himself got such stimulus from reading that he was baffled for a time by the failure of his sons to develop an attachment for the classics. In 1874 Garfield wrote in his diary of how he had read to his children from a translation of *Iphigenia in Tauris,* and that at one stage nine-year-old James "had left the room crying" at the prospect of Iphigenia's being sacrificed to assure a wind that would carry the Greek ships to Troy. One wonders whether the tears were those of compassion or boredom.

Photographs of Garfield in his late forties show a man of imposing physical build, with thinning hair on top and a touch of gray in his beard. The face is less full than when he first entered Congress, and the beard somewhat more imposing. But most of his contemporaries agreed that the photography of the day did not do him full justice. His carriage, erect to the point of stiffness, would convey to later generations an image of remote dignity and impress Thomas Wolfe as one of a series of "gravely vacant and bewhiskered faces" which "swam together in the sea-depths of a past intangible." [19]

Notwithstanding his reputation for scholarship, Garfield gradually dropped his preoccupation with self-improvement. In the mid-70s, he took up cards and became quite skilled at euchre and whist. When Congress was in session, close friends such as

Swaim and Rockwell were frequent visitors for dinner, a cigar, and a few rounds of cards or billiards. Although Garfield was never more than an occasional social drinker, he resisted periodic attempts by temperance groups to get him to foreswear his high-ball, and he was critical of the edict which banned wine from the White House table during the Hayes administration.

With the Ohioan destined to be his party's next presidential candidate, what could be said of Garfield's personality and character? Certainly not all observers were impressed with Garfield's intellectual attainments. Historian James F. Rhodes spoke of his "broad though superficial intelligence," while a fairly close friend, journalist Don Piatt, limited himself to the observation that Garfield, without being either deep or original, "had a most suggestive mind." [20] As might be expected from a teacher-turned-legislator, Garfield's thinking tended to be analytical rather than creative. But his memory was prodigious, and his enthusiasm for ideas marked him as one of a handful of intellectuals who have reached the White House. The post-Civil War era was a raw, acquisitive age, and there were few in either House of Congress who looked beyond the everyday scramble for patronage and railroad routes. Garfield had his lapses, but he appears to have tried to identify the important issues, and to address his appeals to reason rather than emotion.

The Ohioan had more than his share of wholehearted admirers. President Hayes, of all people, saw him as the complete man. ("If he were not in public life he would be equally eminent as a professor in a college, as a lecturer, as an author, an essayist, or a metaphysician.") [21] Senator Hoar of Massachusetts was even more impressed, writing of Garfield, "We have no other example in our public life of such marvelous completeness of intellectual development." [22] But even among his friends there were those who felt, with Albert Riddle, that Garfield had "some little thing wanting to completeness." To some he conveyed an impression of vacillation. John Sherman felt that Garfield's will power was not equal to his charm, writing that "he easily changed his mind and honestly veered from one impulse to another." [23] This charge is not altogether fair, for although Garfield sometimes shifted his ground he was also capable of holding to his views with considerable tenacity, as on subjects as diverse as Fitz-John Porter and fiat money. Nevertheless, it would appear that Garfield's friends regarded a lack of decisiveness as perhaps his most conspicuous shortcoming.

As a soldier, Garfield had faced up to decisions courageously. On the political issues of the postwar era, however, Garfield was uneasy where he could find no useful precedents, and in a matter such as Johnson's impeachment he ended up taking a purely partisan position. He brought an open mind to the viewpoints of his colleagues, and the affair of the salary grab is a conspicuous example of Garfield's being pressured into taking action which was against his better judgment. Yet once he was convinced of the rectitude of his position, his tenacity was fearful to behold.

Much of Garfield's difficulty stemmed from his sensitivity to criticism. "He rushes into a fight," observed Jeremiah Black, "with the horns of a bull and the skin of a rabbit," [24] It was this thin-skinned quality which made Garfield self-conscious; he required approbation, and in the absence of it he was prone to despondency. The pages of his diary abound with comments concerning the reception accorded his speeches. But appearances were also important to Garfield, and from the time of his defeat for the colonelcy of the Seventh Ohio on that black day in 1861 he was careful not to appear to be courting promotion or applause. The warfare between Garfield's ambition and his sense of propriety often led to becoming acts of modesty, as in his offer to stand down as congressman in deference to Ben Wade.

Garfield's difficulties in 1873 could not be attributed to a thin skin; in fact, they were an outgrowth of his insensitivity to certain ethical considerations. They did, however, reflect his tendency to be unduly influenced by others. With stocks and bonds being all but traded on the floor of Congress, Garfield put aside any scruples he may have had about obtaining a loan from Oakes Ames. Since a Republican colleague saw nothing wrong in representing the De Golyer Company, Garfield had no hesitation about filling in on his behalf. On balance, one suspects that Garfield represented as honest a politician as one could expect in the Gilded Age. With Albert Riddle, however, the biographer misses that extra bit of discrimination that would have set Garfield apart from his colleagues of the Grant era. For all his industry, Garfield accepted the mores of the period in which he served, and did little to change them. His phase as a quasi-reformer did not last beyond 1872, and was all but eclipsed from 1876 on as his role became that of a party strategist.

Although Garfield's attitude on financial and tariff matters has typed him as a conservative, it is noteworthy that he himself did not espouse a conservative credo. In facilitating the country's industrial expansion he and his colleagues liked to think of themselves as breaking new ground. One of Garfield's strongest accolades was to refer to a speech or an action as "bold." After having read a biography of Samuel Adams, the Boston revolutionary, Garfield noted in his diary that he himself retained his faith in radicalism, since "only radicals have accomplished anything in a great crisis." [25]

Whether bull or rabbit, Garfield was remarkably successful as a party leader. His highly effective work on behalf of Hayes in 1876 has already been noted. The same tendency to defer to others which kept him from being an independent force in the House increased his effectiveness in party caucus. Although he was privately critical of certain of Hayes' policies, Garfield's increased prominence was in part an outgrowth of the fact that he enjoyed the president's confidence. With Hayes having announced that he would not be a candidate for re-election, it was hardly surprising that Garfield came to be mentioned occasionally as a possible successor.

Chapter Thirteen

THE
AVAILABLE MAN

———◆———

As Hayes' term approached its close, there can be no question that Garfield was ready for a change. In his diary he complained anew of overwork, and of the difficulty in providing the president with the votes he needed. He looked longingly toward the Senate where, in his mind, there would be greater influence and a more responsive audience for oratory. He recalled with annoyance the pressure on him to stand down from the senatorial race in 1877, and he does not appear to have been impressed by comments from Hayes to the effect that he, Garfield, might follow him into the White House.

Garfield was no longer the ambitious Union brigadier and he was not courting the presidency. Apart from the fact that the Senate looked like a surer bet, he saw problems in becoming a rival to John Sherman for the role of Ohio's favorite son. He was briefly tempted in the spring of 1879 by the prospect of the Republican gubernatorial nomination. Hayes urged him to seek the governorship, and the governor's mansion in Columbus would have provided, even more than the Senate, a prestigious change of scene such as Garfield desired. But his election as governor might well propel him into the presidential race, and in so doing hasten the confrontation with Sherman that he hoped to avoid. The upshot was that, when Sherman began looking for a means to remove Garfield as a presidential rival, he found his fellow Ohioan quite receptive.

In May 1879, a friend of Garfield was told by Sherman that he would not enter the race for the Senate seat which would become vacant the following year if he were assured of the support of the Ohio delegation for the presidential nomination. Garfield was noncommittal, perhaps because he feared talk of a "deal." After Congress adjourned, however, Garfield accepted a dinner invitation from the secretary, a dinner which was followed by a long drive into the Maryland countryside. In the course of a far-ranging political discussion, Sherman apparently promised to do nothing to interfere with Garfield's campaign for the Senate. Although there is no evidence that Garfield committed himself to Sherman's candidacy at this time, it appears likely that he at least promised to stay out of the older man's way. With the removal of the potential obstacle posed by Sherman, Garfield became increasingly committed in his own mind to a campaign for the Senate. He wrote in his diary in October,

> If I were to act on my own choice, without reference to influences, I would remain in the House of Representatives. But I have resolved to be a candidate for the U. S. Senate for these reasons. *First.* I am, and as leader of the House shall continue to be, too hard worked, and am likely to break down under its weight. *Second.* There are many good men in my District who will think it selfish in me to keep them out of the House when I have a fair chance of promotion. *Third.* I once gave way at the request of the President, and a few fellows of the baser sort said I was afraid to risk my strength in the larger field of the Senate. If I should decline now, I should lose still more in this direction.[1]

Thus, to Garfield, all signs pointed in the direction of the Senate, and when the Ohio state elections went heavily to the Republicans in the fall of 1879 it became assured that the new senator would be from the Grand Old Party. Recognizing opportunity when he saw it, Garfield decided to go all the way, and took the key step of designating agents to lobby on his behalf among the incoming state senators. Although Garfield was widely regarded as having the inside track, the field was a large one, including as it did Garfield's friend ex-Governor Dennison, former Attorney General Alphonso Taft, and President Hayes' college classmate Stanley Matthews. Despite his favorable prospects, Garfield continue to be apprehensive regarding Sherman. According to his diary, Garfield implied to Sherman's brother-in-law that his attitude toward Sherman's presidential candidacy "would depend, in part, upon his conduct towards me in the [senatorial] contest." Such precautions were in character, but probably were unnecessary. At the Republican caucus in January his three rivals withdrew their names, and Garfield was unanimously nominated. There remained only the formality of election by the heavily-Republican state senate. But Garfield, typically, felt no elation. To Hinsdale he wrote,

> I go into the unknown and the untried; and I have this premonition that the Senate is composed of old men whose ideas and opinions are crystallized into fixed and well-nigh unchangeable forms and they are much less likely to be impressed by anything that may be said to them than are the members of the House. Furthermore, a decided majority of all my associates who have gone from the House to the Senate have been measurably lost in its silence.[2]

The year 1879 became 1880, and President Hayes moved into the final year of the presidential term which he had administered with such disregard for political sensibilities that even in his own party he found few mourners. As the wags put it, "Mr. Hayes came in by a majority of one, and goes out by unanimous consent." Congress reconvened in January, following the Christmas recess, and confirmed Hayes' appointment of James Russell Lowell as minister to Great Britain. Otherwise it found little to do. Garfield observed in his diary, "On the whole this session thus far has been the most meek and stupid of any I have known. The late elections have greatly subdued the spirit of the Democracy and they have not yet determined what their plans for the future

187

are to be." [3]

The most popular topic of gossip was, of course, the forthcoming presidential election, in particular the possibility of a third term for General Grant. His world tour had lasted more than two years, and the honors showered everywhere on the "Silent Soldier" had brought him widespread publicity at home. He returned in September 1879 to a frenzy of admiration and acclaim. Grant's disappointing presidency appeared hardly to have dimmed his luster, and Grant was more than willing to be considered presidential timber once again. Roscoe Conkling began preparations to secure the presidential nomination for Grant, but it became quickly apparent that the task would not be easy. Blaine, who had come so close to nomination in 1876, had his hat very much in the ring, and there was also Sherman. These men had their own reasons for opposing Grant, but there was also a popular uneasiness. Was Grant the man for whom the tradition against a third term should be broken? And apart from the key question of Grant's qualifications, there were those who felt that Grant stood for the old order and that with the withdrawal of troops from the South the country had entered a new period, one which required fresh leadership.

In the two decades since Lincoln's election the two conservative parties had become firmly entrenched. There was recognition that social evils existed, but the notion that the federal government should take the lead in grappling with them was a radical concept, one calculated to bring social ostracism. The two major parties looked with some annoyance on the Greenbackers, whose visionary program included demands for reforms such as woman suffrage, a graduated income tax, and the regulation of interstate commerce. Because the major parties were so firmly dedicated to a program of noninterference with the economy, the Greenbackers reached a zenith of popularity at the height of the depression which had begun in 1873. But the return of good times in 1879 made heavy inroads into the reform movement. As for the Democrats, they were prepared to make the "fraud of 1876" their great issue four years later, and did not look for support to fiscal malcontents such as the Greenbackers.

For the most part, the country's reviving economy was matched by an equal political complacency. The *Springfield Republican* editorially complained at the end of 1879,

It had been a commonplace year—one of prosperity and returning comfort in material things, and of the petty and disappointing in political and moral affairs. . . . The questions left to us by slavery, in which we still wallow, are only less grave than slavery itself. . . . It has been a year of standing still rather than of advance. Let us hope that 1880 will reveal the leaders of public opinion in a more courageous attitude.[4]

Yet if 1879 had been commonplace, it had also been prosperous. The relative austerity which had followed the depression year of 1873 had been all but forgotten, and the Greenbackers, notwithstanding their showing of two years previous, showed no signs of broadening their political base. The new year brought no new scandals, and comparatively few happenings. The public vented its wrath upon an unfortunate architect in April, after the front wall of the original Madison Square Garden collapsed, killing four bystanders. Similarly, the press described in macabre detail a maritime disaster in Long Island Sound. Twenty persons died on a foggy night in June when a coastal steamer, the *Narragansett,* burned to the water after colliding with the *Stonington.* For the most part, however, the public focused its attention on the forthcoming election. As convention time drew near, the tone of the press grew more shrill as the papers debated, in emotional and highly subjective terms, the merits of the possible candidates.

The Greenbackers held their convention in early June, and nominated General James B. Weaver for president, but most papers were too preoccupied with the major parties to give the Greenbackers more than passing notice. The *New York Times*— not yet the arbiter of what was "Fit to Print"—divided its front page between articles lauding Grant and those attacking Sherman, Blaine, and the Democratic favorite, Samuel J. Tilden. No holds were barred. Some representative columns were headed as follows:

THE PRESIDENCY AT STAKE

Sherman's Prodigal Use of Money In Ohio;

He Secures the Franklin County Delegation by Hiring
Democratic Voters and Buying Whiskey.

And again:

STEALING TILDEN'S DEVICE

Blaine and Sherman Running Literary Bureaus;

How Some Presidential Aspirants Stab Rivals in the Back.[5]

The *Springfield Republican,* which opposed the boom for Grant, was more moderate in its commentary and endorsed no single candidate. There was a widespread assumption that Grant's managers had victory within their grasp, however, and few were disposed to quarrel with the statement made by the *Times* on May 21 that "no political event can be much more certain than that Gen. Grant will be the nominee of the Republican Party for President of the United States." The *Times'* assumption was based on a widely held belief that the personalities of the candidates, and not party organizations or platform promises, would prove decisive in the election. As early as April, the *Republican's* perceptive editor, Samuel Bowles, deplored what he saw as an absence of positive issues for the forthcoming campaign:

> The truth is, if we look at parties as embodiments of ideas and principles, both the two great parties are in the strict sense of the word *effete.* They are worn out . . . bankrupt in ideas and policies. Each trades mainly on the blunders of its opponent, [and thus both] become mere machines for advancing the political fortunes of their managers.[6]

There was considerable merit in Bowles' argument; elements of both parties were weary of refighting the Civil War every four years and ready to move on to new issues. Henry Grady, publisher of the *Atlanta Constitution* and a leading spokesman for the reviving South, visited New York City in the early months of 1880 and came away with plenty of advice that the South should concern itself less with politics and more with material development. "Fast mails, small farms, . . . new industries," Grady wrote on his return, "these are the channels through which the South

190

can command the respect of the North." [7]

But politics has a momentum peculiarly its own, and both major parties were locked into the issues of the past. Each side thought it held a winning hand, and had no interest in upsetting a very delicate equilibrium. In any case, with the restoration of home rule in the South there was no longer an issue which had truly national appeal. The season of reform was not yet on the land.

In the period before a political convention, probably a dozen "dark horses" are solemnly assured by various admirers and syco-phants that they are uniquely qualified to lead the nation in the perilous years ahead, and that the convention must inevitably turn to them. So it was with Garfield. As early as February 1879, Governor Pound of Wisconsin told Garfield that Wisconsin wanted him, and urged the Ohioan not to commit himself irre-vocably to any other candidate. Garfield had another admirer even more highly placed. According to his diary, the subject of Gar-field's presidential prospects came up in the course of a train trip with President Hayes as early as 1878. Garfield recorded that, as they whiled away the hours between Cleveland and Washington, Hayes urged him to become a candidate for governor, intimating that this was "the surest road to the presidency."

Garfield's mail began to include an increasing number of let-ters urging him to seek the presidential nomination. Although flat-tered by the attention, he kept his eye on the U. S. Senate. He noted in his diary in early February, "While I am not indifferent to the good opinion of men who think me fit for the presidency, I am still wholly disinclined to believe that any result will come out of it other than some general talk. I have so long and so often seen the evil effects of the presidential fever upon my associates and friends that I am determined it shall not seize upon me." [8] Garfield began with some misgivings to work for a state delega-tion solid for Sherman, all the while wondering whether this might not be the year in which Blaine's ambition would be grat-ified. Such satisfaction as Garfield derived from Sherman's can-didacy concerned the votes which were being denied to Grant, whose re-election Garfield continued to view as a political disaster. In view of his understanding with Sherman, however, he found it somewhat disquieting to see his name cropping up more frequently as a possible compromise candidate. On January 26, 1880, Garfield wrote a public letter committing himself to Sherman's candidacy—a letter which, while not effusive, stated that the secretary of the treasury deserved recognition "for the great service he has rendered in making the resumption law a success, and placing the national finances on a better basis."

Such a letter was not calculated to discourage Garfield's coterie of admirers, and it did not. In mid-February a Pennsylvania industrialist, Wharton Barker, advised Garfield that sentiment in his favor was growing in Pennsylvania, and that he, Barker, was going to attempt to organize it. Garfield wrote back that he was not a candidate, that he was working for Sherman in good faith, and that he would not solicit support on his own behalf. He was clearly not ruling out a draft, but was making a genuine effort to carry out his part of the bargain with Sherman. On April 16 he wrote,

> I am between two fires. . . . On many accounts I would be embarrassed to go to Chicago, while on the other hand, I do not wish to shirk the responsibility nor appear to be negligent of Sherman's interest. While I do not think he has much of a chance, if any, of the nomination, I still think, if we want to prevent Grant's nomination, we ought to give Ohio to Sherman. . . .
>
> I will not offer myself as a candidate, nor decline if it is tendered me.[9]

Although the Republican party was under the tight control of a handful of regional bosses, each of whom sought to dictate the convention's choice of the nominee, the political balance was sufficiently close in 1880 that the Republicans could not afford the luxury of a lackluster candidate such as Sherman. Grant, Blaine, Garfield—each of the three had a significant popular following, with Garfield's easily the smallest of the three. But the Ohioan was acceptable to a broad cross-section of the party as the other two were not. And his was a fresh face.

Not the least of the intangibles working in Garfield's favor were two novels published in 1879, both the work of a popular novelist, Albion W. Tourgee. He and Garfield had first met when Tourgee visited Ohio as a boy, and the two had periodically exchanged letters. *Figs and Thistles* was the story of an Ohio lad who put himself through college, rose from private to general during the Civil War, and went on to a distinguished career in the House of Representatives. The life of Tourgee's hero paralleled Garfield's sufficiently closely that the *New York Tribune* later observed, "In his last volume . . . Judge Tourgee has put into the form of attractive fiction something of the lives and loves of President Garfield and his wife." Tourgee's other effort, *A Fool's Errand,* was an outgrowth of the author's own experiences as a political appointee in post-bellum North Carolina. As the title suggests, the book portrayed sympathetically the problems faced by Northerners during reconstruction, and it could be read as justification for the Radical program supported by Garfield. The Ohioan's nomination thus came about not solely because of the convention deadlock, although it was this deadlock which made it possible. Once the search for a compromise candidate began, Garfield could count as assets a "good press" from Tourgee and others; a host of friends in various echelons of the party; and the image of a hardworking, self-made man which permitted the delegates to overlook the scandals of 1873.

If Garfield's nomination came as a surprise, the convention's choice of his running-mate was nothing short of earth-shaking. For the choice of the delegates was one of Roscoe Conkling's chief lieutenants, Chester A. Arthur of New York.

Contrary to the popular belief, then as now, "Chet" Arthur was not a prototype machine politician. The son of a Baptist minister, he had gone into politics less in search of a livelihood than of an avocation. In his pre-Civil War law practice Arthur was associated with a number of cases involving Negro rights, and in 1855 he assisted in obtaining a ruling that Negroes were to be accorded impartial treatment on New York City streetcars. But the image which Arthur cultivated was that of the *bon vivant.* He was poised, urbane, and, according to one account, possessed of "every quality required of a gentleman in his day." In particular, he was noted for his fastidiousness of dress.

To this day, one's impression of Arthur is a two-dimensional one. The aspect of politics which seemed to interest him most was administration, which in his day meant the distribution of patronage, and he never appeared especially ambitious for national office. There could hardly be a greater contrast to Garfield than his running mate. Whereas Garfield was a product of rural Ohio, Arthur was the city boy. Where Garfield even in his forties was alert for new opportunities and challenges, the New Yorker tended to be lethargic. And while Garfield liked to think of himself as an idealist, Arthur had no illusions about his political role.

Until Grant had appointed him collector for the Port of New York, Arthur was not even well-known in his own state. Invariably he inherited most of Conkling's enemies, and his tenure as collector was never a smooth one. Initially he was paid a percentage of the revenue which he collected, a practice which provided Arthur with a salary in the neighborhood of $40,000 a year. In 1872, however, it developed that the government had lost some fees as a result of bad bookkeeping, and following an investigation Congress passed a law which put the collector on a flat $12,-000 per year salary.

Arthur continued in his post as collector, and he was a dashing figure at Delmonico's until Hayes saw his opportunity to strike a simultaneous blow for reform and against the Conkling apparatus by giving the New York Customs House a badly needed overhaul. The result was the investigation which brought about the removal of Arthur and his Naval Officer, Alonzo B. Cornell. After a protracted skirmish with Conkling, who attempted to block the appointment of a successor to Arthur, President Hayes succeeded in appointing a collector of his own choice, Edwin A. Merritt.

At the Chicago convention Arthur was constantly at Conkling's side in the fight for the retention of the unit rule, and in the subsequent struggle on behalf of Grant. But when the compromise was reached which put Hoar in the chair and permitted the convention to vote on the unit rule, Arthur went along with good grace, and held the Stalwarts to the letter of the agreement. As the convention went on, Arthur, with his partisanship tempered by courtesy and comraderie, made a far better impression on the delegates than the overbearing Conkling.

Following the nomination of Garfield in the early afternoon of the 8th, the convention went into recess until he could be formally notified of his nomination. That afternoon, Garfield's friend Dennison visited the New York delegation on the candidate's behalf, carrying with him an offer of Ohio's support for any vice-presidential nominee they might wish to select. The day in which a presidential candidate would dictate the choice of his running mate was still far off, and Garfield was giving first priority to conciliating the New Yorkers. The first person to whom the vice-presidential nomination was tendered was Levi P. Morton, whose personal wealth and solid Stalwart credentials were both in his favor. Years later, Morton related that he had checked out the offer with Conkling, who told him to do as he pleased, but that by the time he rejoined Garfield's emissaries the nomination had been offered to Arthur. (When Morton would later reach the vice presidency, it would be as running mate to Benjamin Harrison, who lived out his term.) A newsman, W. C. Hudson, has related how he overheard a heated conversation between Conkling and Arthur in which the latter refused to decline the vice-presidential nomination, insisting that "even a barren nomination would be a great honor." Although it is not clear why Conkling would have taken one line with Morton and another with Arthur, the weight of the evidence suggests that Conkling was still smouldering over Grant's defeat and did not wish any of his New Yorkers to link their names with Garfield.[10] When the balloting for vice president began, no fewer than nine names were placed before the convention. But the vote was not close, and Arthur received the nomination on the first ballot.

Few conventions in American political history have generated as much controversy as the Republican convention of 1880. Initially the surprise centered on the choice of Arthur, who was criticized as a weak selection and as too apparent a sop to the Grant forces. In later years, historians tended to focus on Garfield's conduct. Was he Ohio's fair-haired boy, who had the nomination dropped in his lap, unsolicited, by the weary convention?

Or did he skillfully maneuver for the nomination, in disregard
of his obligation to John Sherman?

Garfield went to the convention fully aware that, in the
seemingly unlikely event that the convention should turn to him,
he might be accused of disloyalty to Sherman. His "visibility" as
one of the anti-Grant leaders, as in his rebuttal to Conkling over
the expulsion of the two delegates, could be cited by those who
professed to see Garfield working in his own interest. But at this
distance it is difficult to see how he could have behaved much
differently, either in the months before the convention or at the
convention itself. Garfield was never enthusiastic about his prospective role as Sherman's manager, but he probably felt that to
decline might jeopardize the arrangement under which he was
to move up to the Senate. While he might have announced in advance that he would not accept the nomination under any circumstances, this would have been presumptuous. No one really
expected it to be offered to him.

Garfield had declared in April, "I will not offer myself as a
candidate, nor decline if it is tendered to me." His subsequent behavior at Chicago was entirely consistent with this attitude; in
fact, his dialogue with Senator Hoar suggests that he was leaning
over backward to assure that his conduct was above criticism. It
is unfortunate that Garfield was unable to keep up his diary on
these key days, but one can assume that the diarist would have approved his own standard of conduct. Although some of Sherman's
supporters were critical of Garfield, the secretary himself was not,
at least not at the time. Dennison advised him that Garfield's conduct had been "frank and manly throughout," and Sherman wired
his congratulations.[11]

Jeremiah Black was in London during all the excitement in
Chicago, and he was torn between his old Democratic loyalties
and the good fortune which had befallen his friend. He ended by
viewing the Republican convention as the agency "by which a
very dear friend will probably reach that great office which makes
ambition virtue"—though he would not have Black's vote in getting there! To Garfield he wrote,

> I am sure that if elected you will try your best to do justice,
> to love mercy, and to walk humbly before God. But to a cer-

tain extent you are bound to fail, for in our country the leader
of a party is like the head of a snake—it can only go as the
tail impels it, and your tail will be a very perverse one.

But the older man's good will was evident, and Garfield's
reply was equally warm:

I know how grounded you are in the ways of political thinking which seem to you just and for the highest good of your
country—and so all the more for that reason I prize your
words of personal kindness. . . . Succeeding or failing I shall
none the less honor your noble character, great intellect and
equally great heart.[12]

Chapter Fourteen

THE TUMULT
AND
THE SHOUTING

———◆·◆———

Samuel J. Tilden had received a quarter of a million votes more than his Republican opponent in 1876 and, as far as the party was concerned, had been deprived of his office by fraud. The presence of Rutherford B. Hayes in the executive Mansion was viewed with a sense of outrage by all Democrats, but by no one more than their titular leader. Yet not all of Tilden's ire was directed against Republicans. As seen from Gramercy Park, the actions of men such as Randall, Thurman, and Bayard, who had conceded the presidency to Hayes in return for an end to reconstruction, had permitted Hayes to be imposed upon the country. Tilden continued to be regarded as the leader of his party, despite a seemingly genuine preference for the life of a country squire. His followers regularly addressed him as "Mr. President," as did communications from Democratic organizations all over the country.

In the four years since the disputed election, it was widely assumed that Tilden would be the Democratic nominee again in 1880. Unfortunately for his admirers, however, he had encountered a series of political reverses. In 1878, discovery of the "cypher telegrams" revealed that someone in Tilden's entourage had attempted to bribe members of the Electoral Commission the previous year. Cyrus Field, among others, had charged Tilden with low standards of business ethics. And to add insult to injury, the government had instituted charges of income-tax evasion. As for a new try at the presidency, Tilden apparently hoped for a draft. Just prior to the Democratic convention at Cincinnati, Tilden entrusted to his brother a long letter to the assembled delegates in which, after acknowledging his qualifications for the presidential office, he blasted the "false count" of four years previous, and then, in a smashing anticlimax, declined to run again on the grounds of poor health. Had Tilden wished to withdraw absolutely, he—like Garfield—could have expressed himself a good deal more forcefully.

Much to Tilden's chagrin, the convention chose to take his letter at face value. In so doing, the delegates appear to have been influenced by a number of factors, including the outcry over the cypher telegrams and Tilden's continued unacceptability to Tammany Hall in New York. What they envisaged was a campaign based in large part on the issue of the "stolen election" but with a more appealing personality at the head of the ticket. The upshot was that the Democrats, like their rivals, turned to a dark horse, who in their case was General Winfield Scott Hancock of Pennsylvania.

Hancock had been a factor in Democratic politics since the close of the war. As the able and colorful commander of the Army of the Potomac's Second Corps, he had been one of the architects of the Union triumph at Gettysburg. A life-long Democrat, he was also a strong Unionist and had, in 1864, voted for Lincoln in preference to his friend McClellan. Following the war, Hancock identified himself with the reconstruction policies of President Johnson; his unwillingness to employ to the full his powers as commander of the military district for Louisiana and Texas brought on him the ire of the Radicals, including Garfield. As

199

one of his party's few bona fide war heroes, Hancock came close to receiving the Democratic presidential nomination in 1868. By 1880, however, the popular Hancock had moved into a portly middle-age; at more than 300 pounds, he had lost something of his martial aura. He appeared in public comparatively rarely, and his nomination at Cincinnati was as great a surprise to the public as that of Garfield.[1]

An election in the late nineteenth century had more in common with those of Henry Clay's day than with what we know today. Of the modern communications media which we now take for granted, only the telegraph was in general use in 1880. Mass media comprised, as they had for previous decades, the press and the stump. But perhaps the most striking difference between an election then and now concerned the behavior of the candidates themselves. Until well into the present century, it was an article of faith that the office must seek the man. If there were an occasion for a speech during a campaign, a few gracious words from the candidate were more than adequate. No major issues were to be discussed; these would be taken care of by other speakers.

With the candidates thus on the sidelines, and in the absence of radio and television, newspapers and orators played a far more influential role than they do today. And except for a few "independent" papers, the press was for the most part both partisan and unscrupulous. A "good press" was conceded to be far more important than campaign biographies and literature, and most of the rumors of an election campaign could be traced back to some party journal. Good speakers were perhaps less important, but hardly to be ignored. The entertainment value of a rally or a torchlight parade was considerable in an era not yet blessed with movies or television. Decades later, Herbert Hoover recalled how his awareness of national politics had come with a torchlight parade in the 1880 campaign. "I was not only allowed out that night," wrote Hoover, "but I saw the torches being filled and lighted. I was not high enough to carry one but I was permitted to walk alongside the parade." [2] Young Hoover was six.

With the conventions behind them, the two candidates prepared for a traditional "front porch" campaign. Garfield's front porch was at his farm in Mentor; Hancock's was at his headquarters on Governor's Island. At these locations, over the next four months, each shook hands with hundreds of visiting delegations, uttered a few words of greeting, and sent the visitors on their way. But with respect to such delegations, Hancock had one advantage: a bay lay between his home and New York City beyond. Garfield, on the other hand, let the nation come to him. "It came in the form of school children, senators, businessmen, suffrage workers, prohibitionists and hot crowds of people who might be classed as more or less mere. . . . It came climbing fences, trampling grass and flowers, shouting and cheering and whistling too. It came singly and in groups large and small, and it came by districts, by crank-notion, by organization, by profession, sometimes even by appointment." [3]

The press reaction to the nominations was almost straight down party lines. The *New York Times* discerned in Hancock's nomination evidence that the Old Confederacy had taken over the party, but heartily approved the Republicans' choice of Garfield and Arthur. The *New York Sun,* Garfield's old bête noire, applauded the choice of Hancock while dusting off its old charges concerning Garfield and the Credit Mobilier. The moderate *Springfield Republican,* relieved at the convention failures of Grant and Tilden, had kind words for both tickets.

> The country can now draw a deep, grateful breath of relief and wait until Messrs. Garfield and Hancock issue their letters of acceptance. The fight is between two brave old soldiers who aspire, the one to extend, the other to gain, his civil leadership. Now let them tell us just what they will try to do for their fellow-citizens. [4]

The "letter of acceptance" was at the time a standard means by which a candidate could elaborate upon his party's platform, or clarify some issue of the day. In 1880, however, the campaign had largely taken shape before either candidate issued his letter. From the day of his nomination Garfield was the target of abuse growing out of the scandals of 1873. Although the Democrats missed no opportunity to harp upon the "fraud" of 1876, their main target was the Republican candidate. In early July the *Sun* alleged that leading Republicans, "whose names would excite surprise if given to the public," were urging that Garfield be replaced at the head of the ticket by a candidate "whose record is not tainted with venality and dishonor." [5]

Before issuing his letter, Garfield was obliged to make the first of two trips East which would loom large in the campaign. Notwithstanding the warnings of friends, Garfield decided to combine a trip to Washington, in order to gather some papers, with a few personal appearances en route. Wherever it stopped his train was enthusiastically received, and in response to the cheers Garfield invariably responded with a few well-chosen words. Party officials gradually lost their nervousness as it became apparent that Garfield was turning rear-platform appearances into a minor art form. As his train pulled into a station—resplendent in bunting since the night before—the band would strike up and local dignitaries would adjust their cravats and top hats. The crowd would watch in good humor as the local party officials and lesser candidates filed on board. Then, as the minutes wore on, clapping and calls for "Garfield" would be heard. The candidate's appearance on the rear platform invariably brought cheers which were rewarded with a brief speech tailored to a group in the audience:

> Comrades of the Boys in Blue, and fellow-citizens of New York, I cannot look upon this great assemblage and these old veterans . . . without remembering how great a thing it is to live in this Union and be a part of it. (Applause). . . .
> Gentlemen, ideas outlive men. Ideas outlive all things, and you who fought in the war for the Union fought for immortal ideas, and by their might you crowned our war with victory. (Applause). . . . We gathered the boys from all our farms, and shops, and stores, and schools, and homes, from all over the Republic, and they went forth unknown to fame, but returned enrolled on the roster of immortal heroes. (Great applause). They went in the spirit of those soldiers of Henry Agincourt, of whom he said: 'Who this day sheds his blood with me today shall be my brother. Were he ne'er so vile, this day shall gentle his condition and elevate the heart of every working soldier who fought in it (applause), and he shall be our brother forevermore.' [6]

Under such a verbal barrage it was easy to forget that it was Hancock, and not Garfield, who in fact turned back the rebel charge at Gettysburg. But it would be unfair to impute a cynical motive to Garfield when he delivered himself of such boilerplate. To him, as to his listeners, the Civil War had been the greatest experience of his generation. In speaking as he did, Garfield was saying little more than what he had written many times in the privacy of his diary.

In Washington Garfield had a long talk with Blaine, and attempted to call on Conkling at his hotel. The senator was out but he returned the call the following day, only to find the candidate not at home. Later in the day, Conkling heard a sordid tale: the candidate had been seen riding in public with none other than the reformer, Carl Schurz. Conkling flew into a rage. Never again would he trust that "angleworm" Garfield! In part as a result of this childish episode, Conkling once again looked upon Garfield with suspicion.[7]

Thus it was with an eye to placating the Stalwarts that Garfield wrote his letter of acceptance. To Whitelaw Reid of the *Tribune* he wrote that "the Grant and the Blaine men will have no cause of complaint about my letter if I can help it." In his letter Garfield went on record as favoring the rights guaranteed by the Constitution, popular education, and sound money, and he fearlessly championed the improvement of rivers and harbors. Most important of all, he implied that he had no desire to upset the various state organizations in matters affecting patronage:

> To select wisely, from our vast population, those who are best fitted for the many offices to be filled, requires an acquaintance far beyond the range of any one man. The executive should, therefore, seek and receive the information and assistance of those whose knowledge of the communities, in which the duties are to be performed, best qualifies them to aid in making the wisest choice.[8]

Garfield's letter was acceptable to Republican party organs, but it drew no cheers elsewhere. The *Nation* called it "a cruel disappointment to those Independents who had hoped to find in it a trumpet-call." [9] The *Springfield Republican* insisted that it read "not like a statesman's plan for government, but like a politician's bid for votes." To add insult to injury, the *Republican* contended that Arthur's letter, which called for a serious study of the question of civil service reform, had been better received than Garfield's.[10] Through all this, Garfield kept his composure. He desired the approval of the independents, who represented a small but conceivably pivotal bloc, but he was obliged to give greater priority to Republican party unity, without which defeat was certain.

At the end of July, it could be said that neither party could claim a significant edge, and all signs pointed to a close election. The electoral lineup was a curious one. With federal troops withdrawn, and with white Southerners still belligerent on the subject of reconstruction, the South was felt almost certain to go Democratic. The Republicans were conceded the edge in much of the East and Midwest, but whereas a Democratic landslide in the South loomed as a real possibility. the Republican edge was everywhere much narrower. Out of the 185 electoral votes required for victory, most papers conceded a minimum of 138 to the Democrats. The Republicans were felt to be ahead in states totaling 144 votes, but by a much smaller margin. Thus the Republicans needed to come up with 41 additional votes from "doubtful" Northern states such as Ohio, Indiana, New York, and New Jersey.

On the positive side, Garfield's friends were coming to the conclusion that Democratic charges of corruption on the part of the Republican candidate were having little impact. On the subject of the Credit Mobilier, for instance, the *Springfield Republican* observed that judging by Garfield's "splendid service" in Congress, "it is more reasonable to credit Oakes Ames . . . with a confounded memory than to believe that Garfield perjured himself." [11] The *Nation* took a similar view. But one of the Republicans' greatest assets was the new respectability that Hayes had given the party. In a key address delivered at Indianapolis, Carl Schurz saw a new Democratic administration as "hundreds and thousands of politicians, great and small but all hungry, rushing for seventy or eighty thousand places." Under Hayes, on the other hand, the Republican party had regained its old vigor:

It is true that parties are apt to degenerate by the long possession of power. The Republican party cannot expect to escape the common lot of humanity; but no candid observer will
deny that within a late period the Republican party has
shown signs rather of improvement than deterioration; and
that it possesses the best share of the intelligence, virtue and
patriotism of the country. . . .
The Democracy may in the course of time gain the confidence of the people . . . [but only] when it will no longer
find it necessary to discard the ablest of its statesmen and to
put a general of the army, who has never been anything but a
soldier, in nomination for the presidency, to make for itself a
certificate of loyalty to the settlements of the great conflicts of
the past.[12]

It might have been expected that, with a strenuous campaign
ahead, both parties would have harmonized their differences and
buckled down to the election. Neither party demonstrated any
such cohesiveness, however, and by late July Garfield was actively
concerned at the lassitude within the G.O.P. His consultation
with Blaine and Schurz had antagonized the Stalwarts to an extent which Garfield found hard to understand. When it became
apparent that Garfield's letter of acceptance had made no real impression on the Grant men, party officials began to suggest that a
personal visit to New York might be necessary. The candidate
was willing, but fearful of the effect that such an obvious wooing
of the Stalwarts might have on independents; could not Conkling
come to Ohio, as Grant was planning to do? But William E.
Chandler, a member of the Republican National Committee,
urged that Garfield take the initiative, noting that "it is worth
while perhaps to stoop a little to conquer much."

The most aggressive of Garfield's advisors was the secretary of
the Republican National Committee, Stephen W. Dorsey, who
until the previous year had been senator from Arkansas. Earlier,
Garfield had provided the National Committee with the names of
four possible chairmen, one of whom, ex-Governor Marshall Jewell of Connecticut, had subsequently been chosen. But Jewell was
not popular with the Stalwarts, and as the need for party unity became more apparent a Grant man, John A. Logan, was invited to
choose a secretary for the National Committee. Logan's choice

was Dorsey, whose Senate seat had been a casualty of post-recon-
struction political realignments in Arkansas. Although the *Nation*
had characterized him as "one of the most disreputable of the carpetbag senators," Dorsey was a man of keen insight and relentless
energy.

Two days after Chandler's letter to Garfield, Dorsey came
down strongly in favor of the trip to New York:

> I have been told within the past four or five hours that
> when this question was suggested to you you made the natural
> inquiry as to what these people wanted to see you about. My
> reply to that is that they want to know whether the Republi-
> cans of the State of New York are to be recognized as a por-
> tion of that part of the Country or whether the 'scratchers'
> and Independents and 'featherheads' are to ride over the
> Republican party of this State as they have for the past four
> years. . . .
>
> Now in my judgment, I think you are far in advance of any-
> one of them upon all the questions that they seem so doubtful
> about . . . [and] that a discussion of thirty minutes with the
> persons named will settle for all time the doubt which exists in
> their minds. . . .
>
> I am not sure that Gov. Jewell concurs with me in any part
> of this. I am rather inclined to think that he does not, but I
> cannot see for the life of me what good Gov. Jewell can do
> you or the party by running out to Mentor on next Friday
> and bustling about the Country and producing none of the re-
> sults which you and I and every practical man know to be the
> essentials of success.[13]

This was not a communication which could be readily ignored. Reluctantly, Garfield agreed to go to New York. He left
Mentor on August 3, allowing time for more than twenty rear-
platform appearances in the course of the two-day trip to New
York City. At Albany, the candidate was joined by Governor Cornell, "Chet" Arthur, Hamilton Fish, and Chauncey Depew.

On his arrival in New York, Garfield rode through great
crowds to the Fifth Avenue Hotel, where he set up a temporary
headquarters. That evening, in a private discussion with influential New Yorkers, Garfield characterized New York as the "dark-
est spot" in the campaign picture, and asked for their help. It

was agreed that a special fund should be raised to attempt to carry the state, and Levi Morton was placed in charge. The following morning, at the home of his friend Whitelaw Reid, Garfield conferred with Jay Gould. The candidate noted in his diary that they had discussed the campaign, and added, "I think he will help." [14]

The crucial meeting of the trip began that afternoon in the gilded parlors of the Fifth Avenue Hotel. There Garfield played host to the New York Republican establishment, including Logan, Sherman, and, of all people, James G. Blaine. But despite assurances by his aides that he would be present, the object of Garfield's attention, Conkling, failed to show. After an awkward wait, the meeting heard a series of presentations concerning the mechanics of the campaign.

Later in the day, the candidate again closeted himself with Conkling's acolytes. Exactly what was said at this smaller meeting has never been clearly established, largely because Senator Tom Platt, the only one present who left a record of the meetings, was a notoriously unreliable witness. The talks were held in Morton's rooms, with Morton, Arthur, and Platt among those present. Platt wrote later in his autobiography that Garfield, when asked how he might reward the Stalwarts for supporting him in the election, "replied with great earnestness, and at some length."

> He declared that he knew that the dominant power in the State of New York was the friends of Grant and Conkling. . . . He did not wish to change the order of things, but desired us to take hold with zeal and energy and insure his election. If this was done, he assured us that the wishes of the element of the party we represented would be paramount with him, touching all questions of patronage.[15]

The last sentence is the key one, and had Garfield in fact spoken so unequivocally, his subsequent course with respect to patronage in New York State would be difficult to justify. In fact, however, Garfield had no need to go so far. What he was prepared to tell the New Yorkers was (and here Platt's account is probably accurate) that he did not intend to continue Hayes' vendetta against the Conkling faction. Garfield himself appears to have regarded his consultations as somewhat inconclusive. On August 9 he wrote in his diary, "Very weary but feeling that no serious mistake has been made and probably much good has been done. No trades, no shackles and as well fitted for defeat or victory." Once back in Mentor he inquired of Whitelaw Reid, "Do you know how Arthur, Platt or Cornell are feeling since the conference? I do not hear from either of them." [16]

Fortunately for Garfield, the Democrats also were having troubles in New York State. Tammany Hall was hardly more pleased with Hancock than it had been with Tilden four years before, and the Democrats, as usual, lacked the financial resources of their rivals. Right up to election day neither candidate could be sure of where he stood in the country's most populous state, whose 35 electoral votes could and would prove decisive.

In an era in which the term "floating vote" referred to that part of the electorate whose votes could be purchased, each party was highly dependent on the campaign funds which it could raise for key states. By August both parties were feeling the pinch, but the Republicans had far greater resources than their rivals—a situation which was to continue into the twentieth century. One special source was then available only to the party in power: the contributions of officeholders who owed their positions to political preference. On August 18 Dorsey wrote to Garfield,

> I have just returned from Washington, where I have been for some days to arrange details in regard to the campaign in Indiana. I succeeded in securing the assistance that is essential in every department but one in Washington. I regret to be obliged to say that, in my opinion, the Secretary of the Treasury is acting very badly towards the party and its candidates, and the action of the President in many respects is most damaging to our cause. . . .
> It seems to me that the results of the whole campaign are centered for the time being in Indiana and Ohio. I believe that I have consummated arrangements which, added to the general drift in our favor, [are] almost certain to give us Indiana.[17]

As to private sources of revenue, long before the tariff emerged as an issue in the campaign the business "interests" of the country were solidly behind Garfield. Among the party's leading contributors were financiers Jay Gould, Chauncey Depew, Levi P. Morton, and John D. Rockefeller. On September 1, Morton wrote to Garfield, "It's getting to be hard work to raise any larger amounts for Indiana in view of the importance of carrying our own state, but I shall spare no effort in that direction." [18]

Chapter Fifteen

A NEAR THING

With his return from New York, Garfield settled down in Mentor to wait out the campaign. His role, however, was in no sense a passive one. Until late August he sought in effect to direct the Republican campaign almost single-handedly, assisted only by the faithful Stanley-Brown. Although the secretary gave the morning mail a preliminary screening, each day Garfield would personally pen replies to letters from party workers, admiring citizens, and autograph seekers across the country. Much as Garfield disliked disrupting his normal routine, it was apparent that he required assistance. As a result, Garfield's Washington secretary, G. U. Rose, was brought to Mentor, and that latest marvel, a telegraph wire, installed at the farm. Rose joined Stanley-Brown in a little office which had been set up in a one-room building next to the farmhouse. To gain some degree of privacy, Garfield himself moved into a back room on the second floor which was turned into an office.

For relaxation, Garfield sought to keep up his work around the farm. In his diary, notes about repairs on the farmhouse and the hauling of oats are interspersed among comments concerning visiting delegations. In his search for a degree of privacy, however, the candidate was handicapped by the absence of convenient hotel facilities in which he could house guests, and by the fact that the Lake Shore Railroad ran across the farm itself. Garfield could hardly go outdoors without wondering whether the next train might not bring a new delegation or, as likely, some dignitary who would have to be put up for the night. His boyhood friend Fuller has described the scene at Mentor:

> We arrived at the farm of Mr. Garfield about 10 o'clock. I found him in the little office, dictating to two stenographers while in one corner of the room lay a pile of newspapers sufficient to fill a large wagon-box. He had about five thousand unanswered letters and telegrams, and was busily employed upon them. He gave some rapid directions to his secretaries, put on his coat and hat and led me to the carriage which I had hitched at the gate, jumped in himself and made me do so, and taking the lines drove into the yard and down the long lane which leads back north through the farm and across the Lake Shore Railroad. . . . He showed me the improvements he had made on the farm and others he had planned which were yet to be made; pointed out a fine peach orchard he had planted; stopped a few minutes to give directions to his foreman as to some hay which had been out and which he thought sufficiently cured to be put into the barn. When we reached the yard, he ordered a hired man to put up the horse as he said that we were going to stay to dinner.[1]

Apart from his own popularity, Garfield's greatest contributions to the Republican campaign were his thorough knowledge of the issues and his familiarity with who in his party was best equipped to debate these issues. The restraints on a candidate's personal appearances, however, were particularly galling to a skilled debater, who was obliged to see his political record turned into a major campaign issue. Moreover, as the campaign progressed, the attacks on Garfield grew in intensity. Dana's *New York Sun* wrote,

> *Harper's Weekly* says that the Democrats have invited a blackguard campaign. . . . But how have the Democrats invited a blackguard campaign?
> By publishing the condemnation of the Republican candidate in the very words of the Republican members of a Congressional Committee who investigated his conduct in their official capacity.

To call a thief a thief; to call a swindler a swindler; to call a witness who testifies falsely under oath a perjurer: this is not blackguardism.

If anyone has invited a bitter and disagreeable, scurrilous campaign, the Republicans have done it by nominating such a candidate.[2]

By September, "329"—the amount of dividend allegedly paid to Garfield by the Credit Mobilier—had become canonized in campaign graffitti. It was painted everywhere: on sidewalks, doors, fences, and, on at least one occasion, on the steps of Garfield's home in Washington. Nor did the disparagement of the Republican candidate end with the Credit Mobilier. The *Washington Post* attacked him for having left the Army in 1863, and in so doing having opted for "a comfortable seat in Congress to a life in the tented field."

In the absence of more momentous issues, both parties waged their campaigns on issues of the past. The Democrats, for their part, blasted the "fraud" of 1876 almost as much as they attacked Garfield personally, and allowed no one to forget that the Republican candidate had been a member of the notorious Electoral Commission. A campaign song set to a tune from *H.M.S. Pinafore,* not only made this point but poked fun at contemporary eulogies of Garfield's log-cabin upbringing:

> When I was a lad I scarce went to school,
> But bossed the career of a towpath mule;
> I urged him from spring until late in the fall
> To pull a big boat on the raging canal.
> My urging of that mule was so ef-fi-ci-ent,
> That now I am a candidate for President.
>
> I rolled up my trousers as high as could be,
> And relied upon that mule to educate me;
> I soon learned many of his tricks and ways,
> Which helped me very much at the counting in of Hayes.
> At the counting in I was such an in-stru-ment,
> That now I am a candidate for President.[3]

The Republicans were equally guilty of warming over old issues. Through most of the campaign Republican orators charged, with some truth, that the Democratic-oriented Old Confederacy was once more in the hands of the rebel brigadiers. The fact that the Democrats had opposed the resumption of specie payments came in for mention, as did the platform reference to a tariff "for revenue only." The Republicans seemed themselves divided as to how to treat the end to reconstruction. To many Republicans, the entire period had been a political debacle, with the party finally having had to abandon its Southern allies, black and white alike. Some were not yet reconciled to the result. In Gloucester, Massachusetts, the Great Agnostic, Robert Ingersoll, claimed that the Civil War had settled nothing and reminded his audience that there were states "where it is a crime to vote the Republican ticket." Ingersoll added, with considerable insight, that "there is not a southern state where a man can vote as he pleases without running the risk of social ostracism." [4]

In both the number and quality of their speakers, the Republicans were a good deal better off than their opponents. Both parties used a large number of professional orators—it was estimated in October that each party had about thirty speakers stumping Indiana—but the Republicans had most of the big names. Hancock, unlike Garfield, made almost no public appearances during the campaign, and among those Democrats who spoke fairly widely only Randall, Bayard, and Seymour were men of national reputation. By way of contrast, the Republicans were able to call on Grant, Blaine, Arthur, Conkling, Schurz, Hoar, Depew, John Hay, Mark Twain, and Benjamin Harrison, to name only a few. Clearly one of the stars was Ingersoll, who in one memorable address claimed full credit on his party's behalf for the country's new-found prosperity:

> I belong to the party that believes in good crops; that is glad when a fellow finds a gold mine; that rejoices when there are forty bushels of wheat to the acre. . . . The Democratic party is a party of famine; it is a good friend of an early frost; it believes in the Colorado beetle and in the weevil.[5]

Despite the seeming vulnerability of his record, Garfield made a strong candidate. This was not immediately apparent, for until election day there was no way of knowing how many people would credit the charges against him. But in most respects, the Ohioan was a model choice; his humble birth and his rise from poverty were a bit of folklore thoroughly in keeping with the Horatio Alger tradition. Many undoubtedly agreed with Governor Long of Massachusetts, who said of Garfield, "To my mind he is the ideal candidate—soldier, scholar, statesman . . . a man who from his mother's knee, through hardship and toil and poverty, through his self-made course in college and in the larger school of life, has lain no stain on his conscience . . . and to whose virtues friends and foes, Republicans and Democrats alike, do testify." [6] It was hard to believe that anyone with a life story as inspiring as Garfield's could be dishonest, and apparently few people did. But to be on the safe side, many Republican orators sought to eliminate the question of personalities from the campaign. John Hay insisted that *both* Garfield and Hancock were good men:

> Between now and November they both will be charged with plenty of petty little infamies, but nobody will believe a word of it. The Democrats know that General Garfield is an able, patriotic and honest man of great capacity, unsullied character and blameless life. The Republicans know that General Hancock is a gallant soldier and an accomplished gentleman. Both of them have private characters without stain.[7]

In 1880, three bellwether states had the somewhat unsettling practice of holding their gubernatorial elections well in advance of the November elections. Over a period of years, Maine, Ohio, and Indiana had almost invariably voted in November as they had in September or October for their governors, and as a result the local contests in these states took on a psychological importance out of proportion to the number of electoral votes these states would cast for president. The boast that "As Maine goes, so goes the nation" was already entrenched in political folklore.

Maine, the stamping-ground of James G. Blaine, had been regarded as safely Republican in 1880. There was strong Greenback sentiment in the state, but the Republicans were confident. Thus, when a Democratic governor was narrowly elected on September 13, thanks to an informal alliance between Democrats and Greenbackers, the result was highly unsettling to the G.O.P. But

Maine proved to be a cloud with a silver lining. The prospect of Democratic-Greenback victories elsewhere was appalling to many business interests, as well as to the Republican rank and file. On September 17, Governor Foster of Ohio wrote to Garfield, "The effect here of our reverse in Maine has been very favorable. The businessmen of Columbus seem to have suddenly awakened. A movement is on foot to call a meeting of businessmen of the city, who will probably pass strong resolutions upon the situation and try to influence their brethren all over the state to engage actively in the canvass." [8]

Both Ohio and Indiana were to vote on October 12. The former was conceded to be strongly Republican, though in the first flush of their success in Maine some Democrats spoke wistfully of carrying Garfield's home state. Indiana was felt to be leaning toward the Democrats, though by a narrow margin. The *Springfield Republican* viewed the contest for Indiana with obvious distaste, observing that "in Indiana both parties are equally unscrupulous and equally accustomed to the use of money in politics."

Well before September Dorsey had recognized the importance of a Republican success in Indiana and had singled out that state for special attention. As early as August Dorsey was shipping in out-of-state Republican journals, particularly the *New York Tribune,* and urging that the National Committee obtain them in greater numbers. Meanwhile, he was developing an elaborate organization of his own, independent of the regular G.O.P. organization. By dividing the state into sixteen districts, and each district into smaller units by county and town, Dorsey's well-manned machine was able to monitor developments right up to election day, and to ascertain exactly what effort on the part of the Republicans was required. The Pinkerton detective organization, engaged for just this purpose, kept the Republicans informed concerning opposition moves. On September 1, Dorsey wrote to a colleague,

> There is only one question about carrying Indiana, and that is the question of money, and the majority we get will keep pace with the amount we expend.
>
> If the Democratic party can put up any jobs on us this year, with such an organization as we have, I, for one, will be will-

ing to throw up the sponge. They have money, and are using it very freely in several portions of the State, but I do not believe they can spend $25 without my knowing it.[9]

When Ohio and Indiana voted, the result was much as might have been expected. Ohio went Republican by 20,000 votes, a majority somewhat larger than had been anticipated. Indiana went Republican by some 7,000 votes out of 225,000 cast. The Democrats immediately raised the cry of fraud, but no one paid much attention. The Republicans had emitted similar cries of anguish after the Maine debacle and no one had cared much then, either. The G.O.P. coup was complete, and both Ohio and Indiana were to provide majorities in November almost identical with those of October. On October 16, Garfield wrote to a well-wisher, "The victory in Ohio and Indiana grows greater every way and ought to be decisive of the contest." [10] He was right.

Having gained an edge with their gubernatorial victory in Indiana, the Republicans proceeded to capitalize on the errors of their opponents as the Democrats strove to make up lost ground. On October 11, General Hancock was quoted in a Democratic newspaper on the subject of the tariff. The tariff was, according to the Democratic candidate, a problem of little interest to the federal government. He went on to refer to it as "a local question . . . that the general government seldom cares to interfere with." To the extent that each state had its own tariff interests, Hancock was quite right. But since Congress had been debating tariffs for years, the General's remarks invited ridicule. Republican speakers, who had maintained all along that Hancock was not very bright, jumped on his tariff interview as evidence of his ignorance of civil matters. Thomas Nast, the cartoonist, pictured the Democratic candidate on a platform, turning to inquire of his neighbor, "Who is Tariff, and why is He for revenue only?" [11]

In the final weeks, excitement reached a peak. Businessmen determined that the country must have a Republican administration, and the *Springfield Republican* reported that in New Jersey new business ventures were being made contingent on a Republican victory. In one instance, the owners of a foundry were said to have promised to reopen with an enlarged work force in the event of Garfield's election. Perhaps feeling that such developments presaged a last-minute surge to the Republicans, the Democrats blundered in a way which produced far more harm than had Hancock's remarks. On October 20, an obscure New York City journal, paradoxically named *Truth,* published a letter ostensibly from Garfield to one H. L. Morey of the Employers' Union of Lynn, Massachusetts. The letter, marked "Personal and Confidential," expressed the view that the importation of Chinese labor was desirable "until our great manufacturing and corporate interests are conserved," and added further that "companys [*sic*] have the right to buy labor where they can get it cheapest."

The letter caused an immediate sensation. No one knew where it had come from; the editor of *Truth,* one Joseph Hart, claimed to have found it on his desk. At Democratic headquarters, members of the National Committee examined the letter and pronounced it genuine. Garfield just as quickly denounced it as a forgery, though he was not as certain as he sounded, and privately he requested that a check be made in his letterbook in Washington. But handwriting experts were summoned and within a matter of days had concluded that the Morey letter was a clumsy forgery. Two misspellings, "companys" and "employes," tended to confirm their findings, as did the fact that the envelope bore a stamp rather than Garfield's congressional frank. Finally, the Republicans were able to produce evidence that no such person as H. L. Morey had recently resided in Lynn, Massachusetts.

By election day it was common knowledge that the Morey letter was a fabrication. John Sherman, just finishing a week of stumping in the East, advised Garfield that "the movements of [Democratic Chairman] Barnum and especially the Morey letter have reacted against the Democratic party as they ought to do." [12] Not even the loss of Indiana hurt the Democrats more than did this demonstration that the party which for four years had harped upon its rival's misdeeds had endorsed, if not actually fabricated, a spurious attempt to portray the Republican candidate as supporting the unrestricted importation of Chinese labor. Even the

Garfield-hating *New York Sun* was chagrined, writing that "if a party requires such infamous aids . . . [it] deserves to perish." *

In New York, with Tilden's once-firm hand slack at the reins, all was discord among the Democrats. An attempt to reconcile the competing factions appeared to be making progress in September, only to become unstuck over the issue of a candidate for mayor of New York City. Not until October 18, when the election was only two weeks away, were the Tammany and anti-Tammany groups able to agree on a candidate: William Russell Grace, a Roman Catholic businessman. The nomination of Grace brought a religious issue into the campaign with a vengeance, for many Protestants feared that control of the Board of Education by Catholics would bring the diversion of public funds to parochial schools. Some Democrats chose to support the Republican nominee, a Protestant, and the result served to narrow the traditional Democratic margin in the city.

On November 2, with both parties making the usual predictions of victory, the country went to the polls. It had not been a notably inspiring campaign, and with the difficulty in reaching polling places in many rural areas, the percentage of eligible voters who went to the polls was probably not much above 50 per cent.

For Garfield, the last few days before the election had brought a lull. He busied himself with work around the farm, and on election day itself "arranged for ploughing and seeding garden east of house and starting a new one in rear of engine house." By six o'clock in the evening the first returns were in, being taken down by each of two telegraphers. Friends and newsmen came by from as far away as Cleveland. Garfield wrote in his diary, "By eleven P.M. it became evident that we had carried New York. At twelve we gave supper to about twenty-five friends. At

---

* To this day, no one knows who wrote the Morey letter. The Republican National Committee put one of its minions in charge of an investigation, but his search was unsuccessful, as was the Republican attempt to connect the letter with the Democratic National Committee. On October 28, a reporter for *Truth* was arrested, but the case against him was dropped when nothing could be proved except that he enjoyed dabbling in manuscripts. See Caldwell's *Garfield*, pp. 307–08.

three A.M. we closed the office, secure in all the northern states except New Jersey and the Pacific States, which are yet in doubt." His Democratic rival, in contrast, went to bed early. Mrs. Hancock has related how, at seven o'clock, her husband "yielded to the extreme weariness and prostration that ensued from his five months' labors and went to bed, begging me under no circumstances to disturb him, as the result would be known sooner or later. . . . At 5 o'clock on the following morning he inquired of me the news. I replied, 'It has been a complete Waterloo for you.' 'That is all right,' said he, 'I can stand it,' and in another moment he was again asleep." [13]

As the votes continued to come in, however, it became apparent that the Republican victory had been a narrow one. Although the last few weeks of the campaign had seemingly pointed to a Democratic debacle, the parties were too closely balanced for any such outcome. The Republican ticket received 4,454,416 votes to 4,444,952 for their opponents—a margin of less than 10,000 votes, and as such the narrowest popular margin in any presidential election up to this day. The fact that the Greenbackers polled over 300,000 votes made Garfield a "minority" president-elect, but Republicans were no less joyful on account of this.

The electoral vote was less close, with the Republicans carrying 214 votes to 155 for their opponents. Each ticket carried nineteen states, but the Republicans carried the important ones— New York, with the 35 electoral votes that meant the margin of victory, plus such states as Pennsylvania, Illinois, Ohio, and Indiana. The Democrats carried the entire South, and established the tradition of the Solid South which was to last well into the next century. Outside the South, however, Hancock could carry only four states.

For all his forebodings, Garfield had proved to be a strong candidate. Of the five presidential elections from 1876 through 1892, the Democrats outpolled the Republicans in terms of the popular vote in every year except one, 1880. Even allowing for the Democrats' blunders, it was apparent that Garfield had more than measured up to his party's hopes. The question was, however, whether Republican unity could be established on a permanent basis, or whether it would continue to be an election-year

219

phenomenon only.

The congratulations poured in, and the city of Cleveland adopted Garfield as one of its own, draping the streets with red, white, and blue bunting. One of Garfield's warmest letters came from Indiana's Benjamin Harrison. "You must know how sincerely I rejoice over your success," he wrote. "Outside your own family I am sure no man in the country can be happier than I am over your elevation to the presidency. Whoever else *might* have been elected, you have been—and this justifies those who were not of the 'mystic 306.' " [14]

The Voting

GARFIELD			HANCOCK		
	ELEC.			ELEC.	
STATE	VOTE	MAJORITY	STATE	VOTE	MAJORITY
California	1	—	Alabama	10	34,964
Connecticut	6	2,656	Arkansas	6	18,339
Illinois	21	40,716	California	5	78
Indiana	15	6,642	Delaware	3	1,142
Iowa	11	78,082	Florida	4	4,310
Kansas	5	61,748	Georgia	11	48,384
Maine	7	8,868	Kentucky	12	42,762
Massachusetts	13	53,245	Louisiana	8	26,430
Michigan	11	53,744	Maryland	8	15,191
Minnesota	5	40,588	Mississippi	8	40,896
Nebraska	3	26,456	Missouri	15	55,042
New Hampshire	5	4,058	Nevada	3	881
New York	35	21,033	New Jersey	9	2,010
Ohio	22	34,227	North Carolina	10	8,334
Oregon	3	671	South Carolina	7	54,241
Pennsylvania	29	37,276	Tennessee	12	20,514
Rhode Island	4	7,416	Texas	8	98,535
Vermont	5	27,251	Virginia	11	44,566
Wisconsin	10	29,751	West Virginia	5	11,148
Colorado	3	2,803		155	
	214				

As Garfield tackled his mail, he ran across a letter from John Sherman calculated to give one pause, for Sherman was forwarding a letter from a resident of Michigan expressing concern lest Garfield be the target of an assassination attempt. In reply Garfield advised his colleague that he did not anticipate danger on that score, "though I am receiving what I suppose to be the usual number of threatening letters on that subject. Assassination can be no more guarded against than death by lightning; and it is best not to worry about either." [15]

An incidental casualty of the 1880 campaign was Garfield's friendship with William S. Rosecrans. However questionable his wartime correspondence behind Rosecrans' back, Garfield had retained a real affection for his wartime commander and had been able to assist him in small ways over the years. Periodically, however, Charles A. Dana had attempted to drive a wedge between the two by publishing in the *Sun* insinuations to the effect that it was a letter of Garfield's that had brought about the sacking of Rosecrans after Chickamauga, and denying that his own despatches to Stanton had urged any such step. In a column in the *Sun* over his initials, Dana raised the issue once more in November 1879, denying any role in Rosecrans' replacement and attributing it once again to Garfield.

In an exchange of letters with Rosecrans the following spring Garfield offered at one stage to rebut Dana in print, assuring Rosecrans once more that there was "no particle of truth" in Dana's charge. Garfield eventually decided against a public rebuttal; he had successfully ignored Dana in the aftermath of Credit Mobilier, and he may have concluded that it would be unwise to challenge him on a lesser matter. There the matter might have rested had not Rosecrans become a Democratic candidate for the House at the same time that Garfield was running for the presidency. During the campaign Garfield heard tales of "Old Rosey's" having assisted in circulating copies of the Morey letter in California, and read newspaper reports which quoted Rosecrans as having referred to him as a "thief." What appears to have bothered Rosecrans most were the effusive campaign biographies of Garfield, which gave the Ohioan credit for all that went right with the Army of the Cumberland and Rosecrans the blame for what did not. Rosecrans was never noted for his discretion, and he appears to have been provoked into some harsh statements concerning the Republican candidate.

On December 9, Rosecrans wrote a friendly letter to Garfield, indicating regret for some of his statements and expressing the hope that "we stand on the old ground of cordial regard which existed between us before the election and which began in that fraternity of patriotism with which you were admitted to my military family." The response was frigid. Garfield quoted back to Rosecrans a statement in which he had publicly disassociated himself from his wartime praise for Garfield, observing that in the space of seventeen years "many a splendid young man had descended from honor to infamy, and mortified admiring friends . . . by being put in the penitentiary." This was strong language, and "Old Rosey" was asking quite a bit in assuming that Garfield would forgive and forget. In any case, in his last letter to his old chief Garfield characterized Rosecrans' campaign statements as "an insuperable barrier to the resumption of our old relations." They never met again.[16]

Chapter Sixteen

THE SPOILSMEN: ROUND 1

For the president-elect, the end of a long campaign brought no relief. To be sure, the character of his mail changed. Gone were the fervid expressions of support and the press clippings which told of Republican doings in remote corners of the country. But the volume of letters was unchanged. On the heels of thousands of congratulations came letters full of unsolicited advice, requests for favors, and admonitions. Garfield once again found himself grappling with a mountain of correspondence, assisted only by his two secretaries.

The character of his visitors, however, underwent a subtle metamorphosis. There were no more delegations of Farmers for Garfield and Arthur from the great prairie states, to be received on the front porch and sent on their way. The new visitors generally came singly or in pairs, and they had favors to seek rather than support to pledge. Garfield appears to have determined from the outset not to make any promises with respect to the secondary offices which would be at his disposal. But he had no experienced assistant to screen his visitors, and anyone who was known to the president-elect or his family, or who brought a sufficiently impressive letter of introduction, was assured of a hearing. The fact that Garfield was noncommittal on matters of patronage, and close-mouthed on the subject of his cabinet choices, made a hospitable climate for rumors. And with the election past, Garfield's plans regarding the politically sensitive chore of picking a cabinet became a prime subject for speculation in the press.

In this rather Byzantine atmosphere, Garfield turned to the question of picking a cabinet which would be satisfactory to the disparate factions of his party. In applying himself to this task, he was bound by a combination of political precedents and his own predilections. A president's cabinet was expected to reflect a suitable geographic distribution and, at the same time, accord "recognition" to those elements which had contributed most to the common cause in the campaign. A president-elect might personally prefer to place emphasis on other qualities in his subordinates: administrative capacity, perhaps, or personal congeniality. In practice, however, geographic and factional distribution were most often the controlling factors.

In Garfield's view, and in that of most political observers, there were two cabinet posts of special importance. These were State and Treasury—the two most senior departments, whose chiefs could trace their provenances to Thomas Jefferson and Alexander Hamilton. The State post had traditionally been the most prestigious portfolio; it was not unusual for a secretary of state to be referred to as his president's "premier." As for the Treasury Department, it had been instrumental in more key policy decisions in the 1870s than had State. In considering the various possibilities for his cabinet, Garfield made a clear distinction between State and Treasury and the lesser cabinet posts. Charting out some cabinet possibilities in his diary, Garfield allocated only the top two posts to specific individuals; the remainder he allocated by state, with one post reserved for the South as a whole. (The latter was a somewhat grudging concession to the Republican organization in the Old Confederacy, an organization almost moribund since the end of reconstruction.) In a December 30 letter to Burke Hinsdale, Garfield outlined in highly pragmatic terms why he would not repeat Hayes' action in appointing a former Confederate to his cabinet:

> I have no doubt that the final cure for the Solid South will be found in the education of its youth and in the development of business interests, but both of these things require time. . . . Patronage to Democrats has been tried and has proved a dreary failure. Rebel Democrats appointed to office by Republicans take one of two courses—either they suffer complete ostracism by their neighbors, or they become more fierce assailants of the Republican party to keep themselves in good standing at home. In fact, the "Solid South" accepts all patronage at the hands of Republicans as an admission of our weakness and their superiority.[1]

Not surprisingly, Garfield was receiving a barrage of advice as to how to cope with his problems. John Hay wrote to Whitelaw Reid, "If you go to Mentor, give our great and good friend all the wisdom you have got on the cabinet question. He will need it." Hay, like no small number of Garfield's friends, feared that the new president would prove easily imposed upon. But in the country at large, there were great expectations for the new administration. President Hayes spoke for many when he observed to Garfield in January, "It is generally supposed that Blaine will be in the State Department. The saving clause in the whole business is *the faith that you will be President.*"

At some time in November, Garfield reached the decision which would dog him through his brief presidential term: he determined, as Hayes had anticipated, to offer the State post to his friend Blaine. The opportunity to do so in person arose when Garfield concluded that he should go to Washington to look after the closing of his house. On November 23, he and Crete arrived at the Baltimore and Potomac station, where they were met by Rockwell, Robert Ingersoll, and a small group of well-wishers. Garfield asked that there be no ceremony. Hayes had sent his carriage, and the Garfields, together with Rockwell, went immediately to I Street. The following day, Garfield began a back-breaking schedule with a call on the president.[2] In the course of a breakfast with Blaine, he all but promised him the top post in the cabinet. Garfield reconstructed the conversation in his diary:

'If I should ask you to take a place in the cabinet, what would be your probable response, and before you answer, please tell me whether you are, or will be, a candidate for the presidency in 1884. I ask this because I do not propose to allow myself or anyone else to use the next four years as the camping-ground for fighting the next presidential battle.' He replied that he would not again seek a nomination. . . . He then asked me if I really wanted him in my cabinet. I answered that if I should find it possible to make a cast of a cabinet in which he would be a harmonious factor, it would be personally very agreeable to have him with me. . . . We both agreed that only the State or Treasury Departments would be desirable for him.[3]

On the same day, Garfield sought out Levi P. Morton, the Wall Street financier who had seen fit to decline the vice-presidential nomination at Chicago. Garfield probably had in mind offering him an unspecified post in the cabinet, and in so doing discharge his obligations to the Conkling machine. In any case, Garfield was considerably annoyed when he found that Morton believed the Treasury Department to have been promised to the Conkling faction. "This was not my understanding," Garfield wrote in his diary, "and seems wholly inadmissible. It would be a congestion of financial power at the money centre, and would create jealousy at the West." In other words, Garfield did not want a secretary of the treasury from Wall Street. The trip to Washington left him despondent, and he saw the closing of his house as an ill omen for the future. "I did not know how strongly I had become attached to the little Washington home. I have probably taken my final leave of it as a home. I cannot expect as much happiness in any other house in Washington." [4]

Garfield returned to Mentor to an avalanche of advice from James G. Blaine. Not until December 20 did the Plumed Knight formally accept what was by then understood to be the State Department portfolio. As early as December 10, however, there were danger signals. On that date Blaine forwarded to his friend a fascinating analysis of the Republican party—an analysis which concluded that "with you as President I could do much to build up the party as a result of a strong and wise policy." Examining the Grand Old Party, Blaine came up with the not-surprising conclusion that it was divided into three parts. The first and most important part was the "Blaine section," important because it was dominant in the traditional areas of Republican strength. On the other hand, the Stalwarts were seen to be strong primarily in the South, where they could no longer deliver electoral votes. Ignoring the fact that it may well have been the Stalwarts who delivered to Garfield the key state of New York, Blaine went on to denounce the Grant men as "rule or ruin leaders" who should not be coddled but who must be destroyed:

> These men are to be handled with skill, always remembering that they are harmless when out of power and desperate when in possession of it. . . . Of course it would not be wise to make war upon them. Indeed, that would be folly. They must not be knocked down with bludgeons: they must have their throats cut with a feather.[5]

The third section of the party, according to Blaine, was composed of the reformers, a collection of upstarts, "conceited, foolish, vain, without knowledge . . . of men." Blaine saw them as no particular threat to anyone. "They can be easily dealt with," he concluded, "and be hitched to your administration with ease."

Not since William H. Seward had offered to relieve Lincoln of the burdens of the presidency had anyone in Blaine's position been quite so forward with his chief in attempting to set the tone of a new administration. In fairness to Blaine, he may well have put aside his immediate presidential ambitions, in accordance with the condition Garfield had set on his tender of the State post. The urge to dominate, however, was not so easily thrust aside. The tone of this and subsequent letters suggests that, subconsciously at least, Blaine sought a merging of political fortunes in which he would retain the role of senior partner. In any case, his analysis of the Stalwarts took no account of the fact that they as well as the Blaine men could claim a fair share of credit for securing Garfield's election.

Garfield, like Lincoln, avoided any direct rebuke to his precocious secretary. But Lincoln was a master of human relation-

ships, who was able to demonstrate to Seward his clear intention
of running his own administration. Garfield, however, was convinced of Blaine's good will and partially because of this failed to
recognize the need to establish a new relationship with his old
colleague. His replies to Blaine's letters were generally apprecia-
tive but noncommittal. In the end Garfield's cabinet would be his
own, and as for Blaine's suggestions he rejected many more than
he accepted. But nothing that Garfield wrote challenged Blaine's
basic assumption that he, Blaine, would be the prime mover of
the new administration.

Meanwhile, with word of Blaine's prospective appointment
having leaked to the press, the Stalwarts were all the more insis-
tent that they should have nothing less than the one portfolio of
comparable prestige, the Treasury Department. But Garfield, for
reasons which he regarded as sound, remained unwilling to name
an Eastern banker to that post. The president-elect was paying a
high price for having chosen to make Blaine the cornerstone of
his cabinet. Not only had he underestimated the temper of the
Stalwarts but, by promising Blaine the State portfolio at the outset, Garfield had greatly reduced his options.

On December 13, two of Conkling's henchmen came to Mentor to reopen the subject of Morton and the Treasury Department, arguing this time that Morton's senatorial prospects—he
was a candidate in New York—had been injured because of the
assumption that he would be joining Garfield's cabinet. Garfield
stood his ground, replying that one reason he was holding back
the names of his cabinet was to avoid interfering in the senatorial
elections about to take place in several of the state legislatures. In
the latter half of December, Garfield began using Stephen Dorsey
as an intermediary in dealing with the New Yorkers. Dorsey professed sympathy with Garfield's views concerning the Treasury
post, and appears for a time to have coaxed Conkling over to a
more conciliatory frame of mind. In a letter to Garfield on December 16, Dorsey quoted Conkling as having spoken in a friendly
fashion concerning the Ohioan, and as having expressed a belief
that Morton might be satisfied with a cabinet post other than
Treasury. Here, at last, was a glint of hope. "Important letter
from New York," Garfield wrote in his diary, "indicating that Mr.
Conkling is really desirous of sustaining my administration. It

ought to be true. I will try to make it so without surrendering the proper control of any function I should hold." [6]

The fragile flower of a Garfield-Conkling reconciliation had not yet begun to bloom when it wilted under a wintry blast from Maine. Abandoning his feather for the bludgeon, Blaine chose this time to challenge Conkling on his own turf. On January 3, an editorial appeared in Reid's *New York Tribune* which, written as it was "by authority," was interpreted as having been drafted by Blaine with Garfield's concurrence. The editorial stated that the president-elect was taking no part in the New York senatorial race, but added that "the incoming administration will see to it that the men from New York and from the other States, who had the courage at Chicago to obey the wishes of their Districts . . . shall not lose by it. The Administration . . . will not permit its friends to be persecuted for their friendship." [7]

Here was blunt warning that the new administration would look after the interests of Blaine's friend William H. Robertson, who at Chicago had defied Conkling and had supported first Blaine and then Garfield. To the Stalwarts, the editorial was like a red flag to the bull. Inasmuch as Garfield knew nothing about the letter until it was published, this was clearly the time to curb his ambitious secretary-designate, by a public repudiation if necessary. Incredibly, Garfield did nothing. In a piece of rationalization remarkable even for Garfield, he wrote to Reid that "the article is all right, and may do good. Of course, that class of announcement should be used sparingly, but I want the country to know that I will not meddle in the Senatorial contest." Needless to say, Conkling saw the matter in a different light. "What was the meaning of that article," he asked, "but that the men who had voted faithfully for Grant need expect no quarter from the administration, while the men who had basely violated their pledges by abandoning Grant for Garfield were to be rewarded for their treachery?" [8]

Meanwhile, Garfield continued to be harassed by a variety of lesser problems. To his wife, off visiting in New York City, he related one of them:

> Yesterday we had trial of our patience. A Kentucky woman, a Disciple who had lived less than two years in Cincinnati, came at noon armed with a couple of Disciple letters of recom-

mendation and modestly wanted to be made [Post Mistress] of Cincinnati. She dismissed her driver before she came into the house and we apparently had her on our hands for five hours. Fortunately, the express was an hour late and we got her off at 2:30. She was greatly grieved not to have seen 'Sister Garfield' and still more grieved that 'Brother Garfield' would not give her the P. O.[9]

Only weeks before the president-elect had devoted part of his morning to one visitor, only to discover that the sole purpose of his call was to sell a life insurance policy. Although Garfield had the self-made man's distaste for large staffs and secretarial spearbearers, he appears to have concluded vaguely that something would have to be done about the handling of visitors and correspondence. He acknowledged to Whitelaw Reid that he badly needed a "private secretary," and that he had in mind making the position one comparable to cabinet rank in terms of prestige. Actually, Garfield had one particular person in mind for the post: Lincoln's one-time secretary, John Hay. On Reid's suggestion he wrote to Hay directly. "I am casting about me," Garfield wrote, "to find someone who will help to enliven the solitude which surrounds the Presidency. The unfortunate incumbent of that office is the most isolated man in America." Although Garfield portrayed the position in glowing terms, the latter declined, writing that "the constant contact with envy, meanness, ignorance, and the swinish selfishness which ignorance breeds needs a stronger heart and a more obedient nervous system than I can boast." Garfield tried again, and even urged Blaine to use his influence to make Hay change his mind. But the poet was not to be won over, and contented himself with a letter of appreciation and admonition:

It is a comfort to know that you go into the Presidency with the best equipment possible. Besides the qualities that are personal to you, you know more of the past and present of government, more history, and more politics than any man since the younger Adams, and you are free from his peculiar infirmities of temper. 'One thing thou lackest yet' and that is a slight ossification of the heart. I woefully fear that you will try too hard to make everybody happy—an office which is outside of your constitutional powers.[10]

The latter half of January brought new pressure from the Stalwarts for the Treasury portfolio, as Governor Cornell and Senator Tom Platt came to Mentor as emissaries of Conkling. The visit came at a time when Mrs. Garfield was still in New York, a house guest of Garfield's and Blaine's friends, the Whitelaw Reids. It is a commentary on the aura of conspiracy which surrounded the cabinet negotiations that Garfield was apprehensive over what construction might be placed on his wife's visit. He wrote to Crete that when Cornell and Platt asked to see her, "I would have given an arm to have had you here. Then, one of them remarked, they understood Mrs. G. was in N. Y. at a private house and I knew Mr. Conkling knew that you were the guest of his enemy." The meeting with Cornell and Platt was inconclusive, but Garfield made use of it to float a trial balloon, asking of his guests their opinion of Judge Charles J. Folger, who was later to be a member of Arthur's cabinet, for attorney general or secretary of the treasury. The New Yorkers spoke highly of Folger, but maintained that he could not be spared from his post on the state court of appeals. Perhaps whimsically, Garfield raised the possibility of a cabinet post for Conkling himself. As with Folger, the two Stalwarts maintained that Conkling could not be spared. Garfield wrote Blaine of his conversation, including his mention of a cabinet post for Lord Roscoe. "If it seems best to make the tender," he wrote, "what would you say of exchanging seats—you for the Treasury, he for State?" In writing as he did, Garfield all but confessed his error in tying himself down with Blaine in the State Department post. But Blaine did not take the hint, and recoiled from the suggestion: "His appointment would act like strychnine upon your administration—first, bring contortions and then be followed by death." Garfield dropped the subject, and did not raise it again.

As if to remind the president-elect of his obligations, the Stalwarts organized a highly publicized testimonial dinner for Stephen Dorsey on February 11. The party was held at Delmonico's in New York City, with Grant, Arthur, and others vying with one another in their praise for Dorsey as the Republican "architect of victory." Arthur in particular was in good form as he ruminated on the subject of the recent election:

Indiana was really, I suppose, a Democratic State. It had been put on the books always as a State that might be carried by close and perfect organization and a great deal of—— [laughter, and cries of 'soap']. I see the reporters are present, and therefore I will simply say that everybody showed a great deal of interest in the occasion and distributed tracts and political documents all through the State.[11]

Garfield, apprised of the dinner, called it "a curious affair," which it certainly was. At minimum, it appeared designed to underscore the Stalwarts' contribution to the election success. Blaine viewed it as a device to enable Dorsey to obtain an appointment in the Post Office Department "through which channel there are cunning preparations being made by a small cabal to steal half a million a year during your administration." Whether Blaine was aware of Dorsey's activities in connection with the "star route" mail frauds, of which more would be heard, is not entirely clear.

For two wearying months, Garfield had been drawing up, changing, and eventually discarding various potential cabinet slates, all of which began with the name of Blaine. Not until late February, on the eve of his departure for Washington, did he have even a fairly firm list. As secretary of war he had determined on Robert T. Lincoln, who was acceptable to party leaders in Illinois and whose very lineage—he was the president's son—was expected to bring a certain luster to the cabinet. From Pennsylvania he chose Isaac Wayne MacVeagh, a champion of reform who appears to have been rendered palatable by his status as Senator Don Cameron's brother-in-law. In the end, MacVeagh would prove to be one of the ablest of Garfield's inner circle.

As his "Western" cabinet secretary Garfield had considered Benjamin Harrison of Indiana. In the course of an interview at Mentor, however, Harrison turned him down. Subsequently Garfield chose Senator Samuel Kirkwood of Iowa, who had gained a reputation while combatting Copperheads as wartime governor of his state. As his "Southern" representative, Garfield was undecided as between an old colleague of the Forty-second Ohio, Don Pardee, who had taken up residence in New Orleans, and another transplanted Northerner, Louisiana lawyer William H. Hunt. In the end the nod would go to Hunt, who had been recommended by President Hayes, and Pardee was rewarded with a federal judgeship.

Considering how a president-elect was bound by the traditions of cabinet-making, Garfield was not doing badly at assembling an able cross section of his party. But he was no closer to resolving the Treasury impasse in February than he had been on election day. In a meeting with Conkling at Mentor, Garfield reiterated that he had not ruled out a Stalwart for the Treasury Department, and he inquired again concerning the availability of Judge Folger. Over Blaine's objections he offered the post to Folger, only to have the New Yorker decline, perhaps under pressure from Conkling. With time running out, Garfield turned again to Morton in connection with the Navy portfolio. On February 28 Morton wired his acceptance, and Garfield breathed what proved to be a premature sigh of relief.

As the time of his departure for Washington drew near, Garfield felt more strongly than ever the pull of home and neighbors. Although hard work and the passage of time had lent considerable polish to the "pulpy boy" of Garfield's youth, the president-elect remained a sentimental soul, prone to looking backward with nostalgia and forward with more than average trepidation. On February 7 he wrote to his friend Austin,

> It is a great grief for me to go away without visiting you once more, in your own house, before I leave. In fact, few people would believe that I go away with great sadness, but such is the fact. I know I am bidding goodbye to my old freedom and to my many good friends whose countenances and counsel I shall miss, and, worst of all, I know many of them will be disappointed in me and many will be alienated. But I feel sure that our friendship of so many years will not be shattered or dimmed by time nor by the whirl of events.[12]

The Garfields left Mentor on the last day of February. The morning was spent in packing and in issuing final instructions concerning the management of the farm. "The crowd of callers increased," Garfield wrote that night. "At twelve-fifteen, the last load left the house. Several hundred people at the depot. A. L. Tinker made a speech to me and I said a few farewell words to my neighbors." [13]

Garfield left Mentor thinking that his cabinet problem was in hand. No sooner had he reached Washington than he found that his troubles were by no means over. There were rumbles of discontent over Morton's portfolio, and Blaine inveighed against Garfield's tentative choice of William Windom as secretary of the treasury. On the morning of March 1, everything became unstuck. Morton, under heavy pressure from his New York colleagues, belatedly informed Garfield that he could not accept the Treasury post. Garfield, after insisting that Morton put his declination in writing, interviewed another Stalwart, Postmaster Thomas James of New York City, in connection with the Post Office Department. James, a one-time newspaper publisher who had administered his city post with marked efficiency, was prepared to accept Garfield's tender without clearing his action with Conkling.

Word of James' acceptance triggered the Stalwarts' wrath once more. Garfield had scarcely finished breakfast on March 3, the day before his inauguration, when he received word that Conkling and Arthur had to see him at once. Receiving them in his suite at Riggs House, Garfield submitted to a torrent of abuse. According to one account, Conkling "stormed up and down the room, charging Garfield with treachery to his friends in New York and asserting that he was false to his party." Garfield, sitting on the side of his bed, listened to the tirade in silence.

The frantic, disorganized pace of this final week took its toll in terms of Garfield's inaugural address. As far back as December he had attempted to approach the problem with the same thoroughness with which he had tackled his major presentations in Congress. For a brief period he attempted to read all the inaugurals of his predecessors as background for his own. Then, as time became more pressing, he turned over the task of summarizing the inaugurals to an assistant, T. M. Nichol. By mid-February he had concluded that past inaugurals, "except for Lincoln's, are dreary reading. Doubtless mine will be also." He began a first draft in January, but could work up little enthusiasm and pronounced himself "jaded." He was sufficiently dissatisfied with the result that he snatched what time he could on the first three days of March to recast it entirely. A reporter for the *Washington Star,* commenting on the number of callers at Riggs House, observed that "even Gen. Garfield's strong physique shows signs of weariness." With a characteristic burst of energy, Garfield wrote on past midnight of his inauguration eve. Finally he noted in his diary, "I wrote the last sentence at half-past two o'clock A.M. March 4." [14]

Earlier in the evening, after dinner with Mark Hopkins and before his speech-writing marathon, Garfield and Hopkins dropped in on a group of his old Williams classmates at the Wormley Hotel. Here once again Garfield appeared impressed with the loneliness of the presidency; replying to remarks by Hopkins, Garfield struck a nostalgic note:

> Tonight I am a private citizen. Tomorrow, I shall be called to assume new responsibilities and, on the day after, the broadside of the world's wrath will strike. It will strike hard; I know it and you know it. You may write down in your books now, the largest percentage of blunders which you think I will be likely to make, and you will be sure to find in the end that I have made many more than you have calculated, many more. This honor comes to me unsought. I have never had the presidential fever, not even for a day, nor have I it tonight. I have no feeling of elation in view of the position I am called upon to fill and I would thank God were I today a free lance in the House or the Senate. But it is not to be and I will go forward to meet the responsibilities and discharge the duties which are before me with all the firmness and ability I can command.[15]

There was snow on the evening of the 3rd, and the next day dawned cold and blustery. The city was packed with visitors, who overflowed the wooden sidewalks and turned the snow into slush. But neither the wind nor the cold had much effect on the inaugural festivities. Gordon's Cafe, at Pennsylvania Avenue and First Street, was "gaily decorated from top to bottom with a variety of flags and banners," while W. T. Atkinson's dry goods store, two blocks toward the White House, featured "a large gilded eagle, with shields." The *Washington Star* office displayed "evergreen wreathes interspersed with bunting," while M. W. Galt, the jeweler, had his store "handsomely adorned from top to bottom" with "flags, shields and many novel devices." [16]

At 11:00 A.M., following breakfast with Rhodes and Hinsdale, Garfield rode with President Hayes and Vice President-elect Arthur to the Capitol. Notwithstanding the brisk weather, newsmen estimated that some 15,000 persons had gathered on the grounds around the East portico. When Arthur spoke briefly after taking his oath of office, Senator Conkling was seen to applaud "vigorously," and Senator Blaine "no less heartily." Chief Justice Waite then administered the oath to Garfield, who upon its completion turned to kiss his mother, who was in the seat of honor on the platform. Never before had a mother witnessed her son's inauguration as president, and Garfield's gesture was the sentimental highlight of the day.

Following an introduction by Senator George H. Pendleton, Garfield delivered his inaugural "slowly & fairly well, though I grew somewhat hoarse towards the close." The first portion of his address was largely historical, and chronicled the growth of the nation in its first hundred years. Garfield saw the Civil War as having rendered decisions from which there could be no appeal. "The supremacy of the Nation and its laws should no longer be the subject of debate." He implicitly acknowledged, however, that the issues arising out of the emancipation of the Negro had yet to be resolved:

> The elevation of the Negro race from slavery to full rights of citizenship, is the most important political change we have known since the adoption of the Constitution. . . .
> The emancipated race has already made remarkable progress. With unquestionable devotion to the Union, with a patience and gentleness not born of fear, 'they have followed the light as God gave them to see the light.' . . .
> It is alleged that in many communities Negro citizens are practically denied freedom of the ballot. In so far as the truth of this allegation is admitted, it is answered that in many places honest local government is impossible if the mass of uneducated Negroes is allowed to vote. . . .
> So far as the latter is true, it is no palliation that can be offered for opposing the freedom of the ballot.

The crowd stirred when the president, toward the close of his address, touched on the subject of civil service reform.

The Civil Service can never be placed on a satisfactory basis until it is regulated by law, for the good of the service itself. . . . I shall, at the proper time, ask Congress to fix the tenure of minor offices of the several Executive Departments, and prescribe the grounds upon which removals shall be made during the terms for which the incumbents have been appointed.[17]

A number of onlookers compared the incoming and outgoing chief executives and concluded that it was Garfield who looked somewhat the worse for wear. Benjamin Harrison thought that Hayes looked "sweet and lamblike," but that Garfield looked "worn." [18] Nevertheless, the inaugural speech was followed by the traditional military parade. Sherman and Sheridan were there, and so was Garfield's campaign opponent, General Hancock, who drew a generous round of applause. When the last of the marchers had tramped down Pennsylvania Avenue the stage was set for the Inaugural Gala at the National Museum (the present Smithsonian Institution). More than 150 musicians, including the Marine Band of John Philip Sousa and a German band brought in from Philadelphia, provided the music. Tickets, at $5 each, had been purchased by more than 5,000 people. For one dollar more, merrymakers could enter a temporary pavilion adjoining the main hall where they could feast on pickled oysters, chicken salad, roast turkey, roast ham, beef tongues, ice cream, cakes, lemonade, fruits, and relishes.

All agreed that the presidential couple cut a handsome figure. Mrs. Garfield wore "a rich mauve satin trimmed with point lace," while Mrs. Hayes wore "a soft finished ivory-tinted silk combined with plain satin and trimmed with pearl passementerie." [19] It was another late night for the Garfields, but the next morning brought good news. William Windom accepted the offer to be secretary of the treasury, and at long last Garfield had a full cabinet.

Chapter Seventeen

A NEW
ADMINISTRATION

---◆---

The city of Washington in 1881 still had about it the aspect of a rather unkempt small town. The permanent population was less than 200,000, and even this figure was subject to fluctuation depending on whether or not Congress was in session. The telephone had begun its portentous infiltration of the government offices—the Chesapeake and Potomac Telephone Company had begun operations in 1878—but the number of instruments was still negligible, and the messenger boy was still the primary means of communication between government departments.

Sanitation in the city was rudimentary. According to one survey, fewer than a third of the houses in Washington and neighboring Georgetown had sewer connections, and in the hot midsummer much of the city was actively malodorous. The water system was incomplete; many families continued to obtain water from cisterns and public wells. And behind the White House, the mosquito-infested marsh which ran from Seventeenth Street to the Long Bridge was still the eyesore which it had been in Lincoln's day.

Although the Capital retained its transient atmosphere, it also had year-round residents who lent a certain air of permanence. On Lafayette Square, within sight of the White House, the Henry Adamses were a permanent fixture. Viewing the Executive Mansion much as a family heirloom, Adams had a contempt for the new generation of politicians which had inspired his anonymous novel of the Gilded Age, *Democracy*. Nearby lived one of the Capital's resident financiers, William W. Corcoran. Although Corcoran's pride was his collection of old letters and manuscripts, his gift to the city of its only art museum had placed him foremost in the ranks of civic leaders. Near Scott Circle lived another leading citizen, Professor Alexander Graham Bell. The Capital even had a resident hippie, the poet Joaquin Miller. The long-haired "Poet of the Sierras" lived in a log cabin on Sixteenth Street; he was prone to boast that "the President's house is at one end of Sixteenth Street, and mine is at the other."

As for the White House itself, the Garfields inherited a drafty old mansion which had not had a complete renovation since the time of James Monroe. There were some thirty-one rooms in all, including parlors, offices, and a library which had been begun by President Fillmore. Furnishings were generally worn and rarely matched. Maintenance was casual, and the staff waged a running battle with bedbugs and mice. When the front portico received one of its infrequent hosings, the result was a shower of spiders which had spectators ducking for cover.

There were, of course, certain compensations. From the second floor library there was a fine view of the Potomac, and on a clear day one could see from Fort Washington to the south to Georgetown up the river. And there was no denying that the old mansion exuded a certain grandeur. A contemporary newsman, Frank Carpenter of the *Cleveland Leader,* set down his impressions:

> Let us take a walk through the President's house. A door-keeper with a face like that of a statesman, and a form that would have made him a member of the giant guards, had he lived years ago in Prussia, opens the doors. They turn silently on their hinges of polished brass and we step in upon the tiled floor of the great vestibule. . . .

At the left is the entrance to the hall leading to the East Room, which is probably the largest parlor in the United States. Eighty feet long and forty feet wide, it was originally intended for a banqueting hall, but now it is used solely for receptions. . . . From its richly decorated beams hang enormous chandeliers, each one of which is made up of six thousand pieces of Bohemian glass, and cost five thousand dollars. When the chandeliers are lighted, the eight massive mirrors, set into the walls of the vast room, reflect the brilliant lights, which bring out the richness of the old-gold satin furniture and the beauty of the soft mosslike carpet. . . .

The Green Room, which adjoins the East Room, and the Blue Room and the Red Room are furnished like parlors, in the colors indicated by their names. Full-length portraits of the Presidents hang on the walls of the long promenade upon which these rooms open, and at its end is the spacious doorway into the conservatory, which is filled with the plants and flowers of the tropics amid coral rockery. Here palm trees, orchids and ferns, roses of a hundred different varieties, lemon and orange trees bloom away while the wintry winds blow outside and the temperature stands at zero. During receptions, the guests wander with oh's and ah's into this tropical paradise, meeting at intervals the guards who keep watchful eyes upon their fingers.[1]

As the first family completed their move from Riggs House to this dilapidated wonderland, Garfield took satisfaction from the favorable reception accorded his cabinet by the press. The Blaine appointment, predictably, occasioned considerable tongue-wagging, but it had been so long rumored that it came as something of an anticlimax. The *Washington Star,* while expressing reservations concerning Windom and James, observed that "the general expression of opinion is that President Garfield has succeeded in organizing a good working cabinet and one pretty well balanced . . . as regards the various divisions of the Republican party." Although Garfield, since his rebuff by Hay, had no private secretary as such, most observers were impressed with young Stanley-Brown, whom the *Star* described as "a pleasant and genial young man of about 22 or 23 years old." Socially, the new administration was felt to be for the most part unknown quantity. "The only members whom we know," wrote Mrs. Henry Adams, "are

Wayne MacVeagh and Lincoln. . . . The former is a square out-
and-out Independent . . . a great talker and laugher. We have
seen him from time to time unmuzzled; how he will appear as an
official I am curious to see." [2]

Meanwhile, the new president was not finding it easy to get
organized. When the family went to church on their first presidential Sunday, they found the Campellite church on Vermont
Avenue full of curious onlookers. The White House was scarcely
more private. "The fountains of the population seem to have overflowed, and Washington is inundated," grumbled Garfield.

> Again and again we were compelled to shut the doors, with
> the file of people extending to the avenue. I received several
> thousand in the East room. This was the easiest part of the
> day's work, for these callers were pleasant, kind people who
> wished to see me & shake hands before going home. But the
> Spartan band of disciplined office hunters who drew papers on
> me as highwaymen draw pistols were the men with whom I
> had to wrestle like a Greek.[3]

Thus forewarned, Garfield turned to the touchy matter of appointments. As a favor to Hayes, Garfield once again sent to the
Senate the nomination of Stanley Matthews as justice of the Supreme Court. Matthews had been rejected a year before, largely as
a result of Hayes' own unpopularity, but this time there was no
hitch. A second appointment which bore Garfield's personal
stamp was that of ex-Senator Blanche Bruce as registrar of the
treasury. There was no "Negro vote" in 1881, but Garfield
wanted to recognize his party's abandoned wards; hence he appointed the former Mississippi legislator to the most prestigious
executive position yet occupied by a member of his race. A few
appointments Garfield made on impulse. After reading Lew Wallace's *Ben Hur* with much enjoyment, Garfield noted in his diary,
"I am inclined to send [Wallace] to Constantinople, where he
may draw inspiration from the modern east for future literary
work." Wallace had been slated to go to Paraguay, but Garfield
succeeded in having the assignment changed.

Appointments such as these afforded satisfaction to the gran-
tor. But they were very much the exception. Much of Garfield's

day was spent in contact with greedy office-seekers: minor party functionaries seemingly convinced that it was through their efforts alone that Garfield had gained his election victory. No one could have satisfied the horde, but Garfield, as a Republican successor to a Republican president, had comparatively few offices to fill. One of his callers was a zealous but little-known party worker from New York City, Charles Guiteau. Physically slight and nervous in manner, Guiteau sought the post of minister to Paris as reward for his authorship of a campaign pamphlet, "Garfield Against Hancock." According to Guiteau's later testimony, the president received him courteously, but was noncommittal concerning the Paris post. It was callers like Guiteau that forced Garfield to change his routine. In late March Stanley-Brown was formally installed in the outer office as private secretary, and new rules were laid down with respect to visitors. On March 21 Garfield was able to write, "Made a new rule, that I would see only members of the Government and Congress until twelve. . . . This gave me some relief from the crowd of last week." [4]

It was all very frantic living in the Executive Mansion, but it was also rather exhilarating. Having watched her husband dutifully tending his diary for most of their married life, Mrs. Garfield also began to keep a journal in the White House. The Garfields' first major social affair was a reception for the diplomatic corps on March 10. Crete found it rather nervewracking; she noted in her journal that "for two hours we shook the hands of the passing crowd, without a moment's intermission." Garfield himself took it all in stride, finding it in fact "very pleasant. [Crete] grows up to every new emergency with fine tact and faultless taste."

St. Patrick's Day was set aside for the Irish, and several fraternal societies paraded by the White House portico. Although refreshments were not served, the thirsty paraders were a reminder of a dilemma which the Garfields had inherited from their predecessors. Under the austere regimen of "Lemonade Lucy" Hayes, the White House had undergone four dry years. Garfield was disinclined to maintain the White House as a symbol of the temperance movement; at the same time he was reluctant to make any sharp break with Hayes' practice at a time when the new administration was being observed on every hand. Following their first dinner, Garfield noted in his diary, "We gave a dinner to Dr. Hopkins of Williams College. . . . A very pleasant party and a good dinner *sine vino*." But when a ladies' temperance delegation came by the White House to present a portrait of Mrs. Hayes, Garfield's remarks reflected a degree of tact and a greater degree of embarrassment:

> . . . . What you have said concerning the evils of intemperance meets my most hearty concurrence. I have been, in my way, and in accordance with my own convictions, an earnest advocate of temperance, not in so narrow a sense as some, but in a very definite and practical sense. These convictions are deep, and will be maintained. Whether I shall be able to meet the views of all the people in regard to all the phases of that question remains to be seen, but I shall do what I can to abate the great evils of intemperance.[5]

The patronage situation in New York came again to the fore in late March, and set in motion the train of events which would bring the Garfield administration to a tragic close. The president met with Conkling on March 20 for more than two hours; that night he wrote in his diary, "I adopted many of his suggestions, but I told him that I must recognize some of the men who had supported me at Chicago. He wanted me to give them foreign appointments. I said they did not deserve exile but rather a place in the affairs of their own state."[6]

The immediate outcome of the conference was that Garfield sent to the Senate on March 22 a group of nine Stalwarts for appointment to federal posts as collectors and judges in New York state. The reaction was not long in coming. Garfield noted in his diary that "in the evening, while we were at dinner, Blaine came, and expressed great distress at the NY appointments." In the conversation which ensued, Blaine was not able to win Garfield over completely, but he succeeded in shaking his confidence as to the wisdom of his appointments. Garfield commented to his wife, "I have broken Blaine's heart with the appointments I have made today. He regards me as having surrendered to Conkling. I have not, but I don't know but that I have acted too hastily." After noting this comment in her journal, Mrs. Garfield added significantly, "He has decided, on account of the Secretary's anxiety, to send in another batch of appointments tomorrow which will very thoroughly antidote the first." [7]

True to his word, Garfield dropped his bomb on the 23rd, sending to the Senate a group of appointments headed by that of William Robertson to be collector for the Port of New York. Once again, Garfield took a step which was possibly desirable for the wrong reasons and with little regard for the consequences. Not surprisingly, in light of his stated views on the subject, Garfield did not wish to be shackled by the tradition of senatorial courtesy in appointing some of his own supporters to federal posts. Although Garfield might have balked at the analogy, he was in effect continuing the struggle against encroachments on the Executive which had been waged by Lincoln and Andrew Johnson more than a decade before. But Garfield was fighting not on grounds of his own choosing but on ground chosen by Blaine. And Garfield's attempt to assert his independence of the senatorial bosses was further complicated by the personalities involved.

By naming Robertson as collector, Garfield was ousting an able public servant, General Merritt, for no apparent reason other than to please Blaine. In the end, the choice of Robertson not only infuriated the Stalwarts, but alienated Garfield from the reformers whose good will was otherwise his. The impression everywhere was that the Robertson appointment was the work of Blaine, while the resulting ouster of Merritt prompted the *Nation* to say of Robertson, "His appointment was made on Boss principles and . . . to all appearances by a Maine Boss instead of a New York Boss." [8]

This adverse reaction was somewhat unfair to Garfield, who had informed Conkling before the appointment of his intention to recognize non-Stalwart elements in New York. Moreover, Merritt did not become a public charge, but was appointed by the president to be consul general in London. The whole episode, however, was a reminder that Garfield lacked finesse in sensitive personnel matters, and that his reliance on the secretary of state in such matters could be a serious liability. Nevertheless, having made his move Garfield determined to ride out the storm. In his diary he noted, "Instead of waiting for the long two years contest over the NY Collectorship which will attend the remainder of Gen. Merritt's term, I appointed Merritt Consul Gen to London, & Judge Robertson Collector of New York. This brings the contest to an early close, & fully recognizes the minority element." [9]

As busy as he was in connection with the patronage war in New York, Garfield came gradually to the conclusion that he would have to do something about his living quarters. On April 9 he noted in his diary, "C. and I drove out . . . to the Library of Congress, to . . . ask Mr. Spofford to look into the history of the White House and its contents, of which little appears to be known." Friends came to call a week later, and Mrs. Garfield related how "we sat down to a good rattling talk over the dilapidated condition of this old White House, and I think I have enlisted both Mr. N. and Mr. H. to support me or rather the President in making a plea to Congress to rebuild during the summer following this." [10] Meanwhile, however, the first family found time and opportunities for recreation in the Washington spring. They enjoyed carriage rides in Rock Creek Park, while the president took pleasure in a billiard table he had installed on the second floor of the old mansion. David Swaim, who had been appointed judge advocate general by Hayes as a favor to his successor, was a frequent visitor to the billiard room, as was the ubiquitous Rockwell.

When he could tear away from office-seekers, Garfield sought to come to grips with policy matters, particularly those in the area of finance. Toward the close of the Hayes administration, Congress had passed a Funding Bill, designed to retire some $200,-000,000 worth of 6-per-cent bonds which dated back to the Civil War. Hayes vetoed the bill, reportedly at Garfield's urging, in part because of a rider which would have provided that banks could use only the new bonds as security for bank notes. As a result of the veto, however, the new administration was faced at the outset with the necessity of working out a new means of redeeming the old bonds and floating a new issue.

Garfield considered and then rejected the possibility of calling a special session of Congress to enact new legislation. The Senate had not even been able to organize itself, so close was the division between Democrats and Republicans, and both parties were seeking the support of Senator Malone of Virginia, whose adherence to the G.O.P. would at least give them a tie which could in turn be broken by Vice President Arthur. In this situation Garfield elected to send Secretary Windom, assisted by Mac-Veagh, to sound out Wall Street concerning the possibility of a new loan under the provisions of existing legislation. On April 4 the two cabinet officers returned with a proposal for two new series of bonds. A circular went out to holders of the old bonds, informing them that the bonds should be redeemed after July 1, but offering the option of the holder's keeping the bonds after that date and receiving 3½-per-cent interest. Comparatively few bonds were presented for redemption, and the Garfield administration succeeded in reducing interest on the public debt by almost half.

A peripheral area in which Garfield took a special interest concerned American participation in the International Red Cross. The redoubtable Clara Barton had sought this goal for years, and had repeatedly petitioned the Hayes administration to accredit the American Red Cross as representing the United States in the parent body. Invariably she had run afoul of the Department of State, where Assistant Secretary Frederick W. Seward opposed American participation in such projects. With this background of frustration, Miss Barton sought out President Garfield in the first weeks of his administration. The president greeted her as an old war comrade, remarking with a smile, "We fought together in the Civil War, didn't we?" After hearing her plea, Garfield gave her a note to Blaine, indicating that he was favorably disposed to her request. Blaine also received her cordially; himself an activist in foreign affairs, he had little sympathy with Seward's approach. Miss Barton was so impressed that she wrote to a colleague, "I have made greater progress in the 13 little days which have followed the inauguration . . . than I have been able to accomplish in the whole four years of previous effort." [11]

Garfield was less qualified in foreign affairs than he was in financial matters, but he inherited no serious problems in the field of foreign relations. In any case, Blaine was proceeding within his State Department sphere with the same drive and energy that he brought to matters outside his immediate responsibility. For all his seeming preoccupation with domestic politics, Blaine brought to the State post a grasp of international developments which was matched by few individuals in either party. For better or worse, he was one of the first "dollar diplomats," and he demonstrated a keen awareness of the potential benefits to be derived from American investment abroad, especially in Latin America. He was perhaps the first secretary of state since William H. Seward to view the United States as a two-ocean power.* The secretary was keenly interested in the prospect of an isthmian canal across Central America, and in assuring American control over any canal which might be developed. Garfield described in his diary a cabinet meeting in which "Blaine read an important . . . note to several of our leading ministers in Europe on the neutrality of the South American isthmus, holding that the United States has guaranteed its neutrality and denies the right of other, especially European powers to take any part in the guarantee." [12]

Historians have given Blaine full marks for the characteristically activist policy which he pursued toward Latin America during the brief months of the Garfield administration. Motivated in part by the prospect of developing new and stable markets for American industry, Blaine invited the republics of Latin America to meet in Washington the following year to discuss ways of keeping the peace in the Western Hemisphere. (When Blaine saw his plan come to fruition nearly a decade later, under a different Republican president, the emphasis would be as much on tariff reciprocity as on peacekeeping.) In contrast to his ill-advised domestic forays into the area of New York state politics, Blaine worked closely with Garfield and kept his chief fully informed regarding foreign policy developments.

The most critical problem faced by the new administration, apart from the patronage war in New York, was a holdover from

---

* In December 1881, Blaine in effect urged an extension of the Monroe Doctrine into the Pacific, writing, "In thirty years the United States has acquired a legitimately dominant influence in the Northern Pacific, which it can never consent to see decreased by the intrusion therein of any element of influence hostile to its own. The situation of the Hawaiian Islands, giving them the strategic control of the Northern Pacific, brings their possession within the range of questions of purely American policy, as much so as that of the Isthmus itself." Ruhl J. Bartlett, ed., *The Record of American Diplomacy*, p. 359.

the Hayes administration. Very shortly after his inauguration Garfield was informed, possibly by Blaine, of the discovery of serious malfeasance in the Post Office department. From the first it was apparent that the affair could have explosive political ramifications. Assistant Postmaster Tom Brady was said to be involved, as was Jay Hubbell, to whom Garfield had directed an inquiry during the campaign in which he asked how government employees were doing in their contributions to the Republican campaign fund. When Garfield first spoke of the matter to his postmaster general, no ringing mandate for a cleanup was forthcoming. Meeting with James on March 9, the president ordered an investigation "aimed at a system and not at men." He added, however, that "if the inquiry should disclose the fact that any person or persons had been guilty of corruption or fraud, that person or those persons must be handed over to the Department of Justice." [13]

When James completed his report, it detailed the most costly frauds perpetrated against the government since the "Whiskey Ring" of Grant's day. It seemed that for most of Hayes' term, a ring headed by Brady and the formidable Stephen W. Dorsey had successfully padded bills for contract mail delivery in undeveloped parts of the West. Those contractors engaged were to deliver the mail with "certainty, celerity, and security"—an injunction which led the contract routes to be marked with three asterisks, and later to become known as the "star routes." When the contracts were tendered, the Dorsey-Brady syndicate invariably were low bidders. Subsequently, in collusion with Post Office officials, rates for service on the "star routes" were drastically hiked on grounds that better or more frequent service was being provided. Thus on one group of twenty-six contracts, for which the Post Office had initially budgeted $143,169 per year, rates were raised to such an extent that the government eventually paid over $600,000 for "improved service" over these same routes.

Garfield's first reaction was to express surprise that frauds of such a magnitude could have escaped the notice of his predecessor. But James' preliminary investigation convinced him that drastic action was called for; he noted in his diary on April 9 that "great frauds" had been uncovered in the Post Office department and he promised himself that "I will clear out the contract office." [14] But even then Garfield was not aware of all the implications of the scandal. Breaking the news to his chief, MacVeagh told Garfield on April 22 that "these proceedings may strike men in high places; that [they] may result in changing a Republican majority in the United States Senate into a Democratic majority; that [they] may affect persons who claim that you are under personal obligations to them for services rendered during the last campaign." [15] He then confirmed the rumors of Dorsey's involvement.

According to MacVeagh's later testimony, Garfield walked across the room, reflected for a moment, and then directed him to proceed with the investigation. "I have sworn to execute the laws," he declared, "Go ahead regardless of where or whom you hit." It is a commentary on the times that the "star route" offenders, like those of the "Whiskey Ring," looked to the White House for protection. But Garfield was not Grant and the investigation proceeded, to the chagrin of the Stalwarts who viewed the persecution of Dorsey as further evidence of the president's ingratitude. To the country at large, however, there was welcome evidence that the president recognized the obligations imposed by his office.

Thomas James was clearly one of the "sleepers" of the new cabinet. His honesty and capacity for work were a reminder that association with one of the political machines of the 1880s did not corrupt one absolutely. James had been elevated by Conkling to the head of the New York City Post Office in 1873 at a time when its operations were a national scandal. One of his first tasks had been the delivery of several hundred bags of undelivered mail, and over the years he had turned his operation into a model of its kind. As he undertook an even more sensitive house cleaning in Washington he carried with him the blessings of the *New York Times,* which editorialized in June, "Mr. James took charge of a great department in which fraud had prevailed for years. . . . He has proceeded slowly but surely. Three months are gone, and the annual expenses of the 'star route' bureau have been reduced by nearly $800,000." [16]

Chapter Eighteen

CONFRONTATION
AND VICTORY

The refunding problem and the "star route" affair would themselves have provided an eventful beginning for the new administration. Nevertheless, the reverberations of the Robertson appointment so overshadowed everything else that Garfield's
contemporaries, like later chroniclers, could recall little of his
term except the patronage war with Conkling. Similarly, the constitutional aspect of the struggle became obscured by debate as to
who was directing administration policy, Garfield or Blaine. In-
tentionally or otherwise, the inventive Blaine conveyed the impression that he spoke for the administration; when he stormed to
the White House to protest the Stalwart nominations, it was soon
the talk of Washington, and in the salons of the nation's capital
the Robertson appointment was widely regarded as a reflection of
Blaine's domination of the administration. Few bothered to remember that Garfield had himself taken dead aim on the matter
of senatorial courtesy long before he was being talked of as a presidential candidate himself, most notably in his 1877 article for *Atlantic* when he characterized legislative pressure for appointments

as a "serious crippling" of the powers of the Executive. If this had been Garfield's view while in Congress, it was hardly likely that he would feel less strongly when he was himself in the White House, a target of Conkling's wrath.

Where Garfield and Blaine parted company was over how to assert the president's prerogatives. Blaine, the gut fighter, sought the political destruction of the Grant faction, viewing it as a threat both to himself and his chief. Garfield, on the other hand, had not forgotten his campaign obligations to the Stalwarts, and he was prepared to honor them if he could do so without abandoning his own supporters in New York. His strategy was sounder than his tactics. Conkling had little following outside of New York, and the country at large was fully prepared to grant Garfield the "honeymoon" period due an incoming president. But in seeking to displace the able and popular Merritt, Garfield reduced what could have been a crusade for good government to a quarrel over political spoils in which the president was dependent for popular support on Conkling's continued display of arrogance and bad manners.

The president's failure to "sell" his case threatened at one time to disrupt his own cabinet. On March 25, James and MacVeagh, two of his most promising appointees, met with Garfield to protest the Robertson appointment and to submit their own resignations. James pointed out that Robertson was an anathema to the Stalwarts, and that such a controversial appointment was hardly consistent with Garfield's pledge to consult with Conkling. MacVeagh took a similar tack, and added that he was personally offended by the choice of Blaine's friend William E. Chandler as soliciter general. Chandler had the reputation of a manipulator, and had incurred the wrath of MacVeagh some years ago by a personal attack on the Pennsylvanian. Since both James and MacVeagh saw Blaine at the root of their respective problems, they had determined to make a joint appeal to the president.

This new crisis saw the president at his conciliatory best, making the best of the bad hand which he had dealt himself. To mollify MacVeagh he secured Blaine's agreement to a face-saving arrangement in which Chandler's nomination would not be withdrawn, but would go forward on the understanding that Chandler would step down following his confirmation in favor of a less controversial nominee. In response to James' *démarche* Garfield agreed to meet once more with Conkling in an attempt to resolve their impasse. As the two cabinet officers were about to take their leave, Garfield came from behind the dark mahogany Executive desk and put an arm around the shoulder of each. "Having Conkling come over this evening," he told James. "I will see that the members of the Cabinet are present and it will go hard if we do not settle all this matter before we separate." [1] Garfield must have winced at the prospect of another of Conkling's tirades, but the gesture was well worth the effort. When Conkling failed to keep the appointment, he lost the support of James, his one adherent in the cabinet.

Although Conkling had managed to unite Garfield's official family the president still faced problems in the Senate. On one hand, Conkling had antagonized numerous senators who might otherwise have been allies in a matter in which all had an interest. Nevertheless, in early April Garfield felt obliged to warn "several senators" that the vote on Robertson was a test of "friendship or hostility to the administration." Even some friends of Blaine were sensitive on the issue of senatorial courtesy; Senators Hale and Frye, both close to the secretary of state, conceded a degree of sympathy for Conkling and asked Garfield if the Robertson appointment could not be withdrawn. The impasse over Robertson added heat to an already complicated situation in the upper House. In it were 37 Republicans, 37 Democrats, and 2 independents. Since one of the independents, Davis of Illinois, threw in his lot with the Democrats, it was not until late March, after the G.O.P. had secured the vote of "independent" Malone with promises of patronage, that the Republicans were assured of the votes necessary to organize the Senate. In retaliation, the Democrats initiated a filibuster which effectively closed the Senate to business until early May. Few Republicans were anxious to come to grips with the Robertson affair, however, and many regarded the filibuster as a blessing in disguise.

With the senators thus at loggerheads, the time was ripe for compromise proposals on Robertson. Most of these centered on a withdrawal of his name in connection with the collectorship, in return for Conkling's approval of some less controversial choice. Perhaps on Blaine's urging, Robertson let it be known from Albany that he would not ask that his name be withdrawn. Garfield, in turn, met with Senator "Black Jack" Logan of Illinois to spurn any compromise.

> I summed up the case [to Logan]. . . . 1. The Robertson appointment is mine, not another's. 2. The office is national, not local. 3. Having given all the other places to Conkling's friends, he is neither magnanimous nor just in opposing this one friend of mine. He has raised a question of veracity with me and it shall be tried by the Senate.[2]

Garfield's determination to hold fast was the product of a number of factors. Although slow to anger, Garfield had a stubborn streak which made him loathe to back down in a fight once he was committed. He would never admit that he might have been mistaken about Fitz-John Porter, and he was not about to admit any mistake with respect to Robertson. In any case, Garfield's course had won him widespread if sometimes grudging support in the country at large, and his mail was overwhelmingly favorable on the Robertson issue. It is of interest that, for all this, the president's friends feared he would prove too conciliatory. Whitelaw Reid wrote to Hay, for forwarding to the White House, that "this is the turning point of his whole administration. . . . If he surrenders now, Conkling is president for the rest of the term and Garfield becomes a laughing-stock." [3]

Belatedly, Garfield sought to exploit Conkling's unpopularity and to clarify the administration position to the country. In an interview with a reporter from the *Philadelphia Press*, Garfield gave his side of the controversial March 20 interview with Conkling which had immediately preceded the nomination of Robertson:

> It was then definitely stated by the President that the wing of the Republican party in New York which Judge Robertson represents should be recognized in him, the only question being as to the place. Upon this he asked Mr. Conkling's advice. Mr. Conkling thought that Judge Robertson himself would recognize the fact that his professional experience had

not been of a character to fit him for a prosecuting officer. . . .
The collectorship was not discussed at that time except inci-
dentally. Once during the course of the talk, Mr. Conkling
said to the President, 'When are you going to remove Mr.
Merritt?' General Garfield replied in substance, 'That matter
will be taken up soon.' After the interview and after several
nominations had been made in accordance with Mr. Conkling's suggestions, the disposition of Judge Robertson's case
forced itself upon the President's mind in accordance with his
announced policy of making it manifest at the outset of his administration that all elements of the party were to be recognized. Senator Conkling was not consulted as to this nomination, for the reason that the President thought that the general
understanding with Mr. Conkling covered whatever disposition
he might make of Judge Robertson.[4]

Throughout April, Garfield took soundings among the
Republican senators. Their desire for a compromise was painfully
evident, and with the White House pressing for action on the
nearly 300 appointments requiring Senate approval, Senate Republicans took refuge in a party caucus. The immediate result of
the caucus was the creation of a conciliation committee, headed
by Garfield's one-time congressional colleague, Senator Henry L.
Dawes of Massachusetts. The committee first met with Conkling,
only to find him as intransigent as ever. The senators listened—
dismay mingled with awe—as the New Yorker rang the changes
of Garfield's perfidy in the same florid oratory which he had first
employed to the president-elect at Riggs House. At the close of
his peroration, the New Yorker became secretive. "I now say to
you," announced Conkling, in Dawes' account, "that I have in my
pocket an autograph letter of this President . . . which I pray
God I may never be compelled in self-defense to make public;
but if that time shall ever come, I declare to you, his friends, he
shall bite the dust." This was, of course, nothing less than black-
mail. Dawes subsequently wrote that Conkling "raged and roared
like a bull of Bashan for three mortal hours," and he apparently
thought that Garfield should have put a stop to this exhibition.
"For a great man I think our President has some of the weakest,
and Conkling some of the ugliest, streaks I have ever seen. . . .
The one [needs] to be watched like a child, the other like an

assassin." [5] In private conversation with Dawes, however, Garfield dismissed the suggestion that Conkling possessed any damaging material. The letter in question turned out to be Garfield's campaign letter to Jay Hubbell, in which he had implicitly condoned the assessing of government employees, and its existence had long been rumored in Washington. Dawes urged that the president disarm his opponents by publishing the letter. Such a course might have had something to recommend it, but at this point Blaine joined the discussion. "Here, Blaine, is where I have been slopping over again," Garfield remarked, passing over the letter. Blaine urged against publication, and the subject was not pursued further.

With the administration now in command of the votes needed to confirm Garfield's appointments, the Democratic filibuster ran its course. The White House pressed for action, and Garfield's conversations reflected his concern over the major issue involved. He reminded Dawes that he wanted to know whether he was "the registering clerk of the Senate or the Executive of the Government." Responding to a sympathetic letter from former Attorney General Edwards Pierpoint, Garfield employed the same metaphor:

> I have your kind note, warning me of the efforts of certain persons to defeat the N. Y. nominations. I know untiring and passionate are the efforts to break down the independence of the Executive and I thank you for your kind and valuable suggestions. I have no passion or resentment to gratify: but I am anxious to know, early in my term, whether I am to be a registering clerk or President.[6]

On May 4 the filibuster ended and the Senate was at last prepared to consider the president's business. There was, however, one joker. Probably on the initiative of one of the Stalwarts, the Republican caucus decided to consider treaties and "uncontested nominations" before moving on to other business. If this formula had been followed, the Senate could have confirmed all of Garfield's appointees except Robertson, and the president would have been no closer to a favorable resolution of the confrontation than before. But Garfield's response, which may have originated with Blaine, was a master stroke. On May 5, after the Senate had begun confirming Conkling's friends, Garfield sent young Stanley-Brown to the Capitol. On behalf of the president, Stanley-Brown withdrew all nominations previously sent—all except that of William H. Robertson.

Now the ball was in the Senate court, and there was no avoiding a showdown. As for Garfield, his coup brought new expressions of support from a broad spectrum of the country. Within his official family, the atmosphere was one of elation. "Glory to God," scribbled James G. Blaine, "Victory is yours, sure and lasting." Blaine did not overstate; supporters of Conkling and Platt, fearful of not being able to secure pet appointments of their own, began to waver. On May 9, there was another caucus. Conkling once more held forth on the subject of senatorial courtesy and the ingratitude of presidents; he finally endorsed a motion which would cause consideration of Robertson to be postponed until December. More than ever he appeared outraged over the prospect of political reward for Robertson the apostate, and however reprehensible Conkling's behavior, the violence of his passion was a reminder of how thoroughly the Olympian Garfield had misjudged the personality factor. But Conkling's friends in the Senate could no longer help him. On May 12, the *New York Herald* quoted an unnamed senator as predicting that Robertson would be confirmed by "a large Republican majority." The senator went on to grumble that there was hardly a Republican senator "but would be glad to be relieved from voting for the confirmation." With the members of that august body squirming at the prospect of any weakening of the tradition of senatorial courtesy, the confrontation took another of the sudden turns which made it the most memorable political struggle since the Electoral Commission.

On May 16, Vice President Arthur handed the clerk of the Senate two notes, almost identical in substance. In his sing-song voice the clerk read the first note, from Conkling: "Will you please announce to the Senate that my resignation as Senator of the United States from New York has been forwarded to the Governor of that state." A buzz of astonishment filled the chamber as the clerk went on to read an equally terse note from Tom Platt which would tag that worthy for the rest of his days with the nickname, "Me Too Platt." Seeking to proceed as if nothing unusual had occurred, Senator Burnside of Rhode Island moved to present the report of the Foreign Affairs committee. In the aisles, however, the talk consisted of speculation as to Conkling's motives.

If Conkling's resignation was consistent with his flair for the dramatic, that of Platt had a touch of the *opéra bouffe*. Even more than Conkling he cut an improbable figure as a political boss, for Platt had attended Yale for two years, played the violin, and was as unprepossessing in appearance as his colleague was overbearing. In contrast to the virile Conkling, Platt was slightly built, with a pointed face and scruffy sidewhiskers which made a poor showing alongside the full beards then in vogue. And whereas Conkling would carry on a dalliance with no one less than Kate Chase Sprague, Platt's consorts were drawn from ladies of the night.

Platt had no popular following, even in New York, and could never have been elected U. S. senator except in a day when this chore was handled by state legislatures, whose members could be bought and sold. As Conkling's colleague and ally, Platt was in an uncomfortable position in the controversy over Robertson; with him as with other senators, sympathy for Conkling clashed with the politician's desire to get off on the right foot with the new administration. Friends of Blaine were later to allege that Platt had implied that he would support the administration against Conkling and Arthur; in any case one can only imagine the anguish that went into his decision to follow Conkling out of the Senate. But with the departure of the two angry Stalwarts for home to seek vindication in the form of re-election by the state legislature, the main show shifted to Albany and the Senate was able to get down to business.

In this moment of triumph, Garfield chose to be magnanimous. As one more demonstration of his desire to accommodate all factions, Garfield returned to the Senate on May 19 all of his previous nominations except two. In effect, he was adhering to his version of the understanding with Conkling, even though the latter no longer acknowledged it and was no longer in the Senate.

On May 22 he wrote to Cox, "I was greatly tempted to fill the five vacancies with anti-Conkling men, but on the whole I thought it best not to bend from the course I had started upon—to recognize fairly both wings of the party." Blaine, however, was still unreconciled to a conciliatory policy. "Pardon my intense earnestness," he wrote, in an incongruous footnote to his Glory to God message of a few days earlier, "Nobody can beat you, my dear Mr. President, except yourself. . . . Some blunders you know are worse than crimes. I fear this was one." [7] Since Conkling posed a rather tepid threat to Garfield at the time Blaine wrote, one suspects again that the secretary was motivated in large measure by a desire to assure his own succession once Garfield stood down.

Ignoring Blaine's criticism (the most that Garfield could bring himself to do against Blaine was to ignore him), Garfield sought to lay the Robertson matter to rest once and for all. In proceeding with the New York appointments as planned, he hoped that he had made clear to lukewarm supporters such as Godkin of the *Nation* and Bowles of the *Springfield Republican* that he had been motivated by more than a desire to establish a political foothold in the Empire state. But most of all, he was glad to be rid of the affair which had caused him to remark on one particularly dark day, "My God! What is there in this place that a man should ever want to get into it?" The White House gradually lost the aspect of a fortress under siege which it had worn almost since Inauguration Day. The Senate confirmed Garfield's appointments and then adjourned, a development that allowed the First Family to extend some of the hospitality which they themselves so enjoyed. Murat Halstead, the Cincinnati editor, has left his picture of an evening at the White House:

> There was one evening at the White House . . . that none of those present can have forgotten. . . . Mrs. Garfield, whose chilly sensation was supposed to be trivial, was seated before the fire, and she was pale but animated surrounded by a group among whom were several very dear to her. General Sherman arrived and was—as always when his vivacity was kindly [sic] and it never was otherwise with ladies—fascinating. The President was detained for half an hour beyond the time when he was expected and came in with a quick step and hearty man-

ner, and there was soon a flush of pleasure upon his face, that had been touched with the lines of fatigue, as he saw how agreeable the company were. . . . He was well dressed, of splendid figure, his dome-like head erect, adequately supported by immense shoulders, and he looked the President indeed, and an embodiment of power. He was feeling that the dark days were behind him, that he was equal to his high fortune, that the world was wide and fair before him.[8]

The following day the "chilly sensation" to which Halstead alluded developed into a severe case of malaria, and for a time there was concern for Crete's survival. Garfield sent to Kansas for his cousin, Dr. Silas Boynton, and he was himself constantly at his wife's side. After twelve anxious days, the fever appeared to be running its course. "The external heat has abated," Garfield wrote in his diary, "the very birds seem kind to her, in fact the whole world seems anxious to help her back on shore." The convalescence, however, was a protracted one. Not until the end of May did she shake the effects of her illness entirely, and it was some time after that before her recovery was complete.

In early June Garfield took the family, except for Crete, on a three-day river excursion to Fortress Monroe, his first holiday since taking office. On returning, he attended several commencements, including one at Howard University Law School. The fight for survival being waged by Conkling and Platt in Albany seemed far removed from springtime in Washington. But things were not going well for his erstwhile antagonists, and Garfield may have taken a certain satisfaction from an appraisal by the *New York Times,* which observed on June 7 that "the reelection of Conkling and Platt being conceded by their most ardent friends to be an impossibility, the immediate retirement from the contest of the ex-Senators would seem to be demanded equally by considerations of self-respect and party fidelity." On June 18, Garfield left Washington with the entire family for Elberon, New Jersey, where it was felt that the sea air might help Crete to regain her strength. Meanwhile, the *Times'* assessment of the first months of the Garfield administration provided more good reading:

Mr. Garfield has not had to deal with any startling questions, but he has been called upon to meet some of no small importance and of considerable difficulty. The work of his administration in connection with the refunding of the debt has been sagacious and useful.[9]

Even at the shore Garfield could not escape all political burdens, for another visitor at Elberon was General Grant, who was staying at the cottage of his son Jesse. Garfield had never been on close terms with his predecessor, but in recent months their relationship had taken on a distinct chill. Grant had desired that his Boswell, Adam Badeau, be reappointed as naval agent in London while he worked on a laudatory history of Grant's presidency. Garfield, although willing to assist Badeau, had other plans for the London post, and this factor, on top of the struggle beween the administration and Grant's friend Conkling, had brought Grant's anger to the flash point. From Mexico, Grant addressed to Senator J. Percival Jones of Nevada a letter condemning Garfield's course. Probably on instructions, Jones released the letter to the press. Garfield, though he twice wrote to Grant to explain his course in regard to Robertson, made no impression on the ex-president, who still smarted from his defeat for the Republican nomination. Although it had not yet reached the newspapers, Garfield also had wind of a letter from Grant to Badeau which was even more hostile than that to Jones. In it, Grant characterized himself as "completely disgusted with Garfield's course," adding

I will never again lend my active aid to the support of a Presidential candidate who has not strength enough to appear before a convention as a candidate, but gets in simply by the adherents of prominent candidates. . . . Garfield has shown that he is not possessed of the backbone of an angle-worm. I hope his nominations may be defeated.[10]

Garfield called a cabinet meeting at Elberon, and with little else on the agenda the conversation turned to Grant's behavior. Hunt urged that Garfield make no move to call on Grant unless the latter took the initiative. Garfield had no intention of doing otherwise, and in the end it was Grant who bit the bullet. When Garfield held a predeparture reception for visitors to Elberon, Grant came by for what Garfield estimated was "two or three minutes." Appearances had been preserved, however, and Grant had offered, in Garfield's words, "a tardy recognition of the respect due to the office he once held."

On June 27, a well-rested president returned to Washington. He continued to follow closely both the "star route" investigation and the refunding but had hopes that, with Congress in recess, he would be able to travel to Williams to celebrate the twenty-fifth anniversary of his graduation as well as to enroll Harry and Jim in the freshman class. With this trip in mind, he left Crete in Elberon; he planned to pick her up, her convalescence complete, on his way to New England. But Garfield was not to see Williamstown or Mark Hopkins again, though he would make one more journey to Elberon. For down beside the Potomac marshes, sometimes within sight of the White House, a slight, sallow marksman was practicing with the pistol which he intended to use to kill the president of the United States.

Garfield returned to Washington to find the kind of weather which people went to the seashore to avoid. A Washington summer was testimony to the wisdom of the Maryland fathers who had so cheerfully surrendered title to the site of the Federal City. The morning haze usually foreshadowed a day of still and breathless humidity, occasionally broken by an evening shower which often as not left the city little cooler than before. Garfield found no pressing business awaiting him, but he took pleasure in coming up with a diplomatic appointment for Lincoln's old vice president, Hannibal Hamlin. The president knew that Hamlin, who had just retired from the Senate, wanted to spend some time in Europe and had inquired as to whether he might accept a diplomatic appointment. When Hamlin agreed to go to Madrid, Garfield observed to his cabinet that the appointment was one that gave him particular pleasure.

The cabinet agenda on June 30 was a brief one, and conversation soon turned to plans for the holidays. On an impulse Garfield asked the secretary of war to tell of President Lincoln's dream just prior to his assassination. Robert Lincoln was no raconteur, but he recalled to an attentive audience his father's dream in which he saw a corpse lying on a catafalque in the East Room. In the dream, the sound of sobbing had drawn his father from his bed. "Who is dead in the White House?" Lincoln had asked a soldier guarding the catafalque. "The President" was his reply. Garfield then adjourned the meeting, saying his farewells to members of the cabinet who planned to leave for vacation that evening.

Chapter Nineteen

THE TRAGEDY

———◆•◆———

On the morning of July 2, all was in readiness for Garfield's trip to Elberon, and thence to Williamstown. A special parlor car had been added to the 9:30 train from the Baltimore and Potomac depot, and Garfield had invited those of his cabinet who were headed north to join him in the presidential car. It was only a short ride from the White House to the depot, but Harry and Jim, accompanied by the luggage, left the White House about nine. Blaine, who had offered to take the president to the train, stopped by shortly thereafter. When the two reached the depot at Sixth and B Streets it was still only 9:20, and the two continued their conversation in Blaine's carriage. Both men were in a holiday mood. That very morning the forty-nine-year-old Garfield had jumped over his bed on a dare from young Harry; now the president chatted with Blaine while watching the secretary toss his cane in the air and catch it.

At about 9:30 Colonel Jamison of the Post Office Department, who had handled arrangements for the trip, informed Garfield that the train was ready. He directed them to one of two waiting rooms as the most direct route to the platform, and Garfield and Blaine passed into a drab room lined with empty wooden benches. A servant followed with the presidential luggage, but otherwise the waiting room was almost deserted, for the hour was early and the other passengers were on the train. The two men had scarcely passed the first rows of benches when there was the crash of a pistol shot, followed by another. Blaine turned to locate the sound, only to hear the president gasp, "My God, what is this?" and collapse at his feet.

In an instant the depot was bedlam. As a crowd began to form about the fallen man, his assailant was seen to run out the B Street exit toward a carriage which, as it turned out, he had engaged to take him to the jail. Before he could reach the street, however, he was collared by two policemen. "Keep quiet, my friend," the assassin told patrolman Patrick Kearney, for his greatest fear was of a lynching. "I wish to go to jail." It was a comparatively short time before the crowd was moved back and doctors summoned. First to reach the stricken president was Dr. Smith Townsend, the Public Health Officer, who concluded that the president was dying. Garfield, in deep shock and only partially conscious, was moved to a room on the second floor of the depot. There the cabinet gathered and Robert Lincoln, recalling his narrative at the last cabinet meeting, exclaimed, "How many hours of sorrow I have passed in this town!" [1]

The initial examination confirmed that Garfield was critically wounded. His light gray traveling suit was stained with blood. The first of Guiteau's shots, fired at point-blank range, had struck him in the back, fracturing two ribs. The second shot had only grazed his left arm, but on first examination it seemed unlikely that the president could live through the day. A wagon was procured, and Garfield was borne back to the White House on an impromptu bed. Clara Barton was leaving her house on I Street when she saw a crowd streaming downtown; there were wild reports that the president had been shot. Rumor had it that he had been taken to the Capitol, but when she went there she found the gates locked.[2]

Once the populace had recovered from its initial shock at the assault, interest inevitably turned to the identity and motive of the assassin. Charles Jules Guiteau, thirty-nine years old, had been born in Illinois of French Huguenot ancestry. His mother died when he was seven, and young Charles grew up under the erratic guidance of his father Luther in Freeport, Illinois. Profoundly religious, Luther Guiteau was at one time superintendent of schools in Freeport and in general he was a pillar of the community.

The Guiteaus began to move toward the outer fringe of conventional society with Luther's attraction to the communalism of John H. Noyes. A one-time Congregational minister, Noyes became a convert to a doctrine called perfectionism, which maintained that man might attain in his life a degree of holiness sufficient for salvation. In practice Noyes sought to demonstrate the good in man through a utopian form of communal living in which the good things of life, including wives, were shared among members of the community. Noyes' tolerance of polygamy caused him and his followers to be driven out of Putney, Vermont, but a move to Oneida, New York, proved salubrious and the Oneida Community embarked on a period of relative prosperity.[3]

Eventually, the practice of plural marriage would again bring about the downfall of the Oneida Community, and Noyes would be obliged to take refuge in Canada. As a boy, however, Charles Guiteau was impressed with the dark-bearded divine who came to visit his father and to exchange religious revelations. While no one specifically questioned Luther Guiteau's sanity, there were those who knew that one of his brothers had died insane, as had a niece and a nephew.

Young Charles went to school in Freeport until he was twelve, at which time his father married again. Charles bitterly resented his father's remarriage, and relations finally reached a stage where the boy was allowed to go to Chicago to live with his sister and her husband, George Scoville. Later there was a reconciliation, and Charles was prevailed upon to join the Oneida Community. But he was not temperamentally suited for work in the fields, and after spending the Civil War years at Oneida Guiteau left it for New York City. Already he was something of a religious fanatic. He intended, he said, not to give up his work for the Lord, but merely to practice in a greater arena.

Away from Oneida, Guiteau began a hand to mouth existence which would continue up to the time of his assault on Garfield. He first attempted to publish a newspaper, the *New York*

Theocrat, but this failed and for a brief period he returned to the Oneida Community. In November 1866 he left for good, however, and when Noyes failed to refund several thousand dollars which Guiteau said were due him he attempted unsuccessfully to sell an exposé of life at Oneida. Unable to obtain newspaper work, Guiteau read Blackstone and began a career in law. In Chicago, while working as a clerk with a law firm, he married an attractive sixteen-year-old girl named Annie Bunn, who testified at Guiteau's trial that she had been much impressed with her husband's piety. She soon began to have second thoughts, as Guiteau embarked upon what one writer has called "an eleven-year career of cheating merchants, publishers, pawnbrokers and boarding-house keepers."

> Guiteau's tastes were expensive, running to seventy-five-dollar suits and lavish rooms in the best hotels and boarding-houses. Even if he had money, it was unusual for him to pay his haberdasher or his landlord and still more unusual for him to pay in full. Every few weeks, he and his wife either sneaked out of their lodgings under cover of darkness or were evicted, with their luggage held as collateral. If Mrs. Guiteau expressed misgivings about his way of life, as she often did, Guiteau was likely as not to lock her in a chilly hall closet for the night.[4]

Notwithstanding this precarious existence, Guiteau was capable of impressing many of the people whom he met. He had all the wiles of the professional con man, plus a pious demeanor which many people remarked upon and which allowed him on one occasion to borrow $95 from the pastor of the Calvary Baptist Church in New York City, who naturally never saw either Guiteau or his money again. He might have gone on indefinitely as a petty swindler had not his fortunes undergone a series of reversals beginning in 1873. Long attracted to prostitutes, Guiteau contracted syphilis and was divorced by his wife. The *New York Herald* ran an exposé of his activities as a collection lawyer which all but destroyed his practice. Guiteau brought suit against the paper for $100,000 but dropped the suit, according to his trial testimony, because he did not wish to have the *Herald* as an enemy should he ever run for president.

For several years Guiteau dabbled in law, newspaper work,

and preaching. Drawing freely on Noyes' theology, Guiteau, who billed himself as the "lawyer and theologian from Chicago," defended Noyes' contention that Christ's second coming had taken place in the year A.D. 70. He rode trains without a ticket simply by representing himself as a minister; his guise was sufficiently plausible that more often than not he got away with it. But during this period he became increasingly subject to delusions, including one that he was destined to become president.

Guiteau did moderately well with a pamphlet of religious lectures which he modestly entitled *The Truth: A Companion to the Bible*. But sales fell off, and soon the author's lecturing was going badly. Guiteau had always been attracted to politics, and with the 1880 campaign in prospect he went to the Boston Public Library to do research on a speech for General Grant. When the Republican Convention turned to Garfield, Guiteau modified his speech accordingly and began to solicit speaking assignments from Republican leaders in New York. The Republicans were loaded with big-name speakers and had no need for Guiteau, but it is a commentary that he was able to gain access to Chester A. Arthur as many as ten times during the campaign. So Guiteau idled his time away at the Republican headquarters at the Fifth Avenue Hotel, handing out copies of his speech (which he had entitled "Garfield and Hancock") and discussing his job prospects in the event of a Republican victory.

As soon as the gubernatorial elections in Ohio and Indiana pointed to a Republican triumph, Guiteau sent Garfield a copy of his speech, indicating in an accompanying letter that he was a candidate for the Vienna consulate and that he would soon be marrying a wealthy woman who would enable him to represent his country in a suitable style. Guiteau received no reply, but this did not prevent him from journeying to Washington on the day following Garfield's inauguration to join the horde of office seekers who besieged the new president. Amazingly, he even gained entrée to Garfield during that first, frantic week. Guiteau told at his trial how "as soon as General Garfield was at leisure, I stepped up to him and gave him my speech. Of course, he recognized me at once. . . . I told him that I was an applicant for the Paris [sic] consulship. . . . and I left him reading the speech and retired. This is the only interview I ever had with General Garfield on the subject." [5]

When a White House clerk told Guiteau that his appointment had been referred to the State Department, the runaround began. In the absence of any positive developments Guiteau barraged Garfield, Blaine, and anyone else within range with letters and copies of his speech. He attempted naïvely to drive a wedge between the president and Blaine, hinting in letters to each that he was prepared to support the one against the other. In Washington as elsewhere, Guiteau operated out of a succession of boardinghouses, and he thought nothing of listing the president and secretary of state as references. But Guiteau was wearing out his welcome, and running out of boardinghouses. When, in mid-May, he accosted Blaine at the State Department about his pet subject, the secretary grew livid. "Never speak to me again about the Paris consulship," Blaine exploded, but he listened as Guiteau explained that Garfield was certain to want a new man in Paris. "Well, if he will. . . ." Blaine began, trailing off into something noncommittal. To his dying day, Blaine feared that his temporizing with Guiteau may have caused him to place the blame for his misfortunes on the president.

It was several days after this that Guiteau first had the idea of murdering the president:

> I retired about eight o'clock . . . greatly depressed in mind and spirit from the political situation, and I should say it was about half-past eight, before I had gone to sleep, when an impression came over my mind like a flash that if the President was out of the way, this whole thing would be solved and everything would go well. That is the first impression I had with reference to removing the President.[6]

Guiteau claimed to have resisted his "impression," only to have it keep returning, fed by various editorials which saw in the Robertson controversy indications of the imminent collapse of the Republican party. Having slavishly waited on Blaine over the past few weeks, Guiteau next wrote a letter to the president—his last —urging Garfield to demand Blaine's resignation; he closed with a warning that "otherwise you and the Republican Party will

come to grief." Like its predecessors this letter brought no response, and it is doubtful whether Garfield ever saw it. By June 1,
Garfield's fate was sealed, as Guiteau's "impression" pressed on
him:

> All that time, I was kept horrified. Kept throwing it off.
> . . . But it kept growing upon me, pressing me, goading me,
> so, as a matter of fact, at the end of two weeks my mind was
> thoroughly fixed as to the necessity for the President's removal
> and the divinity of the inspiration. I never had the slightest
> doubt as to the divinity of the inspiration from the first of
> June.[7]

On June 6, Guiteau visited O'Meara's Gun Shop at Fifteenth
and F Streets and asked to see a heavy revolver displayed in the
window, a .44 caliber British Bulldog with a white bone handle.
Guiteau was short on cash and did not buy it that day, but after
borrowing money from a cousin he paid O'Meara ten dollars for
the pistol, a box of cartridges, and a penknife. He could have
saved a dollar by selecting the same model pistol with a wooden
handle but, Guiteau testified, he chose the more expensive model
because it would show to better advantage in a museum.

The assassin then began a bizarre period of four weeks in
which he alternated between target practice along the Potomac
and actual stalking of the president on the streets of Washington.
When Garfield attended services at the National City Christian
Church on June 12, Guiteau stood at the rear of the congregation.
He decided not to shoot then for fear of injuring a bystander.
Six days later, when he read that the president would be accompanying his wife to Elberon, Guiteau decided that he would shoot
him at the railroad depot. In what amounted to a rehearsal for
July 2, Guiteau went to the station and actually approached his
victim. But he had trouble getting up his nerve, and did not
shoot; later he would testify that he had held back out of sympathy for Mrs. Garfield. On July 1, Guiteau followed the president
to Blaine's house on Fifteenth Street, but again his nerve failed
him. ("It was a very hot and sultry night, and I felt tired and wearied by the heat, so nothing was done about it then.")

On the following morning Guiteau arose at five in his room

at Riggs House, took a short stroll around the park, and had breakfast at seven. He then went up to his room and wrote two letters. In one of them he gave his incredible rationale for the assassination:

Washington, July 2, 1881

To The White House:

The President's tragic death was a sad necessity, but it will unite the Republican party and save the Republic. Life is a fleeting dream, and it matters little when one goes. A human life is of small value. During the war thousands of brave boys went down without a tear.

I presume the President was a Christian and that he will be happier in Paradise than here.

It will be no worse for Mrs. Garfield, dear soul, to part with her husband this way than by natural death. He is liable to go at any time any way.

I had no ill-will toward the President.

His death was a political necessity.

I am a lawyer, theologian and politician.

I am a stalwart of the stalwarts.

I was with General Grant and the rest of our men in New York during the canvass.

I have some papers for the press which I shall leave with Byron Andrews [correspondent of the *Inter-Ocean*] and his co-journalists, at 1420 N.Y. Ave., where all the reporters can see them.

I am going to the jail.

Charles Guiteau [8]

At nine o'clock Guiteau, like Garfield, took a carriage for the station. Half an hour later he fired his two shots and told Patrolman Kearney and his partner, "I am a Stalwart and Arthur is president now!"

For two days, Garfield's life hung in the balance. The crowds which milled about the White House gates alternated between hope and despair, and the ambiguous bulletins issued by the president's physicians did little more than add to the rumors. By Monday, expressions of regret were pouring in from all over the world. Queen Victoria sent a telegram to Mrs. Garfield, and Prime Minister Gladstone a personal letter. The emperors of

Russia, Austria, and Germany sent messages, as did the kings of Denmark, Norway, Sweden, Belgium, Portugal, Italy, and Spain. On July 5, the patient took a turn for the better. He was able to retain food for the first time since the shooting, and no longer complained of pains in his legs. His physicians made a fairly complete examination of the wound and concluded—erroneously as it turned out—that the bullet, after entering the small of the back to the right of the spinal column, had deflected downward, penetrated the peritoneal cavity, and lodged in the front wall of the abdomen. In an era before antibiotics, the greatest danger to the president, once he survived the initial shock, was from blood poisoning. But in the absence of accurate information as to the location of the bullet, his surgeons were reluctant to probe for it, and the treatment which they were able to provide became little more than intensive nursing care.

From Elberon, Mrs. Garfield rushed back to Washington by special train. Once the initial crisis was passed, the White House settled into a routine. The sick room was No. 18, a corner room on the south side of the second floor overlooking the Potomac. It also overlooked the city's mosquito-laden canal, however, and concern over the president's contracting malaria led his doctors to give him regular doses of quinine. Unable to do much else for their patient, the attending physicians insisted on almost complete quiet in the sick room. Crete, sometimes accompanied by one of the children, usually visited once in the morning and again in the afternoon. Others who had some entrée to the patient included Swaim, Stanley-Brown, and Rockwell, and the cabinet wives were allowed to visit in rotation and to assist in fanning the patient. Although the doctors were able to impose silence, the heat proved a more difficult problem. An initial attempt to cool the room by forcing air through moistened sheets proved ineffective. Not until mid-July, after the basement of the White House had been turned into a machine room, were Navy engineers able to come up with a forced-air system which proved capable of keeping the room's temperature in the upper seventies on all except the hottest days.

On the apparent assumption that one could not have too many physicians for so distinguished a patient, Garfield was never

271

attended by fewer than three doctors. A few days after the assault, Garfield selected Dr. D. W. Bliss to take charge of his case, and to choose his associates. Bliss was about sixty years old, and had compensated for partial baldness with a pair of flowing gray sideburns. He was a competent physician and a member of the District Board of Health, but his garrulousness and sense of self-importance would become increasingly embarrassing to the president's family as time went on.

Bliss chose three other doctors to assist him. One was the surgeon general of the army, Joseph K. Barnes, who had assisted in treating Lincoln after Booth's assault. Bliss also chose another Army physician, Dr. J. J. Woodward. His third choice among local physicians was Dr. Robert Reyburn, a prominent surgeon and teacher of medicine. Bliss shortly requested the services of two out-of-town specialists in internal medicine, Dr. D. Hayes Agnew of Philadelphia and Dr. Frank H. Hamilton of New York. Bliss was in almost constant attendance upon the president, but the supporting cast changed throughout the long summer. As time went on, Crete brought in two of the Garfield family doctors, the president's cousin, Silas Boynton, and a female homeopath, Dr. Susan Edson of Cleveland. It was all very much a committee operation, and one can only conjecture what might have occurred had Garfield's case required any controversial decisions on the part of his attending physicians.

Throughout his long illness Garfield demonstrated a fortitude which won the admiration of all who saw him. He constantly ran some degree of fever, and was never entirely free from discomfort, but he was generally able to sleep with the aid of small doses of morphine. Once he weathered the first two or three days, Garfield maintained a philosophical and even good-humored view of his situation. In an apparent allusion to Grant's letter to Senator Jones, Garfield remarked to his attendant on one occasion, "I wish that I could get up on my feet; I would like to see whether I have any backbone left or not." About a week after the shooting, Garfield inquired if there had been any word from Jeremiah Black. One of the doctors recalled that Black had sent one of the first telegrams received after the shooting and subsequently had called in person at the White House. The president was clearly touched, commenting with some emotion, "That almost pays for this." [9]

By any reasonable standard Garfield was disabled in terms of the performance of his duties, and Guiteau's assault might well have produced a constitutional mechanism for dealing with the question of presidential disability. In actual fact, the combination of Arthur's recent opposition to Garfield, together with Guiteau's declared intent of putting Arthur in the White House, made everyone loathe to come to grips with the problem. When the vice president paid his respects at the White House on one occasion, the members of Garfield's cabinet who were present were barely civil. In part to forestall the question of disability, Blaine at one time presented Garfield with an extradition paper to sign. At it turned out, this was Garfield's only official act performed after the shooting.

Arthur played his difficult role with circumspection, spending much of his time in New York rather than Washington and playing no part in the speculation as to the degree of the president's disability. Grant, however, was more forthcoming. He was widely quoted as telling a reporter in Chicago that Garfield was "clearly disabled," but he conceded that the Constitution did not specify how this determination should be made. Arthur, he declared, could hardly take the initiative on his own. Grant felt that the president's physicians should attest to the cabinet as to his incapacity, and that the cabinet should then invite Arthur to act as president.[10] In the end nothing was done, in part because there were no problems facing the country in that summer of 1881 which could not be either deferred or handled within the various departments.

One of the most remarkable aspects of Garfield's illness was the persistence on the part of his physicians in issuing optimistic, often misleading, bulletins about his condition. From July 5 until the 23rd, the patient did appear to be recovering, although the danger of infection was still manifestly great. From the 23rd on, however, it was evident that the wound was not draining properly and that secondary areas of infection had developed. Nevertheless, the medical bulletins—generally issued three times a day— exuded good cheer, while providing little hard information beyond the patient's temperature, pulse, and respiration. On top of this, the loquacious Bliss was fond of granting press interviews. As late as August 23, by which time the president had wasted away from some 210 pounds at the time of the shooting to 135 pounds, Bliss had the following dialogue with a reporter from the Associated Press:

> 'How is the President doing today?'
> 'He is doing nicely.'
> 'How much food has he swallowed since last morning?'
> 'He has had about 18 ounces and a half of liquid nourishment since one o'clock last night, not including the enemata.'
> 'Has there been any change in the septic condition of the blood?'
> 'I think there are evidences that the septic condition is passing off.' [11]

If Bliss's interviews were less than candid, neither were they in particularly good taste. When a reporter from the *Washington Star* commented in late August that "some people say that prayer has saved the President," Bliss replied, "They may think so. In my opinion it was whiskey. I have received a number of letters today abusing me for using stimulants."

Not everyone was as sanguine as Bliss. After Burke Hinsdale visited the White House in late July he sent a wire to friends in Cleveland warning that the president was by no means out of danger, and adding, "I do not think it wise for people to settle down to a belief that he is." In New York, Cyrus W. Field proposed a fund for Mrs. Garfield in the event of the president's death, and subscribed himself for $25,000. When Garfield was told of this he was deeply moved. "How kind and thoughtful," he told Bliss. "What a generous people!" [12]

In point of fact, the outpouring of sentiment for the president and his family was remarkable for one whose political career had generated so much abuse. Part of this was the result of admiration for the patient's courage and good cheer. Partly it was recognition of the tragedy in which Garfield had risen so far, only to spend so brief a time at the summit of his career. In any case, the fallen president was someone in whom the country took pride;

the *New York Times* commented that "every heart felt a tender pride in hearing that the wounded and possibly dying President had preserved the bearing of a soldier in the presence of peril and pain as great as though he had fallen on the battlefield." One Ziba H. Potter, an Ithaca, New York attorney who knew Garfield only indirectly, poured out his grief to a friend in Paris:

> By advices rec'd from Washington this morning I am pained to inform you that our beloved President will probably die. . . . If he dies, my Country will lose one of its brightest and most illustrious young men and one whose place can never be filled. To say that all the people love him, North and South, East and West, but feebly expresses the true state of public devotion.[13]

Two political casualties of this outburst of affection were Conkling and Platt. Faced with a widespread popular revulsion against political spoilsmen, the two Stalwarts went down to a rousing defeat in their bid for re-election as the Albany legislature chose in their place two friends of the administration. It was several days before Garfield heard of this development, and when he did the president was characteristically generous. "I am glad it is over," he told Bliss. "I am sorry for Conkling. He has made a great mistake in my judgment. I will offer him any favor he may ask, or any appointment he may desire." [14]

One person among many who flooded the White House with advice and tenders of assistance was the inventor of the telephone, Alexander Graham Bell. At a time when public attention centered on the location of the bullet, Bell set out to see if he could not develop a mechanism which would locate the bullet and permit its removal. At the end of July Bell declared himself ready, although Garfield's surgeons had by that time given up any idea of probing for the bullet, not only because of the president's weakened condition but because the main threat of infection was recognized as coming from the track of the bullet rather than from the ball itself. Nevertheless, there was sentiment for trying out Bell's device, an "induction balance" which proported to locate metal objects on a principle not unlike that of a twentieth-century mine detector. The experiment was carried out on August 1, to the patient's intense interest. Bell's tentative (and erroneous) conclusion supported the surgeons' view that the ball had lodged near the front wall of the abdomen. Bell conceded, however, that his readings could be influenced by the shape of the bullet, and he concluded that in the absence of knowledge as to the shape of the bullet its location could not be pinpointed with accuracy.

By the latter half of August it was evident to all except the most determined optimists that the fight was a losing one. The president's digestion, a source of difficulty even in good health, all but collapsed as he underwent a recurrence of his earlier sieges of nausea. He developed an infection of the parotid gland which, although lanced by the surgeons, left one side of his face partly paralyzed. On August 25, General Sherman wrote to his brother that the president's condition was "absolutely critical," that he was so weak as to be unable to survive another relapse. The following day brought a cautious admission that the patient was at times delirious. Possibly to scotch the more extreme rumors, Rockwell told a reporter on the 26th that Garfield was "sometimes a little incoherent" on awakening, but he added that "at all other times his mind is as clear as ever." [15]

Garfield for his part longed for a change of scene. The doctors were hesitant, for each crisis and recovery had left the patient weaker and more wasted than before. But in the end logic gave way to sentiment, and it was agreed that the president could be moved to Elberon where, all hoped, he would benefit from the therapeutic effects long attributed to the sea air. The result was a major logistical operation. First, the White House accepted the offer of an Englishman, Charles G. Franklyn, for the use of his twenty-room residence on the beach at Elberon. Then Wayne MacVeagh made arrangements with the Pennsylvania Railroad for a special train and for the laying of a special track from the main line to the Franklyn cottage. Working through the nights in the glare of engine headlights, work crews completed the 3,200-foot spur in time for the move, scheduled for September 6.

The evacuation came none too soon, for a new heat wave settled on the Capital. Blaine, who each day summarized the medical bulletins for the benefit of American diplomatic representatives abroad, wired James Russell Lowell in London that "this has been the hottest day of the season, and the heat has told upon the President." On the morning of the 6th, arrangements for his removal were complete. The crowds which still gathered around the bulletin board at the Pennsylvania Avenue gate saw a large American Express wagon pull into the grounds and stop under the portico. At six there was a stir as the president was borne out of the vestibule on a stretcher and carried up a wooden ramp into the wagon. As the vehicle left the grounds, all eyes strained for a look at the patient. Those who could see him were divided in their reaction; the bedclothes sufficiently disguised Garfield's wasted physique that some were encouraged by what they saw.

The crowds along Pennsylvania Avenue were quiet and respectful. At the depot, the same station where he had been struck down two months before, the president was taken onto the special train and placed on a bed designed to minimize the motion of the carriage. Garfield spoke little during the eight-hour trip, for his voice was too weak to be heard above the noise, but on two or three occasions he managed a brief wave to the crowds that lined his route. By three o'clock the Presidential Special was in Elberon, where a fresh retinue of attendants had prepared a room overlooking the sea. The president's eleventh-hour transfer to the shore captured the imagination of the country and gave new hope to many. Special prayer services were held in many parts of the country, and in Cleveland all business was suspended between ten o'clock and noon.

Garfield stood the trip well, a fact which gave rise to one final surge of false optimism. Although no one was yet prepared to say it, the president was clearly dying of blood poisoning and was beyond the reach of either the sea air or the ministrations of his physicians. Yet the bulletins continued to focus on his pulse and respiration, to the exclusion of more relevant symptoms. On September 8, a reporter remarked to Bliss concerning his apparent good cheer. "I should think I was," the physician replied, "why the man is convalescent!" When the reporter expressed surprise Bliss repeated his statement, asking a colleague, Dr. Hamilton, for corroboration. Dr. Hamilton nodded his agreement.[16]

At Elberon Garfield did experience one of his periodic rallies. Even the level-headed MacVeagh was encouraged, although he was fully aware of the long odds against recovery. On September 11, however, Garfield took another turn for the worse, and it was ascertained that he had developed pneumonia in the right lung. This was duly minimized in the evening bulletin, although Silas Boynton took a serious view, ascribing the lung condition to blood poisoning. Alone among the attending physicians, Boynton subsequently made no effort to disguise the patient's deteriorating condition.

Garfield suffered a chill on the morning of September 19, but by afternoon it had passed. At ten o'clock that evening Bliss joined Swaim in the sick room and took the patient's pulse. In reply to Swaim's query he observed that the pulse was not as strong as that afternoon but was still "very good." Bliss left the room and moments later Garfield awakened. The president recognized his old friend Swaim, and stirred slightly "How it hurts here!" he whispered, pressing his hand to his heart. At Garfield's request Swaim procured a glass of water, and raised the patient's head while he drank. Again he complained of severe pain in his chest, and Swaim applied a cool cloth to his forehead. Then Garfield, with a main artery collapsed and hemorrhaging, raised both arms crying, "Swaim, can't you stop this? Oh, Swaim!" and lost consciousness. Swaim, unable to rouse the patient, called the household. At 10:35 the feeble heartbeat stopped.[17]

Although many persons had come to expect the worst, the news that the president had died was the signal for the greatest outpouring of grief since the death of Lincoln. At no time since the Civil War had the nation been so united in sentiment, and even as preparations were made for moving the remains to Washington the very countryside seemed shrouded in black crepe. Newspapers vied with one another in tribute. The New York Times observed that "the silent sick chamber has been for him the greatest arena of his life."

The cabinet gathered at Elberon on the 20th, where they were joined by President Arthur on the following day. The body was brought back to Washington on the 21st, after a team of undertakers had worked through the night to restore the cadaver to a recognizable facsimile of the living man. Those on the funeral train included President Arthur, the Garfield family, the faithful Swaim and Rockwell, and, ironically, Ulysses S. Grant. For the first time the body of a deceased president was returned to lie in the rotunda of the Capitol rather than in the White House, a fitting tribute to Garfield's years of service in the House. The casket lay in state for two days and was viewed by more than 100,000 people. Following a service in the rotunda on September 23, the casket went by special train to Cleveland, which had been chosen by the family as the place for interment.

The bells tolled as the train passed through Baltimore and Pittsburgh, great industrial cities whose growth almost symbolized the policies of Garfield's Republican party. They tolled anew as the train passed slowly across villages and farms, where silent crowds bared their heads as they paid last respects. When someone offered to lower the blinds in order that Mrs. Garfield could have more privacy, Crete demurred, saying that she wished to see the people who had come to honor her husband.

The public funeral in Cleveland was in the nature of a homecoming. Burke Hinsdale was there; so too were Harry Rhodes, Jacob Cox, and John Sherman. The cabinet was in attendance, led by a Blaine who seemingly could not keep himself in fresh handkerchiefs. There were contingents from the Forty-second Ohio and from the Army of the Cumberland, as well as justices of the Supreme Court, delegations from both Houses of Congress, and honor guards from the Army and Navy. Following a huge ceremony in downtown Cleveland, the cortege made its way to Lakeview Cemetery. There Harrison Jones, the wartime chaplain of the Forty-second Ohio, delivered the graveside address, and Hinsdale offered the prayer. A stiff breeze sprang up from the lake as a choir intoned Garfield's favorite hymn, "Ho! Reapers of Life's Harvest." The door of the vault was ordered closed, and an honor guard took up its vigil. Dusk was falling as the great multitude made its way the 3 miles back to Cleveland, walking briskly in the autumn rain.

EPILOGUE

Farewell! the leaf-strewn earth enfolds
Our stay, our pride, our hopes, our fears;
And autumn's golden sun beholds
A nation bowed, a world in tears.

—Oliver Wendell Holmes,
"After the Burial"

———◆———

The services at Lakeview were only the beginning. Across the country and throughout most of the Western world, memorial services were the order of the day. Argentinians produced a memorial volume, "Sorrow of the People of Buenos Ayres for the Death of General James A. Garfield, Late President of the United States." In Liverpool, where Garfield had been an eager tourist in 1869, the Conservative Club was draped in black. But it was in Garfield's own America that a sentimental people reacted most strongly. Party lines dissolved in a sense of common loss, and there was a tacit understanding that Americans were more united in their grief than at any time since the Civil War.

Partially because of this recognition, not even the death of Lincoln brought about a greater outpouring of grief than that of Garfield. Lincoln's martyrdom had come at the end of a bloody conflict, at a time when the country was almost numb to the thought of death. The assassination of Garfield seemed all the more poignant for having taken place in broad daylight, in time of peace, and at a time when expectations for his administration were at a zenith. By the end of the year, few American households

280

were without a glass etching of the martyred president, a lithograph of Garfield and his family, or any of a score of illustrations showing the shooting and its sequel. "Israel's grief for Samuel," observed one Presbyterian clergyman, "was only a small thing compared with America's grief for Garfield. The land of Canaan was not as large as the state of New Jersey." [1]

The last of the official observances took place on February 27, 1882, when President Arthur, both Houses of Congress and distinguished guests gathered in the Capitol to hear James G. Blaine deliver a eulogy of his friend and former chief. It was a potentially awkward situation; the mere fact that the new president was in the audience made the eulogist's task a difficult one. Blaine was himself deeply moved by the occasion, and by having been chosen to deliver the eulogy. His wife told of how long her husband had worked over his speech, writing on one occasion how "for the second time this morning I see him taking . . . a fresh pocket-handkerchief with which he vainly tries to hide his tears." [2]

The result was a classic eulogy, which a generation of schoolboys would in time learn to quote in part or *in toto*. To his attentive audience Blaine recalled his association with Garfield, lauded his qualities as a public servant, and recounted with great restraint the political confrontation which led up to the assassination. Finally, he told of the despairing hope that the president's life might be saved by a change of scene to Elberon.

Gently, silently, the love of a great people bore the pale sufferer to the longed-for healing of the sea, to live or die as God should will, within sight of its heaving billows, within sound of its manifold voices. With wan, fevered face tenderly lifted to the cooling breeze, he looked out wistfully upon the ocean's changing wonders; on its far sails whitening in the morning light; on its restless waves, rolling shoreward to break and die beneath the noonday sun; on the red clouds of evening arching low to the horizon; on the serene and shining pathway of the stars. Let us think that his dying eyes read a mystic meaning which only the rapt and parting soul may know. Let us believe that in the silence of the receding world he heard the great waves breaking on a farther shore, and felt already upon his wasted brow the breath of the eternal morning.[3]

Gradually, public interest shifted from the fallen leader to two trials which were part of his legacy. One of these grew out of the indictment of Dorsey, Brady, and six other Post Office officials for conspiracy to defraud the government in connection with the "star routes." All eight pleaded not guilty and, with the backstage assistance of Roscoe Conkling, carried on a spirited defense. Confessions were recanted, government witnesses disappeared, and charges of jury tampering were freely made by both sides. In the end, the jury stood at 10 to 2 for the conviction of Brady and 9 to 3 to convict Dorsey. In the absence of agreement, however, the government was obliged to seek a new trial.

The second trial, in September 1882, was a repeat of the first. Following a wild three weeks of hearings, "with appeals to patriotism, denunciation of rebels, the intimidation of state's witnesses, and testimonials by cabinet members favorable to the defendants," [4] the jury brought in a verdict of not guilty. Dorsey eventually retired to California where he lived until 1916, protesting his innocence and ascribing his difficulties to the enmity of Wayne MacVeagh and Thomas James.

But the "star route" trials were of minor interest compared to the trial of Garfield's assassin. Although the trial did not begin until November 14, nearly two months after Garfield's death, public interest was at a high pitch. Even before the trial began Guiteau was himself the target of one abortive assassination attempt; during the hearings he would be the target of another. Considering the depth of feeling which his shots had inspired, however, Guiteau had as fair a trial as one could expect.

Guiteau's defense was based on a plea of insanity, and a century later his performance in court alone might have brought an acquittal. Guiteau regularly threw the court into an uproar with impromptu speeches and asides; he once interrupted the proceedings to suggest that members of the jury be taken out for walks to improve their digestion. On another occasion he warned, "I expect an act of God that will blow this court and jury out of this window if it is necessary." [5] But apart from the popular feeling which Guiteau had aroused, the defendant was handicapped by the fact that he objected to being characterized as insane, and he periodically denounced his chief counsel, brother-in-law George

Scoville, for attempting to document his defense. Judge Walter Cox did little to restrain Guiteau's outbursts, on the grounds that since the defendant's mental condition was the central issue the jury should have every opportunity to view it first hand. But here again Guiteau was his own worst enemy; he undercut his defense by telling a government psychiatrist that he knew that if he could convince a jury of his belief that the shooting had been divinely inspired that he would not be convicted.

Guiteau was not only an exhibitionist in court but an indefatigable letter writer. On the day after Garfield died he dropped a note to President Arthur:

> My inspiration is a God send to you and I presume that you appreciate it. It raises you from $8,000 to $50,000 per year. It raises you from a political cypher to the President of the United States with all its power and honors. . . . Never think of Garfield's removal as murder. It was an act of God, resulting from a political necessity for which he was responsible.

Guiteau then listed a number of names as possibilities for Arthur's cabinet, adding, "I took the responsibility of putting you and Senator Conkling into position and feel I have a right to make these suggestions." [6]

On the face of it, the task of proving Guiteau insane would not appear to have been insurmountable. But apart from the fact that they were confronted with an inflamed public opinion, and apart from lapses such as Guiteau's remark to the psychiatrist, Guiteau's attorneys had their problems. In the first place, the yardstick for insanity in the 1880s was the so-called M'Naghten rule, first laid down in England in 1843, which held that a defendant was to be considered responsible if he was aware of the nature of his act and knew it to be forbidden by law. Moreover, although Americans of that day had a fairly high tolerance for eccentric behavior, they were not disposed to regard such behavior as making a man immune from the law.[7]

As the trial drew to a close, Guiteau asked and received permission to address the jury. The Lord had chosen him to remove the president, he said, and nothing that one does in response to divine command can violate any law. In any case, he maintained, nearly everyone was happy over the change of administrations. Finally, Guiteau maintained, with somewhat excessive self-assurance, "to hang a man in my mental condition would be a lasting disgrace to the American people." After predicting a terrible day of reckoning if he were to be executed, Guiteau sang a portion of "John Brown's Body," recited the remainder, and subsided.[8]

For all his threats, Guiteau was found guilty as charged on January 5, 1882. The Supreme Court denied a writ of habeas corpus, and President Arthur declined to grant a reprieve. The date of execution was set for June 30. Guiteau continued his letter writing to the end; he helped to meet legal expenses by selling his autograph for one dollar a card. Only gradually did he come to realize that no pardon would be forthcoming. On June 30, at twelve noon, he was led to the scaffold where some 250 persons, some of whom had paid as much as $300 for admission, had gathered for the day's spectacle. Guiteau did not disappoint them. From the scaffold he read first from the tenth chapter of Matthew ("And fear not them that kill the body but are not able to kill the soul"), but after fourteen verses he put the Bible aside stating that he had a "pathetic hymn" of his own to read. Declaiming in an artificially high-pitched voice, Guiteau gave his valedictory:

> I am going to the Lordy, I am so glad,
> I am going to the Lordy, I am so glad,
>   I am going to the Lordy,
> Glory hallelujah! Glory hallelujah!
>   I am going to the Lordy.
> I love the Lordy with all my soul,
>   Glory hallelujah!
> And that is the reason I am going to the Lord,
>   Glory hallelujah! Glory hallelujah!
>   I am going to the Lord.
> I saved my party and my land,
>   Glory hallelujah!
> But they have murdered me for it,
> And that is the reason I am going to the Lordy,
> Glory hallelujah! Glory hallelujah! . . .[9]

There was another verse, and then silence. The executioner adjusted the hood, and the trap was sprung.

EPILOGUE

Not even Garfield's death could silence the enmity of Charles A. Dana. Only three years before Garfield's election as president, the editor had publicly charged once more that the cause of Rosecrans' removal after Chickamauga had been a private letter from Garfield to Chase. Rosecrans had always accepted Garfield's denials, but with the reservations which, when finally spoken in the heat of the 1880 campaign, had finally ended the friendship between the two men. Rosecrans himself was in the Capitol, as a freshman congressman from California, on the occasion of Blaine's eulogy of Garfield. A somewhat overdrawn allusion by the speaker to the condition in which Garfield had found the Army of the Cumberland triggered a rebuttal by the ever-sensitive Rosecrans, and Dana leaped into the fray. On March 8, 1882, he published in the *Sun* Garfield's July 27, 1863 letter to Chase, in which the Ohioan had poured out his disappointment at Rosecrans' failure to advance. Under the circumstances, a more generous man than Rosecrans might have held his tongue; he knew as well as Garfield the strange malevolence which Dana reserved for those who incurred his displeasure. Instead, Rosecrans characterized Garfield's letter to reporters as "a piece of the blackest treachery," adding, "I had no idea that I was harboring a person capable of such falseness and double-dealing or there would have been a court martial at once." [10]

Curiously, even after printing Garfield's letter of July 27, Dana continued to maintain that there was another letter, written *after* Chickamauga, which brought about Rosecrans' removal. As if to lend credence to this hypothesis, he published a series of Garfield's wartime letters to Chase, obtained from one of Chase's biographers. None of these resembled that which Dana had described, however, and it is evident that the editor was himself confused by the sequence of events in 1863. In retrospect, it appears most likely that Chase and Stanton showed Lincoln Garfield's July 27 letter *after* Chickamauga, employing it as one more reason why Rosecrans should be replaced. By this time Rosecrans had so many enemies in the administration that it is difficult to accept the hypothesis that it was Garfield who brought about his removal. At the same time, one must agree with the conclusion of Rosecrans' biographer that "Garfield had spoken the truth, but not the whole truth." [11] The more honorable course would have been to have coupled his denials of Dana's charges with a more frank explanation of his correspondence with Chase.

There was nothing unusual in a public exchange concerning some forgotten issue of the Civil War, and neither Dana's revelations nor the bizarre details of Guiteau's trial brought any diminution of the luster which surrounded the twentieth president. Instead, the circumstances of the assassination lent impetus to the demand for civil service reform which Garfield, in life, had supported no more than sporadically. Across the country there were public meetings for civil service reform, with Garfield's portrait prominently displayed. Not everyone was carried away by sentiment for the departed; Henry Adams, never a fan of Garfield's, wrote, "The cynical impudence with which the reformers have tried to manufacture an ideal statesman out of the late shady politician beats anything in novel-writing." [12] But popular sentiment concerning the late president ran deeper than either the politicians or the drawing-room dilettantes realized.

In December 1880, Senator George Pendleton of Ohio had introduced a bill to reform the civil service and to end political assessments. Its most conspicuous feature, borrowed from Great Britain, was a provision for competitive examinations in place of the simple "pass exams" which had previously been tendered to those slated for patronage appointments. No action was taken on the Pendleton bill during the turbulent months of the Garfield administration, although Wayne MacVeagh was confident that Garfield's would eventually be a "reform" administration. Even after Garfield's death, when public opinion was clearly aroused, neither party took the lead in pushing the Pendleton bill. Arthur was no reformer, while the Democrats were reluctant to press a bill which might provide tenure to an army of incumbent Republican officeholders. Ignoring demands for reform, Congress took no action on the Pendleton bill and even rejected President Arthur's request for a $25,000 appropriation with which to reactivate the Civil Service Commission.

But signs of a popular revolt were in evidence, and in some quarters they were properly read. In New York, the Democrats chose as their nominee for governor the reform mayor of Buffalo, Grover Cleveland. Another straw in the wind was the 1882 election, which took a heavy toll from among the old guard of both parties. President Arthur was suitably impressed, and in his annual message for 1882 he endorsed the Pendleton bill for the first time. Pendleton himself, who had known and liked Garfield, defended his bill skillfully against those in his own party who thought he should hold off until after the 1884 elections, when the Democrats might have some officeholders of their own. Popular opinion made civil service reform much the same issue that gun-control legislation would become in the 1960s, but in 1882 Congress was itself almost an anti-reform lobby. "We are not legislating on this subject in response to our own judgment," remarked one senator, "but in response to some sort of judgment which has been expressed outside." [13]

Nevertheless, both houses passed the Pendleton bill by substantial majorities and President Arthur signed it into law on January 16, 1883. The first concrete step in the direction of a nonpolitical civil service, the Pendleton bill was something of a memorial to President Garfield. A less sentimental conclusion would be that it demonstrated the effect of an aroused public opinion.

When Crete returned to Mentor following the funeral in Cleveland, she set about her new role with the same fortitude and good sense which she had shown during her husband's illness. The two older boys were off at school, Harry at Williams and James at St. Paul's. The face of the Reserve was changing; John D. Rockefeller's Standard Oil Company was turning Cleveland into one of the great industrial cities of the Middle West. When Garfield's mother finally passed away in 1888, it seemed hard to believe that the Western Reserve which she had known as a young woman had been a virgin wilderness.

In the fall of 1885, the Garfield National Monument Association contracted with a Cleveland firm for a memorial at Lakeview Cemetery. Winner of the architectural competition was George Keller of Hartford, Connecticut. His design called for a circular tower, 180 feet tall, on a square terrace. At the base was a small porch surrounded by bas-reliefs illustrating aspects of Garfield's career. Not much was left to the imagination, and there was some criticism of the panel which portrayed Garfield's horse dropping dead as he reached General Thomas at Snodgrass Hill. But one has the feeling that Garfield himself would have heartily approved his memorial, although he would have been taken aback to learn that it cost $225,000 to build.

Gradually, the generation which recalled the excitement of Garfield's election and the shock of his assassination entered old age, and the twentieth president became but one more statue in the parks of a score of American cities. This bothered Crete, who somehow sensed that the essence of her husband was being lost to posterity. In 1915, three years before her death, she complained to an interviewer that none of Garfield's photographs "suggest at all the way his face lit up in conversation. His face was very responsive, not at all settled or fixed as the photographs invariably suggest." [14] But she took pride in the careers of her children. Among them, Harry went into education, and served for more than a decade as president of Williams College. James became a noted conservationist, and a member of Teddy Roosevelt's cabinet. In one of the first White House romances, Molly eventually married her father's efficient secretary, Joseph Stanley-Brown.

Gradually, Garfield's friends and enemies passed from the scene. Jerry Black survived his young friend by only two years, dying in 1883. Roscoe Conkling never recaptured the political eminence he threw away in 1881; he died in obscurity seven years later, a victim of the great blizzard which struck New York City in the winter of 1888. Some landmarks associated with Garfield's career became victims of the wrecker's ball. In Washington, the Baltimore and Potomac depot gave way to the graceful white dome of the National Art Gallery. In Elberon, the Franklyn cottage was pulled down to make room for a more modern structure, and the painted sign which identified where the Franklyn cottage had stood was relegated to a garage window.

In 1958, one Bruce Frankel, the son of an Asbury Park lawyer, heard about the sign in the garage and about the cottage which had once stood there. Bruce was only eight, but he was interested in American history and concluded that there should be a real marker there. Bruce had collected some $60 from friends and schoolmates when a local monuments manufacturer offered to provide a 3-foot marker free of charge. In 1962 the monument was unveiled. President Kennedy sent a message, and Bruce Frankel shared the limelight with two presidents. It seemed somehow appropriate that Garfield should be the subject of this youthful persistence, a persistence which so recalled his own efforts to get a start in life. As Garfield himself had remarked, "there is nothing . . . in this world so inspiring as the possibilities that lie locked up in the head and breast of a young man." [15]

Appendix A

"A Century of Congress"

by James A. Garfield *

———◆———

Note: Garfield's most ambitious exposition concerning the role of Congress in the American political system was written for Atlantic *magazine in 1877. As was his habit, Garfield put into it a great deal of research, and sought to trace the origins of Congress to the earliest English settlements in North America. The following condensation omits much of the strictly historical material, but retains in its entirety the final section in which Garfield discusses the workings of the Congress which he knew so well.*

We have seen the close of our memorial year, during which societies, the States, and the nation have been reviewing the completed century and forecasting the character of that which has just begun.

Our people have been tracing the footprints of the fathers along the many paths which united to form the great highway whereon forty-four millions of Americans are now marching. If we would profit by the great lessons of the centennial year, we must study thoughtfully and reverently the elements and forces that have made the republic what it is, and which will in a great measure shape and direct its future.

No study of these themes can lead to a just view of our institutions which does not include within its range a survey of the history and functions of the American Congress. Indeed, the history of liberty

* *Atlantic*, vol. XL, No. 237, July 1877.

and union in this country, as developed by the men of 1776 and maintained by their successors, is inseparably connected with the history of the national legislature. Nor can they be separated in the future. The Union and the Congress must share the same fate. They must rise or fall together.

The germ of our political institutions, the primary cell from which they were evolved, was the New England town; and the vital force, the informing soul, of the town was the town-meeting, which for all local concerns was king, lords, and commons in one. It was the training-school in which our fathers learned the science and the art of self-government, the school which has made us the most parliamentary people on the globe. . . .

In the long line of those who have occupied seats in Congress, we should see, here and there, rising above the undistinguished mass, the figures of those great men whose lives and labors have made their country illustrious, and whose influence upon its destiny will be felt for ages to come. We should see that group of great statesmen whom the last war with England brought to public notice, among whom were Ames and Randolph, Clay and Webster, Calhoun and Benton, Wright and Prentiss, making their era famous by their statesmanship, and creating and destroying political parties by their fierce antagonisms. We should see the folly and barbarism of the so-called code of honor destroying noble men in the fatal meadow of Bladensburg. We should see the spirit of liberty awaking the conscience of the nation to the sin and danger of slavery, whose advocates had inherited and kept alive the old anarchic spirit of disunion. We should trace the progress of that great struggle from the days when John Quincy Adams stood in the House of Representatives, like a lion at bay, defending the sacred right of petition; when, after his death, Joshua R. Giddings continued the good fight, standing at his post for twenty years, his white locks, like the plume of Henry of Navarre, always showing where the battle for freedom raged most fiercely; when his small band in Congress, reinforced by Hale and Sumner, Wade and Chase, Lovejoy and Stevens, continued the struggle amid the most turbulent scenes; when daggers were brandished and pistols were drawn in the halls of Congress; and later, when, one by one, the senators and representatives of eleven States, breathing defiance and uttering maledictions upon the Union, resigned their seats and left the Capitol to take up arms against their country. We should see the Congress of a people long unused to war, when confronted by a supreme danger, raising, equipping, and supporting an army greater than all the armies of Napoleon and Wellington combined; meeting the most difficult questions of international and constitutional law; and, by new forms of taxation, raising a revenue which, in one year of the war, amounted to more than all the national taxes collected during the first half century of the government. We should see them so amending the constitution as to strengthen the safeguards of the Union and insure universal liberty and universal suffrage, and restoring to their places in the Union the eleven States whose governments, founded on secession, fell into instant ruin when the Rebellion collapsed; and we should see them, even when the danger of destruction seemed greatest, voting the largest sum of money ever appropriated by one act, to unite the East and the West, the Atlantic and the Pacific coasts, by a material bond of social, commercial, and political union.

In this review we should see courage and cowardice, patriotism and selfishness, far-sighted wisdom and short-sighted folly joining in a struggle always desperate and sometimes doubtful; and yet, out of all this turmoil and fierce strife we should see the Union slowly but surely rising, with greater strength and brighter lustre, to a higher place among the nations.

Congress has always been and must always be the theatre of contending opinions; the forum where the opposing forces of political philosophy meet to measure their strength; where the public good must meet the assaults of local and sectional interests; in a word, the appointed place where the nation seeks to utter its thought and register its will.

CONGRESS AND THE EXECUTIVE

This brings me to consider the present relations of Congress to the other great departments of the government, and to the people. The limits of this article will permit no more than a glance at a few principal heads of inquiry.

In the main, the balance of powers so admirably adjusted and distributed among the three great departments of the government have been safely preserved. It was the purpose of our fathers to lodge absolute power nowhere; to leave each department independent within its own sphere; yet, in every case, responsible for the exercise of its discretion. But some dangerous innovations have been made.

And first, the appointing power of the president has been seriously encroached upon by Congress, or rather by the members of Congress. Curiously enough, this encroachment originated in the act of the chief executive himself. The fierce popular hatred of the federal party, which resulted in the elevation of Jefferson to the presidency, led that officer to set the first example of removing men from office on account of political opinions. For political causes alone he removed a considerable number of officers who had recently been appointed by President Adams, and thus set the pernicious example. His immediate successors made only a few removals for political reasons. But Jackson made his political opponents who were in office feel the full weight of his executive hand. From that time forward, the civil offices of the government became the prizes for which political parties strove; and twenty-five years ago, the corrupting doctrine that "to the victors belong the spoils" was shamelessly announced as an article of political faith and practice. It is hardly possible to state with adequate force the noxious influence of this doctrine. It was bad enough when the federal officers numbered no more than eight or ten thousand; but now, when the growth of the country, and the great increase in the number of public offices, occasioned by the late war, have swelled the civil list to more than eighty thousand, and to the ordinary motives for political strife this vast patronage is offered as a reward to the victorious party, the magnitude of the evil can hardly be measured. The public mind has, by degrees, drifted into an acceptance of this doctrine; and thus an election has become a fierce, selfish struggle between the "ins" and the "outs," the one striving to keep and the other to gain the prize of office. It is not possible for any president to select, with any degree of intelligence, so vast an army of office-holders without the aid of men who are acquainted with the people of the various sections of the country. And thus it has become the habit of presidents to make most of their appointments on the recommendation of members of Congress. During the last twenty-five years, it has been understood, by the Congress and the people, that offices are to be obtained by the aid of senators and representatives, who thus become the dispensers, sometimes the brokers of patronage. The members of state legislatures who choose a senator, and the district electors who choose a representative, look to the man of their choice for appointments to office. Thus, from the president downward, through all the grades of official authority, to the electors themselves, civil office becomes a vast corrupting power, to be used in running the machine of party politics.

This evil has been greatly aggravated by the passage of the Tenure of Office Act, of 1867, whose object was to restrain President Johnson from making removals for political cause. But it has virtually resulted in the usurpation, by the senate, of a large share of the appointing power. The president can remove no officer without the consent of the senate; and such consent is not often given, unless the appointment of the successor nominated to fill the proposed vacancy is agreeable to the senator in whose State the appointee resides. Thus, it has happened that a policy, inaugurated by an early president, has resulted in seriously crippling the just powers of the executive, and has placed in the hands of senators and representatives a power most corrupting and dangerous.

Not the least serious evil resulting from this invasion of the executive functions by members of Congress is the fact that it greatly impairs their own usefulness as legislators. One third of the working hours of senators and representatives is hardly sufficient to meet the demands made upon them in reference to appointments to office. The spirit of that clause of the constitution which shields them from arrest "during their attendance on the session of their respective houses, and in going to and from the same," should also shield them from being arrested from their legislative work, morning, noon, and night, by office-seekers. To sum up in a word: the present system invades the independence of the executive, and makes him less responsible for the character of his appointments; it impairs the efficiency of the legislator by diverting him from his proper sphere of duty, and involving him in the intrigues of aspirants for office; it degrades the civil service itself by destroying the personal independence of those who are appointed; it repels from the service those high and manly qualities which are so necessary to a pure and efficient administration; and finally, it debauches the public mind by holding up public office as the reward of mere party zeal.

To reform this service is one of the highest and most imperative duties of statesmanship. This reform cannot be accomplished without a complete divorce between Congress and the executive in the matter of appointments. It will be a proud day when an administration senator or representative, who is in good standing in his party, can say as Thomas Hughes said, during his recent visit to this country, that though he was on the most intimate terms with the members of his own administration, yet it was not in his power to secure the removal of the humblest clerk in the civil service of his government.

This is not the occasion to discuss the recent enlargement of the jurisdiction of Congress in reference to the election of a president and vice-president by the States. But it cannot be denied that the electoral bill has spread a wide and dangerous field for congressional action. Unless the boundaries of its power shall be restricted by a new amendment of the constitution, we have seen the last of our elections of president on the old plan. The power to decide who has been elected may be so used as to exceed the power of electing.

I have long believed that the official relations between the executive and Congress should be more open and direct. They are now conducted by correspondence with the presiding officers of the two houses, by consultation with committees, or by private interviews with individual members. This frequently leads to misunderstandings and may lead to corrupt combinations. It would be far better for both departments if the members of the cabinet were permitted to sit in Congress and participate in the debates on measures relating to their several departments,—but, of course, without a vote. This would tend to secure the ablest men for the chief executive offices; it would bring the policy of the administration into the fullest publicity by giving both parties ample opportunity for criticism and defense.

CONGRESS OVERBURDENED

As a result of the great growth of the country and of the new legislation arising from the late war, Congress is greatly overloaded with work. It is safe to say that the business which now annually claims the attention of Congress is tenfold more complex and burdensome than it was forty years ago. For example: the twelve annual appropriation bills, with their numerous details, now consume two thirds of each short session of the house. Forty years ago, when the appropriations were made more in block, one week was sufficient for the work. The vast extent of our country, the increasing number of States and Territories, the legislation necessary to regulate our mineral lands, to manage our complex systems of internal revenue, banking, currency, and expenditure, have so increased the work of Congress that no man can ever read the bills and the official reports relating to current legislation; much less can he qualify himself for intelligent action upon them. As a necessary consequence, the real work of legislation is done by the committees; and their work must be accepted or rejected without full knowledge of its merits. This fact alone renders leadership in Congress, in the old sense of the word, impossible. For many years we have had the leadership of committees and chairmen of committees; but no one man can any more be the leader of all the legislation of the senate or of the house than one lawyer or one physician can now be foremost in all the departments of law or medicine. The evils of loose legislation resulting from this situation must increase rather than diminish, until a remedy is provided.

John Stuart Mill held that a numerous popular assembly is radically unfit to make good laws, but is the best possible means of getting good laws made. He suggested, as a permanent part of the constitution of a free country, a legislative commission, composed of a few trained men, to draft such laws as the legislature, by general resolutions, shall direct, which draft shall be adopted by the legislature, without change, or returned to the commission to be amended.

Whatever may be thought of Mr. Mill's suggestion, it is clear that some plan must be adopted to relieve Congress from the infinite details of legislation, and to preserve harmony and coherence in our laws.

Another change observable in Congress, as well as in the legislatures of other countries, is the decline of oratory. The press is rendering the orator obsolete. Statistics now furnish the materials upon which the legislator depends; and a column of figures will often demolish a dozen pages of eloquent rhetoric.

Just now, too, the day of sentimental politics is passing away, and the work of Congress is more nearly allied to the business interests of the country and to "the dismal science," as political economy is called by the "practical men" of our time.

CONGRESS AND THE PEOPLE

The legislation of Congress comes much nearer to the daily life of the people than ever before. Twenty years ago, the presence of the national government was not felt by one citizen in a hundred. Except in paying his postage and receiving his mail, the citizen of the interior rarely came in contact with the national authority. Now, he meets it in a thousand ways. Formerly the legislation of Congress referred chiefly to our foreign relations, to indirect taxes, to the government of the army, the navy, and the Territories. Now a vote in Congress may, any day, seriously derange the business affairs of every citizen.

And this leads me to say that now, more than ever before, the people are responsible for the character of their Congress. If that body be ignorant, reckless, and corrupt, it is because the people tolerate ignorance, recklessness, and corruption. If it be intelligent, brave, and pure, it is because the people demand those high qualities to represent them in the national legislature. Congress lives in the blaze of "that fierce light which beats against the throne." The telegraph and the press will to-morrow morning announce at a million breakfast tables what has been said and done in Congress to-day. Now, as always, Congress represents the prevailing opinions and political aspirations of the people. The wildest delusions of paper money, the crudest theories of taxation, the passions and prejudices that find expression in the senate and house, were first believed and discussed at the firesides of the people, on the corners of the streets, and in the caucuses and conventions of political parties.

The most alarming feature of our situation is the fact that so many citizens of high character and solid judgment pay but little attention to the sources of political power, to the selection of those who shall make their laws. The clergy, the faculties of colleges, and many of the leading business men of the community never attend the township caucus, the city primaries, or the county convention; but they allow the less intelligent and the more selfish and corrupt members of the community to make the slates and "run the machine" of politics. They wait until the machine has done its work, and then, in surprise and horror at the ignorance and corruption in public office, sigh for the return of that mythical period called the "better and purer days of the republic." It is precisely this neglect of the first steps in our political processes that has made possible the worst evils of our system. Corrupt and incompetent presidents, judges, and legislators can be removed, but when the fountains of political power are corrupted, when voters themselves become venal and elections fraudulent, there is no remedy except by awakening the public conscience and bringing to bear upon the subject the power of public opinion and the penalties of the law. The practice of buying and selling votes at our popular elections has already gained a foot-hold, though it has not gone as far as in England.

It is mentioned in the recent biography of Lord Macaulay, as a boast, that his three elections to the House of Commons cost him but ten thousand dollars. A hundred years ago, bribery of electors was far more prevalent and shameless in England than it now is.

There have always been, and always will be bad men in all human pursuits. There was a Judas in the college of the apostles, an Arnold in the army of the Revolution, a Burr in our early politics; and they have had successors in all departments of modern life. But it is demonstrable, as a matter of history, that on the whole the standard of public and private morals is higher in the United States at the present time than ever before; that men in public and private stations are held to a more rigid accountability, and that the average moral tone of Congress is higher to-day than at any previous period of our history.

APPENDIX A

It is certainly true that our late war disturbed the established order of society, awakened a reckless spirit of adventure and speculation, and greatly multiplied the opportunities and increased the temptations to evil. The disorganization of the Southern States and the temporary disfranchisement of its leading citizens threw a portion of their representation in Congress, for a short time, into the hands of political adventurers, many of whom used their brief hold on power for personal ends, and thus brought disgrace upon the national legislature. And it is also true that the enlarged sphere of legislation so mingled public duties and private interests that it was not easy to draw the line between them. From that cause also the reputation, and in some cases the character, of public men suffered eclipse. But the earnestness and vigor with which wrong-doing is everywhere punished is a strong guaranty of the purity of those who may hold posts of authority and honor. Indeed, there is now danger in the opposite direction, namely, that criticism may degenerate into mere slander, and put an end to its power for good by being used as the means to assassinate the reputation and destroy the usefulness of honorable men. It is as much the duty of all good men to protect and defend the reputation of worthy public servants as to detect and punish public rascals.

In a word, our national safety demands that the fountains of political power shall be made pure by intelligence, and kept pure by vigilance; that the best citizens shall take heed to the selection and election of the worthiest and most intelligent among them to hold seats in the national legislature; and that when the choice has been made, the continuance of their representative shall depend upon his faithfulness, his ability, and his willingness to work.

CONGRESS AND CULTURE

In Congress, as everywhere else, careful study—thorough, earnest work—is the only sure passport to usefulness and distinction. From its first meeting in 1774 to its last in 1788, three hundred and fifty-four men sat in the Continental Congress. Of these, one hundred and eighteen—one third of the whole number—were college graduates. That third embraced much the largest number of those whose names have come down to us as the great founders of the republic. Since the adoption of the constitution of 1787, six thousand two hundred and eighteen men have held seats in Congress; and among them all, thorough culture and earnest, arduous work have been the leading characteristics of those whose service has been most useful and whose fame has been most enduring. Galloway wrote of Samuel Adams: "He drinks little, eats temperately, thinks much, and is most indefatigable in the pursuit of his objects." This description can still be fittingly applied to all men who deserve and achieve success anywhere, but especially in public life. As a recent writer has said, in discussing the effect of Prussian culture, so we may say of culture in Congress: "The lesson is, that whether you want him for war or peace, there is no way in which you can get so much out of a man as by training, not in pieces, but the whole of him; and that the trained men, other things being equal, are pretty sure, in the long run, to be masters of the world."

Congress must always be the exponent of the political character and culture of the people; and if the next centennial does not find us a great nation, with a great and worthy Congress, it will be because those who represent the enterprise, the culture, and the morality of the nation do not aid in controlling the political forces which are employed to select the men who shall occupy the great places of trust and power.

Appendix B

Garfield's Inaugural Address

March 4, 1881

Fellow-Citizens—We stand to-day upon an eminence which overlooks a hundred years of national life, a century crowded with perils, but crowned with triumphs of liberty and love. Before continuing the onward march let us pause on this height for a moment to strengthen our faith and renew our hope by a glance at the pathway along which our people have traveled.

It is now three days more than a hundred years since the adoption of the first written Constitution of the United States, the Articles of Confederation and Perpetual Union. The new Republic was then beset with danger on every hand. It had not conquered a place in the family of Nations. The decisive battle of the war for independence, whose centennial anniversary will soon be gratefully celebrated at Yorktown, had not yet been fought. The colonists were struggling, not only against the armies of Great Britain, but against the settled opinions of mankind, for the world did not believe that the supreme authority of government could be safely intrusted to the guardianship of the people themselves. We can not overestimate the fervent love, the intelligent courage, the saving common sense with which our fathers made the great experiment of self-government.

When they found, after a short time, that the Confederacy of States was too weak to meet the necessities of a glorious and expanding Republic, they boldly set it aside, and in its stead established a National Union, founded directly upon the will of the people, endowed with powers of self-preservation, and with ample authority for the accomplishment of its great objects.

Under this Constitution the boundaries of freedom are enlarged, the foundations of order and peace have been strengthened, and the growth in all the better elements of National life have vindicated the wisdom of the founders and given new hope to their descendants.

Under this Constitution our people long ago made themselves safe against danger from without, and secured for their mariners and flag equality of rights on all the seas. Under this Constitution twenty-five States have been added to the Union, with constitutions and laws framed and enforced by their own citizens to secure the manifold blessings of local and self-government.

The jurisdiction of this Constitution now covers an area fifty times greater than that of the original thirteen states, and a population twenty times greater than that of 1780. The trial of the Constitution came at last under the tremendous pressure of civil war.

We ourselves are witnesses that the Union emerged from the blood and fire of that conflict, purified and made stronger for all the beneficent purposes of good government, and now at the close of this, the first century of growth, with the inspirations of its history in their hearts, our people have lately reviewed the condition of the Nation, passed judgment upon the conduct and opinions of the political parties, and have registered their will concerning the future administration of the Government. To interpret and to execute that will in accordance with the Constitution is the paramount duty of the Executive. Even from this brief review it is manifest that the Nation is resolutely facing to the front, a resolution to employ its best energies in developing the great possibilities of the future. Sacredly preserving whatever has been gained to liberty and good government during the century, our people are determined to leave behind them all those bitter controversies concerning things which have been irrevocably settled, further discussion of which can only stir up strife and delay the onward march. The supremacy of the Nation and its laws should be no longer the subject of debate. That discussion, which for half a century threatened the existence of the Union, was closed at last in the high court of war by a decree from which there is no appeal: that the Constitution and the laws made in pursuance thereof shall continue to be the supreme law of the land, binding alike on the States and the people. This decree does not disturb the autonomy of the States, nor interfere with any of their necessary rules of local self-government, but it does fix and establish the permanent supremacy of the Union.

APPENDIX B

The will of the Nation, speaking with the voice of battle and through the amended Constitution, has fulfilled the great promise of 1776 by proclaiming 'Liberty throughout the land to all the inhabitants thereof.'

The elevation of the negro race from slavery to full rights of citizenship, is the most important political change we have known since the adoption of the Constitution of 1776.

No thoughtful man can fail to appreciate its beneficent effect upon our people. It has freed us from the perpetual danger of war and dissolution; it has added immensely to the moral and industrial forces of our people; it has liberated the master as well as the slave from a relation which wronged and enfeebled both.

It has surrendered to their own guardianship the manhood of more than five millions of people, and has opened to each of them a career of freedom and usefulness. It has given new inspiration to the power of self-help in both races by making labor more honorable to one and more necessary to the other.

The influence of this force will grow greater and bear richer fruit with coming years. No doubt the great change has caused serious disturbance to the Southern community—this is to be deplored, though it was unavoidable; but those who resisted the change should remember that in our institutions there was no middle ground for the negro race between slavery and equal citizenship. There can be no permanent disfranchised peasantry in the United States. Freedom can never yield its fullness of blessing as long as law or its administration places the smallest obstacle in the pathway of any virtuous citizenship.

The emancipated race has already made remarkable progress. With unquestionable devotion to the Union, with a patience and gentleness not born of fear, 'they have followed the light as God gave them to see the light.'

They are rapidly laying the material foundation for self-support, widening their circle of intelligence, and beginning to enjoy the blessings that gather around the homes of the industrious poor. They deserve the generous encouragement of all good men.

So far as my authority can lawfully extend, they shall enjoy full and equal protection of the Constitution and laws. The free enjoyment of equal suffrage is still in question, and a frank statement of the issue may aid its solution.

It is alleged that in many communities negro citizens are practically denied freedom of the ballot. In so far as the truth of this allegation is admitted, it is answered that in many places honest local

303

government is impossible if the mass of uneducated negroes are allowed to vote. These are grave allegations.

So far as the latter is true, it is no palliation that can be offered for opposing the freedom of the ballot. Bad local government is certainly a great evil which ought to be prevented, but to violate the freedom and sanctity of suffrage is more than an evil, it is a crime, which, if persisted in, will destroy the Government itself. Suicide is not a remedy.

If in other lands it be high treason to compass the death of a king, it should be counted no less a crime here to strangle our sovereign power and stifle its voice. It has been said that unsettled questions have no pity for the repose of nations. It should be said, with the utmost emphasis, that this question of suffrage will never give repose or safety to the States or to the Nation, until each, within its own jurisdiction, makes and keeps the ballot free and pure by strong sanctions of the law.

But the danger which arises from ignorance in voters can not be denied. It covers a field far wider than that of negro suffrage and the present condition of that race. It is a danger that lurks and hides in the sources and fountains of power in every State. We have no standard by which to measure the disaster that may be brought upon us by ignorance and vice in citizens when joined to corruption and fraud in suffrage. The voters of the Union, who make and unmake constitutions, and upon whose will hangs the destiny of our government, can transmit their supreme authority to no successor save the coming generation of voters, who are the sole heirs of sovereign power. If that generation comes to its inheritance blinded by ignorance and corrupted by vice, the fall of the Republic will be certain and remediless. The census has already sounded the alarm in appalling figures, which mark how dangerously high the tide of illiteracy has arisen among our voters and their children. To the South the question is of supreme importance, but the responsibility for its existence and for slavery does not rest upon the South alone.

The Nation itself is responsible for the extension of suffrage, and is under special obligations to aid in removing the illiteracy which it has added to the voting population. For North and South alike there is but one remedy: All the Constitutional power of the Nation and of the States, and all the volunteer forces of the people, should be summoned to meet this danger by the saving influence of universal education. It is the high privilege and sacred duty of those now living to educate their successors, and fit them, by intelligence and virtue, for the inheritance which awaits them. In this beneficent work section and race should be forgotten, and partisanship should be unknown. Let our people find a new meaning in the divine oracle which declares that 'a little child shall lead them,' for our little children will soon control the destinies of the Republic.

My countrymen, we do not now differ in our judgment concerning the controversies of the past generations, and fifty years hence our children will not be divided in their opinions concerning our controversies; they will surely bless their fathers—and their fathers' God—that the Union was preserved; that slavery was overthrown, and that both races were made equal before the law. We may hasten on, we may retard, but we can not prevent the final reconciliation.

Is it not possible for us now to make a truce with time by anticipating and accepting its inevitable verdict? Enterprises of the highest importance to our moral and material well-being invite us, and offer ample scope for the enjoyment of our best powers.

Let all our people, leaving behind them the battlefields of dead issues, move forward, and in the strength of liberty and restored union win the grandest victories of peace. The prosperity which now prevails is without parallel in our history. Fruitful seasons have done much to secure it, but they have not done all.

The preservation of public credit and the resumption of specie payments, so successfully obtained by the administration of my predecessors, have enabled our people to secure the blessings which the seasons brought.

By the experience of commercial relations in all ages it has been found that gold and silver afforded the only safe foundation for a monetary system. Confusion has recently been created by variations in the relative value of the two metals; but I confidently believe that arrangements can be made between the leading commercial nations which will secure the general use of both metals. Congress should provide that the compulsory coinage of silver, now required by law, may not disturb our monetary system by driving either metal out of circulation.

If possible, such adjustment should be made that the purchasing power of every coined dollar will be exactly equal to its debt-paying power in all the markets of the world. The chief duty of a National Government, in connection with the currency of the country, is to coin and declare its value. Grave doubts have been entertained whether Congress is authorized by the Constitution to make any form of paper money legal-tender.

The present issue of United States notes has been sustained by the necessities of war; but such paper should depend for its value and currency upon its convenience in use and its prompt redemption in coin at the will of the holder, and not upon its compulsory circulation. These notes are not money, but promises to pay money. If the holders demand it, the promises should be kept. The refunding of the National debt at a low rate of interest should be accomplished without compelling the withdrawal of National bank notes, and thus disturbing the business of the country.

I venture to refer to the position I have occupied on the financial question during a long service in Congress, and to say that time and experience have strengthened the opinions I have so often expressed on these subjects. The finances of the Government shall suffer no detriment which it may be possible for my administration to prevent.

The interests of agriculture deserve more attention from the Government than they have yet received. The farms of the United States afford homes and employment for more than one-half of our people, and furnish much the largest part of all our exports. As the Government lights our coasts for the protection of the mariners and the benefit of our commerce, so it should give to the tillers of the soil the lights of practical science and experience.

Our manufacturers are rapidly making us industrially independent, and are opening to capital and labor new and profitable fields of employment. This steady and healthy growth should still be maintained. Our facilities for transportation should be promoted by the continued improvements of our harbors and the great interior waterways and by the increase of our tonnage on the ocean.

The development of the world's commerce has led to an urgent demand for a shortening of the great sea voyage around Cape Horn by constructing ship-canals or railways across the Isthmus which unites the two continents. Various plans to this end have been suggested and will need consideration, but none of them have been sufficiently matured to warrant the United States in extending pecuniary aid.

The subject is one which will immediately engage the attention of the Government with a view to a thorough protection of American interests. We will argue no narrow policy, nor seek peculiar or exclusive privileges in any commercial route; but, in the language of my predecessors, I believe it to be 'the right and duty of the United States to assert and maintain such supervision and authority over any interoceanic canal across the Isthmus that connects North and South America as will protect our National interests.'

APPENDIX B

The Constitution guarantees absolute religious freedom. Congress is prohibited from making any laws respecting the establishment of religion or prohibiting free exercise thereof.

The Territories of the United States are subject to the direct legislative authority of Congress, and hence the General Government is responsible for any violation of the Constitution in any of them. It is, therefore, a reproach to the Government that in the most populous of the Territories this constitutional guarantee is not enjoyed by the people, and the authority of Congress is set at naught. The Mormon Church not only offends the moral sense of mankind by sanctioning polygamy, but prevents the administration of justice through the ordinary instrumentalities of the law.

In my judgment it is the duty of Congress, while respecting to the utmost the conscientious convictions and religious scruples of every citizen, to prohibit within its jurisdiction all criminal practices, especially of that class which destroy family relations and endanger social order. Nor can any ecclesiastical organization be safely permitted to usurp in the smallest degree the functions and powers of the National Government.

The Civil Service can never be placed on a satisfactory basis until it is regulated by law, for the good of the service itself. For the protection of those who are entrusted with the appointing power against a waste of time and obstruction of public business, caused by the inordinate pressure for place, and for the protection of incumbents against intrigue and wrong, I shall, at the proper time, ask Congress to fix the tenure of minor offices of the several Executive Departments, and prescribe the grounds upon which removals shall be made during the terms for which the incumbents have been appointed.

Finally, acting always within the authority and limitations of the Constitution, invading neither the rights of States nor the reserved rights of the people, it will be the purpose of my administration to maintain the authority, and in all places within its jurisdiction, to enforce obedience to all laws of the Union; in the interests of the people, to demand rigid economy in all the expenditures of the Government, and to require honest and faithful service of all executive officers, remembering that offices were created not for the benefit of the incumbents or their supporters, but for the service of the Government.

And now, fellow-citizens, I am about to assume the great trust which you have committed to my hands. I appeal to you for that earnest and thoughtful support which makes this Government in fact, as it is in law, a government of the people. I shall greatly rely upon the

APPENDIX B

wisdom and patriotism of Congress and of those who may share with me the responsibilities and duties of the administration, and upon our efforts to promote the welfare of this great people and their Government I reverently invoke the support and blessing of Almighty God.

Bibliography

MANUSCRIPT AND PRIMARY SOURCES

James A. Garfield Papers, Library of Congress.
Garfield Diaries, Library of Congress. Includes the White House diary of Mrs. Garfield.
Author's Collection of Garfieldiana. Comprises some thirty-five pieces, including fifteen Garfield letters, for the most part unpublished.
Ziba H. Potter letters. A group of five letters by a prominent New Yorker relating to the assassination of Garfield and its aftermath. Author's Collection.
Balch, William R., ed., *Garfield's Words* (Boston: Houghton Mifflin and Company, 1881).
Garfield, James A., "A Century of Congress," *Atlantic*, July 1877.
Hinsdale, Burke A., ed., *The Works of James A. Garfield*, 2 vols. (Cleveland, 1882).
Williams, Frederick D., ed., *The Wild Life of the Army: Civil War Letters of James A. Garfield* (Lansing: Michigan State University Press, 1964).

NEWSPAPERS AND PERIODICALS

New York Times
New York Herald
Nation
New York Sun
The Springfield (Mass.) *Republican*
American Heritage
Williams Alumni Review

BOOKS RELATING DIRECTLY TO GARFIELD

Balch, William R., *The Life of James Abram Garfield* (Philadelphia: J. C. McCurdy & Co., 1881).
Blaine, James G., "The Life and Character of James A. Garfield: Memorial Address" (Government Printing Office, 1882).
Bundy, Jonas M., *The Life of Gen. James A. Garfield* (New York: A. S. Barnes & Co., 1880).
Caldwell, Robert G., *James A. Garfield: Party Chieftain* (New York: Dodd, Mead and Company, 1931).
Fuller, Corydon E., *Reminiscences of James A. Garfield* (Cincinnati: Standard Publishing Co., 1887).
Riddle, Albert G., *The Life, Character and Public Services of James A. Garfield* (1880; Cleveland: W. W. Williams Co., 1883).
Ridpath, John C., *The Life and Work of James A. Garfield* (Jones Brothers & Co., 1881).
Smith, Theodore C., *The Life and Letters of James Abram Garfield*, 2 vols. (New Haven: Yale University Press, 1925).

BIBLIOGRAPHY

GENERAL WORKS

Adams, Henry, *The Education of Henry Adams* (New York: Random House, 1931).

Alexander, DeAlva S., *A Political History of the State of New York* (New York: Henry Holt and Company, 1909).

Anderson, Frederick, Gibson, William M., and Smith, Henry N., eds., *Selected Mark Twain-Howells Letters* (Cambridge: Harvard University Press, 1967).

Badeau, Adam, *Grant in Peace* (Hartford: S. S. Scranton & Co., 1887).

Barnard, Harry, *Rutherford B. Hayes and His America* (Indianapolis: The Bobbs-Merrill Company, 1954).

Blaine, James G., *Twenty Years of Congress*, 2 vols. (Norwich, Conn.: Henry Bill Publishing Co., 1884).

Bowers, Claude G., *The Tragic Era* (New York: The Riverside Press, 1929).

Boykin, Edward, ed., *The Wit and Wisdom of Congress* (New York: Funk and Wagnalls Co., 1961).

Brigance, William N., *Jeremiah Sullivan Black* (Philadelphia: University of Pennsylvania Press, 1934).

Carpenter, Frank G., *Carp's Washington* (New York: McGraw-Hill Book Company, 1960).

Carter, Harold D., ed., *Henry Adams and His Friends* (Boston: Houghton Mifflin Company, 1947).

Catton, Bruce, *Grant Takes Command* (Boston: Little, Brown and Company, 1968).

———*Never Call Retreat* (New York: Doubleday and Company, 1965).

Chidsey, Donald B., *The Gentleman from New York: A Life of Roscoe Conkling* (New Haven: Yale University Press, 1935).

Cortissoz, Royal, *The Life of Whitelaw Reid*, 2 vols. (New York: Charles Scribner's Sons, 1921).

Dennett, Tyler, *John Hay: From Poetry to Politics* (New York: Dodd, Mead and Company, 1933).

Donovan, Robert J., *The Assassins* (New York: Harper and Brothers, 1952).

Fleming, E. McClung, *R. R. Bowker: Militant Liberal* (Norman: University of Oklahoma Press, 1952).

Flick, Alexander C., *Samuel J. Tilden* (New York: Dodd, Mead and Company, 1931).

Franklin, John Hope, *Reconstruction After the Civil War* (Chicago: University of Chicago Press, 1961).

Fuess, Claude M., *Carl Schurz: Reformer* (New York: Dodd, Mead and Company, 1932).

Green, Constance M., *Washington: Capital City* (Princeton: Princeton University Press, 1963).

Hamlin, Charles E., *The Life and Times of Hannibal Hamlin* (Cambridge: The Riverside Press, 1899).

Hancock, Almira R., *Reminiscences of Winfield Scott Hancock* (New York: Charles L. Webster & Co., 1887).

Hesseltine, William B., *Ulysses S. Grant: Politician* (New York: Dodd, Mead and Company, 1935).

Hoar, George F., *Autobiography of Seventy Years*, 2 vols. (New York: Charles Scribner's Sons, 1903).

Hoogenboom, Ari, *Outlawing the Spoils* (Urbana: University of Illinois Press, 1961).

Hoover, Herbert, *Years of Adventure* (New York: The Macmillan Co., 1952).

Howe, George F., *Chester A. Arthur* (New York: Dodd, Mead and Company, 1934).

Hudson, William C., *Random Recollections of an Old Political Reporter* (New York: Cupples and Leon Company, 1911).

BIBLIOGRAPHY

Josephson, Matthew, *The Politicos* (New York: Harcourt, Brace and Company, 1938).

Kane, Joseph N., *Facts About the Presidents* (New York: H. W. Wilson Co., 1959).

Lamers, William M., *The Edge of Glory* (New York: Harcourt, Brace & World, 1961).

Leech, Margaret, *Reveille in Washington* (New York: Grosset & Dunlap, 1941).

Lingg, Ann M., *John Philip Sousa* (New York: Henry Holt and Company, 1954).

MacNeil, Neil, *Forge of Democracy: The House of Representatives* (New York: David McKay Co., 1963).

McPherson, James M., *The Struggle for Equality* (Princeton: Princeton University Press, 1964).

Mayer, George H., *The Republican Party: 1854–1966* (New York: Oxford University Press, 1967).

Moos, Malcolm, *The Republicans: A History of Their Party* (New York: Random House, 1956).

Morgan, H. Wayne, ed., *The Gilded Age: A Reappraisal* (Syracuse: Syracuse University Press, 1963).

Morison, Samuel E., and Commager, Henry S., *The Growth of the American Republic* (New York: Oxford University Press, 1962).

Muzzey, David S., *James G. Blaine* (New York: Dodd, Mead and Company, 1934).

Nevins, Allan, *Abram Hewitt* (New York: Harper and Brothers, 1935).

Nichols, Roy F., *The Stakes of Power* (New York: Hill and Wang, 1961).

Nixon, Raymond B., *Henry W. Grady: Spokesman for the New South* (New York: Alfred A. Knopf, 1943).

Paine, Albert B., *Thomas Nast: His Period and His Pictures* (New York: The Macmillan Co., 1904).

Platt, Thomas C., *Autobiography* (New York: B. W. Dodge & Co., 1910).

Rhodes, James F., *History of the United States from the Compromise of 1850*, 10 vols. (New York: The Macmillan Co., 1893–1925).

Rosenberg, Charles E., *The Trial of the Assassin Guiteau* (Chicago: University of Chicago Press, 1968).

Rossiter, Clinton, *The American Presidency* (New York: Harcourt, Brace and Company, 1956).

Rudolph, Frederick, *Mark Hopkins and the Log* (New Haven: Yale University Press, 1956).

Sandburg, Carl, *Abraham Lincoln: The War Years*, 3 vols. (New York: Harcourt, Brace and Company, 1936).

Schuckers, J. W., *The Life and Public Services of Salmon Portland Chase* (New York: D. Appleton & Co., 1874).

Sherman, John, *Recollections of Forty Years in the House, Senate and Cabinet*, 2 vols. (New York: The Werner Co., 1895).

Sievers, Harry J., *Benjamin Harrison: Hoosier Statesman* (New York: University Publishers Inc., 1959).

Stampp, Kenneth M., *The Era of Reconstruction* (New York: Alfred A. Knopf, 1965).

Stoddard, Henry L., *As I Knew Them* (New York: Harper and Brothers, 1927).

Stanwood, Edward S., *A History of the Presidency* (Boston: Houghton Mifflin Company, 1928).

Stevenson, Elizabeth, *Henry Adams* (New York: The Macmillan Company, 1955).

Stone, Irving, *They Also Ran* (New York: Doubleday, Doran and Company, 1944).

Taylor, John M., *From the White House Inkwell* (Rutland, Vt.: Charles E. Tuttle Co., 1968).

Thayer, William R., *John Hay* (Boston: Houghton Mifflin Company, 1915).

Thorndike, Rachael S., *The Sherman Letters* (New York: Charles Scribner's Sons, 1894).

BIBLIOGRAPHY

Villard, Henry, *Memoirs*, 2 vols. (Boston: Houghton Mifflin Company, 1904).

Wall, Joseph F., *Henry Watterson: Reconstructed Rebel* (New York: Oxford University Press, 1956).

Warden, Robert B., *The Private Life and Public Services of Salmon Portland Chase* (Cincinnati: Willstach, Baldwin and Co., 1874).

White, Leonard D., *The Republican Era* (New York: The Macmillan Company, 1958).

White, William A., *Masks in a Pageant* (New York: The Macmillan Company, 1928).

Williams, Blanche C., *Clara Barton: Daughter of Destiny* (Philadelphia: J. B. Lippincott Co., 1941).

Williams, Charles R., *The Life of Rutherford Birchard Hayes*, 2 vols. (Boston: Houghton Mifflin Company, 1914).

Williams, T. Harry, *Hayes: The Diary of a President* (New York: David McKay Co., 1964).

Woodward, C. Vann, *Origins of the New South* (Baton Rouge: Louisiana State University Press, 1951).

———*Reunion and Reaction* (Boston: Little, Brown and Company, 1951).

MISCELLANEOUS

Bishop, Morris, "The Great Oneida Love-in," *American Heritage*, February 1969.

House of Representatives Report No. 77, Forty-second Congress, third session (Credit Mobilier Report).

Official Proceedings of the Republican National Convention, 1880.

Phillips, John L., "Credit Mobilier," *American Heritage*, April 1969.

Taylor, John M., "General Hancock: Bullets to Ballots," unpublished monograph, The George Washington University, 1954.

———"General Hancock: Soldier of the Gilded Age," *Pennsylvania History*, April 1965.

———"Garfield: Time for Rehabilitation?" *Williams Alumni Review*, Fall 1966

Notes

CHAPTER ONE

[1] George H. Mayer, *The Republican Party: 1854–1966*, p. 199.
[2] George F. Hoar, *Autobiography of Seventy Years*, I, pp. 391–92.
[3] *Official Proceedings of the Republican National Convention*, p. 40.
[4] Matthew Josephson, *The Politicos*, p. 283.
[5] Donald B. Chidsey, *The Gentleman from New York: A Life of Roscoe Conkling*, p. 287.
[6] Mayer, *op. cit.*, p. 174.
[7] *Proceedings, op. cit.*, pp. 179–81.
[8] *Ibid.*, p. 185.
[9] The *New York Times*, June 8, 1880.
[10] *Proceedings*, p. 269.
[11] Hoar, *op. cit.*, I, p. 397.

CHAPTER TWO

[1] Theodore C. Smith, *The Life and Letters of James Abram Garfield*, p. 12.
[2] John C. Ridpath, *The Life and Work of James A. Garfield*, p. 23.
[3] Smith, *op. cit.*, p. 16.
[4] *Ibid.*, pp. 19–20.
[5] *Ibid.*, pp. 21–22.
[6] *Ibid.*, p. 31.
[7] William R. Balch, *The Life of James Abram Garfield*, p. 68.
[8] Smith, p. 39.
[9] *Ibid.*, p. 17.

CHAPTER THREE

[1] Corydon E. Fuller, *Reminiscences of James A. Garfield*, p. 36.
[2] Smith, *op. cit.*, p. 49.
[3] Ridpath, *op. cit.*, pp. 56–57.
[4] Diary, Garfield Papers (January 1, 1853).
[5] Garfield Papers, Library of Congress.
[6] John M. Taylor, *From the White House Inkwell*, p. 81.
[7] Diary, Garfield Papers (June 23, 1854).
[8] For this and the preceding paragraphs concerning Williams, I am indebted to Frederick Rudolph, *Mark Hopkins and the Log*. The quotation is from p. 92.
[9] Smith, p. 77.
[10] *Ibid.*, p. 81.
[11] Garfield to A. Pettibone, September 20, 1854. Garfield Papers.
[12] Ridpath, p. 72.
[13] Smith, p. 101.

NOTES

CHAPTER FOUR

[1] Frederick D. Williams, ed., *The Wild Life of the Army: Civil War Letters of James A. Garfield* (hereafter cited as *Civil War Letters*), pp. xiv–xv.

[2] Ridpath, *op. cit.*, p. 75.

[3] Smith, *op. cit.*, p. 121.

[4] Ridpath, p. 79.

[5] Smith, p. 134.

[6] Garfield to J. E. Jackson and others, September 12, 1859. Garfield Papers.

[7] Newspaper clipping, n.d., Garfield Papers.

[8] Diary, Garfield Papers (December 2, 1859).

[9] Balch, *op. cit.*, p. 107.

[10] Garfield to W. J. Ford, August 6, 1860. Author's Collection.

[11] Garfield, *Civil War Letters*, p. ix. Miss Benedict's appraisal of Garfield's religious meetings is remarkably similar to that of Hinsdale quoted on p. 17.

[12] Diary, Garfield Papers (November 6, 1860).

[13] Smith, p. 158.

[14] Ridpath, p. 85.

[15] Garfield to Rhodes, January 26, 1861.

[16] Balch, p. 122.

CHAPTER FIVE

[1] Garfield to Rhodes, April 13, 1861.

[2] Garfield, *Civil War Letters*, p. 13.

[3] *Ibid.*, p. 16.

[4] Smith, *op. cit.*, p. 176.

[5] Ridpath, *op. cit.*, p. 95.

[6] Smith, p. 183.

[7] *Ibid.*, pp. 60–61.

[8] Ridpath, pp. 109–10.

[9] Garfield to Rhodes, May 1, 1862. *Civil War Letters*, p. 90.

[10] Garfield to Rhodes, May 28, 1862. *Ibid.*, p. 104.

[11] *Civil War Letters*, p. 98.

[12] *Ibid.*, p. 109.

[13] Garfield to Mrs. Garfield, September 17, 1862. *Civil War Letters*, p. 136.

[14] Garfield to Mrs. Garfield, September 20, 1862. *Ibid.*, p. 137.

[15] Smith, p. 241.

[16] Robert B. Warden, *The Private Life and Public Services of Salmon Portland Chase*, p. 489.

[17] Garfield to Mrs. Garfield, October 12, 1862. *Civil War Letters*, p. 159.

[18] Garfield to Mrs. Garfield, October 24, 1862. *Ibid.*, pp. 166–67.

[19] Carl Sandburg, *Abraham Lincoln: The War Years*, II, p. 22.

[20] Garfield to Rhodes, October 5, 1862. *Civil War Letters*, p. 151.

[21] Garfield to Mrs. Garfield, October 31, 1862. *Ibid.*, pp. 171–72.

[22] *Ibid.*, pp. 181, 193.

CHAPTER SIX

[1] William M. Lamers, *The Edge of Glory*, p. 55.

[2] Garfield, *Civil War Letters*, p. 226.

NOTES

[3] Smith, *op. cit.*, p. 276.

[4] Quoted in Garfield, *Civil War Letters*, pp. 217–18.

[5] Edmund Kirke, "Down in Tennessee," quoted in Balch, *op. cit.*, pp. 194–95.

[6] Smith, p. 292.

[7] Garfield to Rosecrans, June 12, 1863. *Civil War Letters*, pp. 281–82.

[8] Smith, p. 296.

[9] Diary, Garfield Papers (June 22, 1863).

[10] The *New York Sun*, March 8, 1882.

[11] Lamers, *op. cit.*, p. 314.

[12] *Ibid.*, p. 351.

[13] Smith, p. 345.

[14] Lamers, p. 411.

[15] *Ibid.*, pp. 412–13.

[16] Garfield to Austin, December 1, 1863. *Civil War Letters*, p. 300.

[17] Garfield to E. B. Taylor, January 9, 1864. Author's Collection.

CHAPTER SEVEN

[1] The *Washington Star*, December 7, 1863.

[2] Garfield to Mrs. Garfield, December 6, 1863. *Civil War Letters*, p. 301.

[3] Smith, *op. cit.*, p. 895.

[4] *Ibid.*, pp. 373–74.

[5] *Ibid.*, p. 382.

[6] John Sherman, *Recollections of Forty Years in the House, Senate and Cabinet*, I, p. 447.

[7] Smith, pp. 375–76.

[8] *Ibid.*, p. 379.

[9] Garfield to Colonel ——, October 12, 1864. Author's collection.

[10] Quoted in Edward Boykin, ed., *The Wit and Wisdom of Congress*, p. 402.

[11] Garfield to Gen. Irvin McDowell, February 3, 1865. Author's Collection.

[12] Smith, p. 383.

[13] Balch, *op. cit.*, pp. 270–73.

[14] Smith, pp. 384–85.

[15] Quoted in James M. McPherson, *The Struggle for Equality*, p. 339.

[16] Smith, p. 392.

[17] Hinsdale, *The Works of James A. Garfield*, I, p. 140.

[18] Diary, Garfield Papers (September 18–20, 1866).

[19] McPherson, *op. cit.*, pp. 365–66.

[20] The *New York Times*, November 8, 1866.

[21] Hinsdale, *op. cit.*, I, pp. 248–50.

[22] Quoted in Republican campaign leaflet No. 26, 1880, "Winfield S. Hancock's Defiance of the Reconstruction Acts."

[23] Diary, Garfield Papers (August 8, 1867).

[24] Garfield to Col. Norton, February 3, 1868. Author's Collection.

[25] Smith, p. 426.

CHAPTER EIGHT

[1] Neil MacNeil, *Forge of Democracy: The House of Representatives*, pp. 309–10.

[2] Henry Adams, *The Education of Henry Adams*, p. 261.

[3] Albert G. Riddle, *The Life, Character and Public Services of James A. Garfield*, p. 83.

[4] Smith, *op. cit.*, p. 411.

NOTES

[5] Leonard D. White, *The Republican Era*, pp. 70–71.
[6] Diary, Garfield Papers (January 8, 1873).
[7] Smith, p. 827.
[8] E. V. Smalley, quoted in Smith, pp. 901–02.
[9] Paoli E. Coletta, "Greenbackers, Goldbugs, and Silverites," in Morgan H. Wayne, ed., *The Gilded Age: A Reappraisal*.
[10] Balch, *op. cit.*, p. 261.
[11] Smith, p. 429.
[12] Balch, pp. 279–80.
[13] *Ibid.*, p. 284.
[14] Garfield to Orlando Morgan, March 22, 1871. Author's Collection.
[15] Mary L. Hinsdale, ed., *Garfield-Hinsdale Letters*, p. 300.
[16] Ridpath, *op. cit.*, p. 240.

CHAPTER NINE

[1] Mayer, *op. cit.*, p. 171.
[2] Smith, *op. cit.*, p. 445.
[3] Garfield to B. A. Hinsdale, December 3, 1871.
[4] Josephson, *op. cit.*, p. 108.
[5] *Ibid.*, p. 105.
[6] Smith, p. 451.
[7] *Ibid.*, p. 462.
[8] McPherson, *op. cit.*, pp. 430–31.
[9] Smith, p. 470.
[10] Kenneth M. Stampp, *The Era of Reconstruction*, pp. 209–10.
[11] Garfield to Orlando Morgan, March 22, 1871. Author's Collection.
[12] Garfield to Jacob Cox, February 29, 1872. Garfield Papers.
[13] Josephson, p. 157.
[14] Garfield to J. B. Burrows, July 29, 1872. Garfield Papers.
[15] Diary, Garfield Papers (November 4, 1872).

CHAPTER TEN

[1] John L. Phillips, "Credit Mobilier," *American Heritage*, April 1969.
[2] The *New York Sun*, September 4, 1872.
[3] William N. Brigance, *Jeremiah Sullivan Black*, pp. 214–15.
[4] The *Washington Star*, November 14, 1872.
[5] House Reports No. 77, Forty-second Congress, third session, p. 129.
[6] *Ibid.*
[7] Smith, *op. cit.*, p. 540.
[8] *Ibid.*, pp. 544–45.
[9] The *New York Times*, February 19, 1873.
[10] Diary, Garfield Papers (March 2, 1873).
[11] Smith, pp. 547–48.
[12] *Ibid.*, p. 551.
[13] Ridpath, *op. cit.*, p. 265.
[14] Smith, p. 557.
[15] Diary, Garfield Papers (December 3, 1873).
[16] Garfield to S. P. Wolcott, April 13, 1874. Author's Collection.
[17] Garfield to Hinsdale, April 20, 1874. Garfield Papers.
[18] Smith, p. 572.

NOTES

[19] Garfield to —— Ordway, October 12, 1874. Author's Collection.
[20] James F. Rhodes, *History of the United States from the Compromise of 1850*, VIII, p. 17.

CHAPTER ELEVEN

[1] Josephson, *op. cit.*, pp. 192–93.
[2] Mayer, *op. cit.*, p. 187.
[3] Rudolph, *op. cit.*, pp. 226–27.
[4] Garfield to J. B. Crandall, January 2, 1872.
[5] Smith, *op. cit.*, p. 803.
[6] Josephson, p. 204.
[7] Garfield to J. Q. Smith, April 16, 1875.
[8] Smith, p. 590.
[9] Quoted in Smith, p. 752.
[10] Smith, p. 765.
[11] Garfield to George W. Steele, May 30, 1876.
[12] Josephson, p. 207.
[13] Smith, p. 596.
[14] Diary, Garfield Papers (June 8, 1876).
[15] *Ibid.* (June 11, 1876).
[16] Brigance, *op. cit.*, pp. 247–48.
[17] Smith, p. 613.
[18] *Ibid.*, p. 615.
[19] Harry Barnard, *Rutherford B. Hayes and His America*, p. 327.
[20] *Ibid.*, p. 334.
[21] C. Vann Woodward, *Reunion and Reaction*, p. 22.
[22] Garfield to Hayes, January 19, 1877.
[23] Smith, p. 632.
[24] Barnard, p. 373.
[25] Diary, Garfield Papers (February 26, 1877).

CHAPTER TWELVE

[1] Barnard, *op. cit.*, p. 427.
[2] *Ibid.*, p. 433.
[3] Garfield to S. P. Wolcott, March 27, 1877. Author's Collection.
[4] Diary, Garfield Papers (March 29, 1877).
[5] Garfield to L. A. Sheldon, February 12, 1878.
[6] Ari Hoogenboom, *Outlawing the Spoils*, p. 151.
[7] Josephson, *op. cit.*, p. 240.
[8] Hoogenboom, *op. cit.*, p. 156.
[9] Barnard, p. 453.
[10] Smith, *op. cit.*, p. 664.
[11] Diary, Garfield Papers (March 4, 1878).
[12] Hoogenboom, p. 165.
[13] Smith, p. 656.
[14] Diary, Garfield Papers (February 22, 1878).
[15] Smith, p. 269.
[16] *Ibid.*, p. 687.
[17] James A. Garfield, "A Century of Congress," *Atlantic*, July 1877.
[18] Frederick Anderson and colleagues, eds., *Selected Mark Twain-Howells Letters*, p. 76.

NOTES

[19] Quoted in Barnard, p. ix.
[20] Smith, p. 775.
[21] Charles R. Williams, *Life of Rutherford Birchard Hayes*, II, p. 239.
[22] Hoar, *op. cit.*, II, p. 17.
[23] Sherman, *op. cit.*, II, p. 807.
[24] Smith, p. 936.
[25] Diary, Garfield Papers (December 16, 1876).

CHAPTER THIRTEEN

[1] Diary, Garfield Papers (October 11, 1879).
[2] Smith, *op. cit.*, p. 692.
[3] Diary, Garfield Papers (December 19, 1879).
[4] The *Springfield Republican*, January 1, 1880.
[5] The *New York Times*, April 19 and 20, 1880.
[6] The *Springfield Republican*, April 22, 1880.
[7] Raymond B. Nixon, *Henry W. Grady: Spokesman for the New South*, p. 182.
[8] Diary, Garfield Papers (February 5, 1878).
[9] Garfield to Harmon Austin, April 16, 1880.
[10] See Henry L. Stoddard, *As I Knew Them*, pp. 118–20; also George F. Howe, *Chester A. Arthur*, p. 109.
[11] Robert G. Caldwell, *James A. Garfield: Party Chieftain*, pp. 291–92.
[12] Brigance, *op. cit.*, pp. 280–82.

CHAPTER FOURTEEN

[1] John M. Taylor, "General Hancock: Soldier of the Gilded Age," *Pennsylvania History*, April 1965.
[2] Herbert Hoover, *Years of Adventure*, p. 9.
[3] Chidsey, *op. cit.*, pp. 301–02.
[4] The *Springfield Republican*, June 25, 1880.
[5] The *New York Sun*, July 1, 1880.
[6] The *Springfield Republican*, August 7, 1880.
[7] Smith *op. cit.*, pp. 996–97.
[8] Balch, *op. cit.*, p. 528.
[9] The *Nation*, XXXI, July 15, 1880, p. 37.
[10] The *Springfield Republican*, July 14 and 22, 1880.
[11] *Ibid.*, July 22, 1880.
[12] *Ibid.*, July 21, 1880.
[13] Dorsey to Garfield, July 26, 1880.
[14] Howe, *op. cit.*, p. 117.
[15] Thomas C. Platt, *Autobiography*, p. 130.
[16] Smith, p. 1015.
[17] Dorsey to Garfield, August 18, 1880.
[18] Morton to Garfield, September 1, 1880.

CHAPTER FIFTEEN

[1] Fuller, *op. cit.*, p. 430.
[2] The *New York Sun*, July 10, 1880.

NOTES

[3] *Ibid.*, September 29, 1880.
[4] The *Springfield Republican*, August 14, 1880.
[5] Josephson, *op. cit.*, p. 289.
[6] The *Springfield Republican*, July 20, 1880.
[7] Tyler Dennett, *John Hay: From Poetry to Politics*, p. 131.
[8] Foster to Garfield, September 17, 1880.
[9] Dorsey to Garfield, September 1, 1880.
[10] Garfield to Edwards Pierpoint, October 16, 1880. Author's Collection.
[11] Albert B. Paine, *Thomas Nast: His Period and His Pictures*, p. 438.
[12] Sherman to Garfield, November 1, 1880.
[13] Almira R. Hancock, *Reminiscences of General Winfield Scott Hancock*, p. 172.
[14] Harrison to Garfield, November 4, 1880.
[15] Sherman, *op. cit.*, II, p. 789.
[16] Smith, *op. cit.*, pp. 865–67.

CHAPTER SIXTEEN

[1] Smith, *op. cit.*, p. 1066.
[2] The *Washington Star*, November 24, 1880.
[3] Diary, Garfield Papers (November 27, 1880).
[4] Smith, p. 1051.
[5] Josephson, *op. cit.*, p. 303.
[6] Diary, Garfield Papers (December 19, 1880).
[7] The *New York Tribune*, January 3, 1881.
[8] Smith, pp. 1055–56.
[9] *Ibid.*, p. 1063.
[10] *Ibid.*, p. 1071.
[11] Josephson, pp. 300–01.
[12] Smith, p. 1090.
[13] Diary, Garfield Papers (February 28, 1881).
[14] Diary, Garfield Papers (March 4, 1881).
[15] Smith, p. 1096–97.
[16] The *Washington Star*, March 5, 1881.
[17] Ridpath, *op. cit.*, pp. 491–95.
[18] Harry J. Sievers, *Benjamin Harrison: Hoosier Statesman*, p. 199.
[19] The *Washington Star*, March 5, 1881.

CHAPTER SEVENTEEN

[1] Frank G. Carpenter, *Carp's Washington*, pp. 53–54.
[2] Elizabeth Stevenson, *Henry Adams*, p. 150.
[3] Diary, Garfield Papers (March 8, 1881).
[4] *Ibid.* (March 21, 1881).
[5] Ridpath, *op. cit.*, p. 503.
[6] Diary, Garfield Papers (March 20, 1881).
[7] Mrs. Garfield, Journal, Garfield Papers (March 22, 1881).
[8] The *Nation*, May 26, 1881.
[9] Diary, Garfield Papers (March 23, 1881).
[10] Mrs. Garfield, Journal, Garfield Papers (April 15, 1881).
[11] Blanche C. Williams, *Clara Barton: Daughter of Destiny*, p. 256.
[12] Diary, Garfield Papers (June 14, 1881).
[13] Smith, *op. cit.*, p. 1157.

NOTES

[14] Diary, Garfield Papers (April 9, 1881).
[15] Smith, p. 1158.
[16] The *New York Times*, June 6, 1881.

CHAPTER EIGHTEEN

[1] Smith, *op. cit.*, p. 1111.
[2] Diary, Garfield Papers (April 6, 1881).
[3] Smith, p. 1115.
[4] *Ibid.*, p. 1120.
[5] Hoogenboom, *op. cit.*, pp. 204–05.
[6] Quoted in John M. Taylor, "Garfield: Time for Rehabilitation?" *Williams Alumni Review*, Fall 1966.
[7] Smith, p. 1136.
[8] *Ibid.*, p. 1172.
[9] The *New York Times*, June 10, 1881.
[10] Adam Badeau, *Grant in Peace*, pp. 533–34.

CHAPTER NINETEEN

[1] Robert J. Donovan, *The Assassins*, p. 48.
[2] B. C. Williams, *op. cit.*, p. 262.
[3] See Morris Bishop, "The Great Oneida Love-in," *American Heritage*, February 1969.
[4] Donovan, *op. cit.*, p. 23.
[5] *Ibid.*, p. 35.
[6] *Ibid.*, p. 39.
[7] *Ibid.*, p. 40–41.
[8] *Ibid.*, p. 46.
[9] Brigance, *op. cit.*, p. 282.
[10] The *Washington Star*, September 7, 1881.
[11] *Ibid.*, August 23, 1881.
[12] Smith, *op. cit.*, p. 1199.
[13] Potter to the Duc d'Orleans, August 26, 1881. Author's collection.
[14] Smith, p. 1196.
[15] Ridpath, *op. cit.*, p. 597.
[16] *Ibid.*, p. 625.
[17] Smith, p. 1200.

EPILOGUE

[1] Charles E. Rosenberg, *The Trial of the Assassin Guiteau*, p. 11.
[2] Smith, *op. cit.*, p. 1205.
[3] James G. Blaine, "The Life and Character of James A. Garfield: Memorial Address," 1882.
[4] Josephson, *op. cit.*, p. 324.
[5] Donovan, *op. cit.*, p. 53.
[6] Guiteau to President Arthur, September 20, 1881.
[7] Rosenberg, *op. cit.*, pp. 54–55.
[8] Donovan, p. 58.
[9] Rosenberg, p. 237.

NOTES

[10] Smith, p. 869.
[11] Lamers, *op. cit.*, p. 445.
[12] Harold D. Carter, ed., *Henry Adams and His Friends*, p. 226.
[13] Hoogenboom, *op. cit.*, p. 251.
[14] Smith, p. 899.
[15] W. R. Balch, ed., *Garfield's Words*, p. 54.

INDEX

INDEX

INDEX

INDEX

INDEX

INDEX

INDEX

INDEX

331

INDEX

INDEX

INDEX

DATE DUE			
MAY 2 3 '74			
MAY 2 3 '75			
MAY 2 4 1977			
DE 3 '84			
ILL 11-28 86			